THE SAINTS OF SOUTH AMERICA

The Saints
of South America

By STEPHEN CLISSOLD

CHARLES KNIGHT & CO. LIMITED
LONDON
1972

Charles Knight & Co. Ltd.
11-12 Bury Street, London EC3A 5AP
Dowgate Works, Douglas Road, Tonbridge, Kent.

SBN 85314 162 2

Printed in Great Britain by
Brown Knight & Truscott Ltd., London & Tonbridge

CONTENTS

The quotation reproduced on p. 113 is from the Poems of St. John on the Cross, published by Harvell Press (1951).

ILLUSTRATIONS

MAPS

THE SAINTS OF SOUTH AMERICA

CHAPTER 1

Saints,
Heroes and Pseudo-saints

ALL nations have their heroes, and some—though they may not always appreciate them—have their saints as well. Heroes are held in honour, whilst the saints, since their glory is not of this world, too often fade into oblivion. We are the poorer for this loss, for saints are remarkable human beings—men and women who made a great impact on their contemporaries and may not be so irrelevant to our own age as we suppose. The very hagiographers and iconographers who have sought to keep their memory green are partly responsible for this neglect, for their pious attentions at times distort or prettify the portrait beyond all recognition. At others, to make sure of our admiration, they lift their subjects bodily out of the stony way of holiness into the world of human heroism. But this is not where the saint belongs. He is not a hero, though his virtues and exertions may be heroic; nor is the hero a saint. Each follows his own calling, has his own qualities, and moves in a world of his own.

The Spaniards, who first brought Christianity to America, are largely responsible for this confusion between saint and hero. The same year that saw the discovery of the New World marked the fall of the last Moslem kingdom in Spain. The epic of the *Reconquista,* which had taken the Christian armies more than 700 years to achieve, ended just as the new epic of the *Conquista* of America began. During those seven centuries, the characteristic temper of the Spaniards and the faith for which they fought were forged. It was a militant temper, identifying the Cross with the Sword, in answer to the militancy of Islam which had seized the Roman-Visigothic Christian kingdoms of the peninsula for the Crescent. Mediaeval Christendom as a whole was familiar with the idea of the Crusade, but nowhere did the crusading spirit so fully pervade the whole life of a people as in Spain. To spread the gospel by the sword, to offer pagans the choice of baptism or death, to win lands and riches for oneself at the expense of the enemies of God—all these things were of the essence of the Spaniard's faith. A good Catholic must perforce become a warrior, the perfect

1

Knight, a Christian paladin, like the national hero El Cid. Ferdinand, the warrior-king who won back Seville for the Cross, was also venerated as a saint.

This militarization of the Christian spirit is strikingly illustrated by the cult of Santiago, Spain's patron saint. Legend had it that it was St. James who first brought the gospel to Spain and that his body was laid to rest at Santiago de Compostela. But legend also transformed the peaceful apostle into a warrior who would miraculously appear on his white charger, flourishing his flaming sword, to help the Christians in their battles against the Moors. He became Santiago Matamoros—St. James the Moor-slayer. In time, there were no more Moors left in Spain to kill; but by then, there was a new pagan enemy —the native inhabitants, or "Indians", of the New World. So when the Spaniards came to America they brought with them the same concept of religion as a crusade, and the same patron saint—Santiago the Moor-slayer. Soon we find accounts in chronicles of the *Conquista,* as they are to be found in those of the *Reconquista,* of how St. James would suddenly appear at a critical moment in some battle against the Indians to give the Christians the victory. López de Gómara, for instance, relates such a miraculous occurrence in Mexico. The old soldier Bernal Díaz del Castillo, who took part in that engagement, comments drily: "It may be as Gómara says; but if so, all I can say is that I, poor sinner, was not worthy to see it. What I did see was Francisco de Morla who came riding up on his chestnut horse with Cortés. . . ." Years later, when the Spaniards were besieged by the Indians at Cuzco, Santiago is again supposed to have appeared in time to turn defeat into victory (Plate 1).

But there was another thread running through the Spanish religious tradition which, though less in evidence than the dominant Santiago-strand, linked it more closely to the heart of the gospel message. This was the purer spirituality which takes the two-fold commandment to love God with all our heart and our neighbour as ourself with a trusting literalness, believing that Christ's disciple should have no other arms but love and that the Kingdom of God is not to be imposed by force. This was the spirit which permitted Christians, Jews and Moslems to live together in amity in certain places for considerable periods during the seven centuries of the *Reconquista,* producing a fruitful cross-fertilization of culture and *mores,* and conversions which stemmed from example and peaceful persuasion. It inspired acts of sublime abnegation, such as those practised by St. Peter Nolasco and his companions of the Order of Mercy, who did not rest content with raising money for the redemption of Christian captives but crossed the straits of North Africa to offer themselves as prisoners of the Moors in their place. The supreme expression of this spirit is to be found in the lives and writings of St. Teresa and the other great Spanish mystics.

The *conquistadores* who set out for fame and fortune in the New World sailed under the banner of Santiago. They held the convenient but sincere conviction that, in winning fresh lands for Spain, they were also winning souls for Christ. Their methods of achieving the one and the other were ruthless. The Indians were called upon to submit to the authority of Spain and to a faith which they could barely understand, or to face extermination as "rebels" and obdurate pagans. Extermination, however, was seldom in the interests of the Spaniards, since they needed the Indians to work the land and operate the mines. A rapid and perfunctory evangelization, as a means of promoting or consolidating their control of the conquered races, was commonly preferred. Some clerics were ready enough with their co-operation, either from cynicism or eagerness to show a high statistical score of conversions, or simply because they saw that large numbers of Indians were doomed to perish through epidemics, hunger or maltreatment, and that the missionaries must act quickly whilst there was yet time at least to save their souls from everlasting perdition.

But the New World was not left wholly to the none too tender mercies of Santiago. In 1617, Teresa of Avila was proclaimed co-patroness of Spain, though diehards like the famous satirist Quevedo, author of "My Sword for Santiago", a spirited defence of the warrior-saint, and himself a Knight of his Order, prevented the proclamation from becoming effective. It was, nevertheless, a gesture in recognition of that other current of purer spirituality within the central Santiago tradition. The latter, indeed, never wholly dominated the thinking of the Crown. From the Testament left by the great Queen Isabel enjoining upon her heirs and officials the welfare, both spiritual and temporal, of her new vassals the Indians, through an unending series of royal instructions, *cédulas* and laws, we note the constant preoccupation of the Crown to ensure that the Catholic faith should be intelligibly preached and freely accepted. The methods prescribed, such as the obligatory reading of the *Requerimiento* or Summons rehearsing the Spaniards' politico-religious version of world history from the creation of Adam to the mandate given by the Pope to their King for suzerainty in the New World, may strike us—as it did many contemporaries—as laughably naive. But the sincerity of the royal purpose could not be doubted; Sword and Cross were to go forward together, and the former was to be wielded as sparingly as possible. Theological jurists like Suárez and Vitoria took pains to lay down enlightened guidelines defining the domain of each and specifying the few occasions when force might justifiably be used in the evangelization and conquest—or pacification rather, for the very word "conquest" came to be proscribed—of the New World.

A few uncompromising souls would have none of this alliance between Cross and Sword. The missionary, they declared, should go amongst the Indians unarmed save for the shield of faith and should preach the gospel without any hint of coercion whatsoever. Such was the passionate belief of the *conquistador* turned friar, Bartolomé de las Casas, who launched heroic but ultimately disastrous attempts at peaceful evangelization, first on the Spanish Main, then in Guatemala. The voice of the Defender of the Indians still rings down the ages denouncing the *conquistadores* for their greed and callousness, thundering excommunication against those who withstood him, and calling in question the whole legitimacy of the Spanish presence in America. Yet, in this fervent forerunner of the anti-imperialists of our own times, there remains something about the very violence of his commitment to the natives' cause, in the intemperance and exaggeration of his language no less than in his indomitable valour, which suggests that the spirit of Santiago he so abhors still survives within him. He would simply have the warrior-saint turn against his own countrymen and belabour them, at least with the flat of his sword, for their sins.

There are other voices which come to us from the early years of conquest and colonization above the cries of "Santiago and Spain!" They reach us more faintly, for they come from those who are given to teaching by example rather than by precept, to prayer rather than polemics. Some of the men and women whose vocations reflect most fully this other, more spiritual aspect of the Spanish religious tradition form the subject of the following pages. Here it is enough to note that they lived within the span of one century, from the mid-sixteenth to the mid-seventeenth. Thereafter, as Spain sank into the long aftermath of her greatness, the religious fervour which had contributed so much to that greatness also flagged. The Church gradually lost her apostolic zeal, caring less and less for the conversion and defence of the Indians and more and more for the acquisition of wealth and the bolstering of the "establishment". From earliest times, as we have noted, the Church had a foot in both camps; Cross and Sword marched together and mutually reinforced one another. Their interests then were, however, by no means always identical, since the Church was the Indians' chief champion against oppressive officials and grasping settlers. As time wore on, the Church became institutionalized, more worldly, and more wholly identified with the colonial power-structure. The age of the saints, whose lot was cast with the humble and whose vocation was to ease the lot of the oppressed, had passed.

But a people needs its saints—at least until society becomes secularized, when it contents itself with mere heroes. The tendency then is to vest those heroes with the halo of the saint, as an earlier age had decked out its saints in the armour of the hero. By the beginning of the 19th Century, when the Creoles demanded emancipation from Spain, the Church—or at least its official hierarchy—had become so much a bastion of the colonial order that the independence leaders tended to be not only anti-Spanish but anti-clerical. This did not, however, save them from often themselves becoming the objects of an almost religious veneration. Thus we find San Martín, the chief architect of Argentine independence, eulogized by his leading biographer as "The Saint of the Sword".

More striking still is the apotheosis of Cuba's national hero—José Martí. Though a confirmed anti-clerical who declared that "Christianity has perished at the hands of Catholicism", Martí was a selfless and noble-hearted man whose sympathies went out everywhere to the poor and the oppressed, and who returned to Cuba from exile to suffer a rebel's death which his admirers do not hesitate to describe as "martyrdom". Moved more by compassion than by hatred or ambition, Martí comes nearer perhaps than any other great public figure to the ideal of the secular hero who has also something about him of the saint. This quality was at once recognized by his countrymen, who invariably refer to him as The Apostle. The titles of the many articles and books which have been devoted to him indicate the sort of cult which his veneration inspires: "Martí—Apostle of Freedom", "Martí—the Saint of America", "Martí—Captain of Archangels", "Martí—Redeemer of the Cubans", "Martí—the Secondborn son of God", and even "Martí—the Christ of America". There are sacramental overtones, too, to the cult. The practice grew up amongst his admirers in the nineteen-twenties of meeting together for a "Martian Supper", when a meal would be taken in common and speeches made in reverent homage to his memory. "Let us eat his flesh to make ourselves stronger, drink his blood to make ourselves worthier", one of his admirers has declared. "Let us receive the sacrament of his creative thought to make ourselves better!"

The Saints are fashioned for all eternity, but the fashion in substitute-saints is forever changing. The cult of the Apostle has now been eclipsed by that of the Guerrillero Heroico. Che Guevara has become more than a mere symbol of the Revolution in Cuba. His bearded features, sometimes accompanied by those of another fallen guerrilla leader, Camilo Cienfuegos, whose head is often shown framed in a wide sombrero as by a halo, preside over every meeting and adorn offices and homes which formerly had their prints of tutelary saints. The two heroes were amongst the 12—the number is symbolic and apparently fictitious, for the official list of the other ten has never been established—who landed in Cuba in 1956 to launch Fidel Castro's guerrilla campaign. The young are exhorted to emulate them in work and play, and to model themselves on Che's "New Man" who strives selflessly (through "moral incentives" rather than for material gain) to build the Socialist community and is ready to die in the performance of his "internationalist duty" (carrying out sub-versive activities in other countries). Che's cult has spread far beyond Cuba. In Bolivia, where he met his death directing guerrilla opera-tions near the village of La Higuera, the intercession of "St. Che Guevara" is invoked in the following anonymous verse :

Santo Che Guevara	St. Che Guevara
Patrón de La Higuera,	Patron saint of La Higuera
Reza por mi Patria	Pray for my country
Que siempre te espera !	Which ever awaits Thee !

To crown the cult, Cuba has now secured a precious relic—nothing less than the severed hands of the Heroic Guerrilla. "Che's hands are preserved perfectly," Fidel Castro has assured his devotees. "The hands in which he carried his weapons of freedom, with which he wrote down his brilliant ideas, with which he worked in the cane-fields. We will make something like a museum for Che"—Castro might more fittingly have said "shrine"—"even if it is only a makeshift affair. Che does not belong to Cuba, but to America. One day, these hands will be where the people of America want them to be. Meanwhile, our people will preserve them and our people will care for them." Nor is Che alone the centre of this guerrilla cultus. Other figures are associated with him, such as the young and brilliant Catholic priest Camilo Torres who, losing patience with the hidebound hierarchy and hope of replacing the ruling "oligarchy" of Colombia by a juster social order, joined a guerrilla band, attempted to ambush an army patrol and was himself gunned down.

The pseudo-saint resembles the authentic prototype in that he appears to identify himself with the needy and oppressed and to dedicate himself to improving their lot. If saints no longer emerge from within the framework of a Church grown estranged from the common folk, the latter will produce their own. They are likely to appear as heretics, rebels, revolutionaries or popular heroes. The social context determines the form which the phenomenon is likely to assume. Argentina, for example, attracted round the turn of the century large numbers of poor European immigrants who, rootless and secularized, formed an amorphous working class which remained unassimilated by the culture and social structure of the nation. This underprivileged mass of *descamisados* or "shirtless ones" was wooed by an army officer, Juan Perón, and carried him to power. Perón's appeal was greatly strengthened by his marriage to Eva Duarte, a woman of humble origins, in whom the *descamisados* saw one of themselves who had made good—fabulously good—reaching a pinnacle of wealth, beauty, power and success which was the fulfilment of every daydream. They delighted in her furs and jewels, much as their pious forebears had delighted in the richly clad, jewel-studded image of the Virgin they would carry in procession. Evita, moreover, was a Lady Bountiful lavishing gifts from her multi-million dollar social fund—sickness and holiday benefits, housing and medical care, presents for children, brides and suppliants of every kind. They called her the Madonna of the Americas, and she was officially styled "Spiritual Head of the Argentine Nation". (Plate 2.) Even before her death from cancer the Union of Workers in the Food Industry petitioned the Pope for her formal canonization. When she died, her ashes were reverently placed in a shrine in the Trade Union headquarters where they were venerated until their disappearance in the upheaval which attended the fall of Perón. One day they may well be returned to her devotees and the cult of the Madonna of the Americas be revived.

Brazil, with its very different racial and social climate, has produced pseudo-saints of a different stamp. In the backward, poverty-stricken North-East, where the people remain ignorant and superstitious and the priests inadequate in numbers and training to give them due pastoral care, popular Catholicism has fused with the African *macumba* cults of the former slaves. The process is described in Da Cunha's masterpiece *The Backlands* which tells the story of Antonio the Counsellor, the half-crazed wandering lay-preacher who led his devotees to form their own settlement at remote Canudos where they defied the godless Republic and awaited the return of the Portuguese martyr-king Sebastian. Friars were sent to Canudos to try to win back the heretics to orthodoxy but failed. Then came the troops, and after an epic and desperate defence Canudos was destroyed.

Other *beatos* and *santos* appeared in the wake of Antonio the Counsellor. The pseudo-saint does not necessarily see himself as a rebel, but the faith he inspires is by its nature subversive of the ecclesiastical and secular order. Another and more ambiguous figure who began to win fame at about the same time as the Canudos episode (1896-7) was Father Cicero, who attracted followers over a wide area centering round Joazeiro in the extreme south of Ceará. The church authorities grew alarmed at the cult of the parish priest and sent him to Rome where the authenticity of the miracles attributed to him was investigated without conclusive results. Father Cicero returned to Joazeiro, which continued to attract vast numbers of pilgrims and grew into a thriving city. Astute disciples attempted, with some success, to manipulate his prestige for political ends. Father Cicero, who survived until 1934, remains an enigma; he himself kept outside politics and inside the Church. The latter refrained from pronouncing on his alleged sanctity, but the common folk continued to remain passionately convinced of it. One can still find in North-East Brazil amulets which have a likeness of the miracle-working priest of Juazeiro on one side and that of the Virgin on the other.

*   *   *   *

These are fascinating byways for the historian, the social anthropologist and the political scientist to explore. Our concern here is rather with the men and women whom the Church, after the lengthy and meticulous enquiry known as the Process of beatification and canonization, has formally declared to be worthy objects for our veneration. Not necessarily, however, suitable in every respect for emulation, since the ways of life to which they felt called led often through regions untrod, inaccessible to later pilgrims, and disturbingly unlike the landscape in which our own lives are set. They form a company diverse in temperament, education, social status and vocation; a Dominican missionary amongst the natives of the Caribbean, a Franciscan amongst those of Tucumán, an Archbishop, a mulatto lay-brother with a gift for healing, three Jesuit martyrs in Paraguay and another who chose the living death of the negro slaves in Cartagena, two young women pursuing lives of mystic contemplation and works of charity in the bosom of their family—a diversity of gifts and callings but each sharing a common quality which may best be described by the unfashionable term "holiness".

The first feature which strikes us as common to these lives is their dedication to those whose need seemed greatest—*los de abajo*, "those below", the underdogs, in the title-phrase of a famous Mexican novel. The lowest strata of colonial society was composed of the Indians, especially those in bondage on the estates of the *encomenderos,* to whom their welfare, spiritual and temporal, was theoretically "entrusted" (*encomendado*) by the Crown, or the *indios bravos* still living in untamed savagery, paganism, and sometimes cannibalism. To these was soon added a still more servile and wretched caste—the negro slaves imported from Africa. To these Indians and negroes the missionaries devoted their principal labours, whilst *el arzobispo santo* spent more than half the 25 years of his ministry travelling through his vast diocese of Lima in the pastoral care of his scattered flock. Martín de Porres, belonging himself to the despised mulatto caste, sought out others still more miserable than himself to lavish his care upon and used his power of healing impartially for the relief of whoever stood in need. Rosa of Lima and Mariana of Quito, confined by the conventions and limitations to which their sex was subject, moved within a narrower range, but turned their own homes into clinic, soup-kitchen or class-room. The saints may belong in spirit to the realms above, but here they are always to be found ministering to *los de abajo*.

Another feature which characterizes all these lives is the balance they maintain between the active and the contemplative. St. Luis Bertrán and St. Francisco Solano leave their monastery cells to undertake immense journeys and the most intense missionary activity, then return once more to the peace of the cloister. St. Martín de Porres, whose days were so crammed with the manifold tasks of the infirmarian that he was credited with the faculty of "agility"—being in two places at once—spent half the night on his knees. St. Toribio, tireless administrator and organizer of councils and synods, traveller on endless diocesan visitations, passed hours in meditation and personal devotions. St. Rosa divided up every 24 hours so as to allow ten for her work as a seamstress and other household duties, two for sleep, and 12 for prayer and contemplation. The Jesuits of Paraguay—explorers, founders of settlements, farmers, masons and catechists—led lives rooted in the practice of St. Ignatius Loyola's *Spiritual Exercises* and in the discipline of unhurried mental prayer. All, in the differing circumstances of their lives, carried out the noble injunction of the Dominican Order—*contemplata aliis tradere*—to bring to others the fruit of contemplation.

The saints whose lives we shall be considering possessed qualities which their pious contemporaries accounted heroic virtues but which may strike us as peculiarities or even abnormalities. Poor as they all were in earthly possession, none lacked a plenteous supply of hairshirts and scourges. Asceticism has become alien to our way of thinking. Though we submit our bodies to discipline for athletic training, we no longer do so for spiritual training. We deny ourselves food for slimming but not for fasting. We even accept that some find sexual satisfaction in masochism, but we find it incredible that men should derive spiritual benefit from mortifying the flesh. The crown of thorns concealed by Rosa's garland of flowers and her bed of shards and stones, the stiff hair-shirts weighing down Mariana's slim figure, the merciless scourgings to which one and all, from Archbishop to lay-brother, submitted themselves as a matter of course—such things seem incomprehensible or even repulsive to us until we understand something of the saint's craving to share in the passion of Christ and the suffering of their fellows and to subdue those temptations of the flesh which they believed stood in the way of their loving union with God.

The vows of poverty, chastity and obedience ring strangely in the ears of the modern world. Poverty is something to be avoided at all costs for ourselves and to be banished as far as possible from the lives of others. The Franciscan concept of Lady Poverty, to be espoused for the treasures of virtue which lie concealed behind her veil, is far from us indeed. Further still is that of chastity, ill at ease in the permissive society where a respect for it would spell the ruin of a dozen industries. Furthest removed of all, perhaps, from our way of thinking is the virtue of obedience. If valued at all, it is less likely to be by the good Christian than by the disciplined Communist who follows out unquestioningly the dictates of his party. In these days of women's lib., we feel little disposed to imitate St. Rosa in subjecting herself so meticulously to her heedless parents that she would not take a glass of water or open her sewing-box without their express command. Or how many of us would wish to pray with St. Peter Claver that we might be blessed with the silent, uncomplaining obedience of the donkey? "If it is slandered, it keeps silent; if it is not fed, silence; if it is forgotten, silence; it never complains however much it is assailed or ill-treated because it has a donkey's patience. This is how the servant of God must behave; I stand before you, Lord, like a donkey."

But lest it be thought that the saints were a self-tormenting, gloomy lot, we should also see them, as they appeared to their contemporaries, God-intoxicated to the point of eccentricity or even folly; St. Francis Solano merrily playing his rebeck to the Indians in the wilderness, or celebrating Christmas "singing, dancing, and ringing a little bell"; St. Martín de Porres filling his monastery with sick cats and dogs and feeding them from the same plate as the kitchen mice, or happily going off to plant olives and medicinal herbs by the wayside for the benefit of future wayfarers; St. Rosa strumming her pious ditties to the guitar in the cool of her garden or singing duets with the nightingales at her bedroom window; the good Archbishop sitting down to picnic with the Indians and giving away all his food and the silver dishes on which it was being served; St. Peter Claver offering his banquets to the beggars and the lepers or squatting contentedly amongst the slaves—these are men and women surprised by a joy which is not of this world. It is related of the Franciscan friar St. Peter of Alcántara that he went through the fields singing his songs of praise aloud, so that those who heard him took him to be mad. "Oh what a goodly madness!" commented St. Teresa, "God grant that we might all behave likewise!"

The biographer who would write of such men and women, stripping the portrait from the layers of legend and moralizing which the piety of years has deposited in order to reveal the fresh colouring and firm contours beneath, sets himself an almost impossible task. Not only does the difference in social conditions, mental processes and *mores* of the age in which they lived make it hard to recreate the scene and assess the personality. The difficulty lies deeper. The saint is, by definition, one whose life is closely knit with God. We can glimpse only a tiny, external fragment of it. To reconstruct the whole from this fragment is like trying to reconstruct a lost symphony from a few surviving grace-notes. Of the favoured few who are vouchsafed the mysteries, fewer still are called to leave some record of the divine intimacies for the inspection of their confessors or the guidance of their fellows. We read of St. Mariana that her confessor once bade her describe her spiritual experience for the edification of her niece; she did so most reluctantly, and when the girl took up her pen to record the mysteries disclosed to her, all recollection of what she had heard was miraculously erased from her memory. Seldom, indeed, does the mystic draw aside the veil before the gaze of the onlooker.

Yet some inkling, nevertheless, is given. We sense a quality about these lives as different from the goodness of decent folk as genius is different from mere talent. A faint, elusive scent comes wafted to us down the ages. Some call it the odour of sanctity.

CHAPTER 2

Missionary to the Spanish Main— San Luis Bertrán

OF all the saints of South America, the one who is furthest removed from us in time, and perhaps in spirit too, is San Luis Bertrán. Even in his native Spain, his most recent biographer tells us, he is now largely forgotten. In South America, where he laboured for only seven years, oblivion is almost total. Time, it seems, is not alone responsible for this neglect. The same writer describes him as "the saint of contrasts". There are ambiguities and contradictions which today obscure the contours of a personality which nevertheless seemed sharp enough to his contemporaries. Saint Teresa was so convinced of his sanctity that she consulted him before embarking on her great work as a foundress. She, like many others, looked upon him as a man wholly committed to the will of God. But just what was this divine will for his own life? Studying such records as have come down to us, we are left with the strong impression that this question continually perplexed him. Hence the ambiguities, the contradictions, the scruples, the sudden decisions followed by as sudden changes of mind. In these tormenting uncertainties, perhaps, we may find that the saint is nearer to us today than might be supposed, however distant the *mores* of the age and the motives of the man.

The Bertráns (their name sometimes appears written as Bertrand or Beltrán) were a well-to-do and respected Valencian family who numbered amongst their forebears St. Vincent Ferrer, the Dominican friar who had won fame more than a century before for his missionary labours, his austerities and miracles, and for the part he played in healing the papal schism. Luis Bertrán's father was a distinguished lawyer who had harboured serious doubts about his vocation and had needed the apparition of St. Vincent and St. Bruno to remove his scruples on this score. From his earliest years, don Juan Luis Bertrán had been a devotee of St. Bruno, founder of the Carthusians, whose life of prayer and penance he thought of emulating in the seclusion of the Porta-Coeli monastery. Instead, he married and sired a child who died in infancy. When his young wife followed their child to the grave, don Juan Luis's thoughts turned again to the cloister and he was actually on his way to Porta-Coeli when the two saints intervened to make clear to him that his vocation was to remarry and remain in the world. They might have added that, if sainthood was not to be his portion, he would at least father one who was destined to become a saint.

Luis, the eldest of several children, was born to don Juan Luis in 1526. He grew up to be a delicate lad whose poor health was a constant worry to his mother. Don Juan Luis was more concerned by the inclination which his son soon began to show for following the religious life. The lawyer seems to have forgotten how strongly he himself had once felt attracted to such a vocation and he did his best to persuade the boy to follow his own profession. But Luis was determined to become a monk. His only doubt was whether he should enter a contemplative or a more active Order. First, he opted for the contemplatives, then finally for the more intellectual Order of Preachers. His father, reluctantly agreeing to let him take the tonsure, thought he had made the wrong choice and wrote that he would rather see him a Carthusian or a Hieronymite. The novice's reply has been preserved. In it he respectfully reminds his father that the Dominican friars occupy themselves with preaching and hearing confessions—"tasks which cannot be performed without contemplation and meditation"—and that although the novice-master had at first expressed doubts about his vocation, he was now convinced that Luis was suited for the Order, and so to turn elsewhere would be "to resist the Holy Ghost".

But Luis was still assailed by set-backs and uncertainties. He suffered a breakdown in health and had to spend four months convalescing at home. By the time he recovered, it seemed to him that he was called to prepare for the defence of the faith against the Lutheran heresy then raging in Germany. Luis set off for the University of Salamanca, but was forced to recognize that he was not cut out for a scholar's life. He was soon back in the Dominican monastery at Valencia where, at the early age of 23, he was entrusted with the exacting duties of novice-master. The young monk had already begun to acquire that reputation for personal sanctity and the cure of souls which was to spread steadily far beyond the radius of his monastery walls.

For the next ten years there is little to relate. In 1555, the peaceful rhythm of the cloistered life was interrupted by the ravages of plague. The monks laboured valiantly amongst its victims in the city, and more than a score of them were themselves struck down. The survivors were dispersed amongst monasteries which were less exposed to the plague and the resulting famine, Fray Luis being assigned to the modest house of Santa Ana de Albaida, some 100 kilometres from Valencia, where he proved himself a vigorous administrator. By the end of the decade he was back again in Valencia instructing his novices. Amongst them was Vicente Justiniano Antist who became his fervent disciple and later biographer. To him we owe a story which illustrates the unsettled nature of the times and the character of our saint.

Valencia, and all the eastern coast of Spain, was then in constant danger of attack by Moslem pirates who would swoop down from their lairs in North Africa to pillage the cities and carry off captives. The danger was all the greater in that large numbers of Moriscos—nominally converted Moslems—were employed as agricultural labourers in those parts and might be tempted to make common cause with the raiders. The effrontery of the latter reached such a pitch that they would land with impunity and swagger through the streets of Valencia demanding ransoms for the Christian prisoners. Antist relates that news of one such raid was brought to Fray Luis whilst he was with his novices in the monastery garden. The Dominican's gentle mien, we are told, changed to righteous indignation, and bidding his charges kneel down, they prayed aloud that God would no longer permit such scandalous affronts to his people, and recited together the verses of the 83rd psalm:—"Hold not Thy tongue, O God, keep not still silence; refrain not Thyself, O God!" The raiders, after parading through the town, re-embarked in their galleys and headed out to sea where a squall suddenly blew up and sent them to the bottom. Fray Luis was filled with mingled exultation and remorse. God had dramatically answered their prayer! But scruples at once began to arise in his mind, not on account of the fate which the miscreants had suffered, but "because he had caused the brothers to pray so vehemently to God to take vengeance on the Moors". Santiago's sword was indeed forever poised above the head of the enemies of the faith; but was it perhaps against Christian charity to be too eager to see it descend?

The mind of Fray Luis, it would seem, was in constant tension between what we have described as the spirit of Santiago and the gentler compulsion of self-sacrificing love. In 1560, the year before the chastisement of the Moors, he had received a letter from St. Teresa. The saint of Avila was about to embark on her reform of the Carmelite Order, but did not wish to take so daring a step without first consulting one whom she considered wiser and more holy than herself. Fray Luis she had never met, but his fame as a man of God gifted with searching spiritual insight had already reached her and she resolved to write to him. After several months' prayer and reflection, Fray Luis penned a confident reply. "I tell you in the name of the Lord to take heart for this great enterprise, for He will assist and favour it. In His name I assure you that 50 years will not pass before your Order will become one of the most illustrious in the Church of God." The man who was so fearful of mistaking the hand of God in his own life could see it clearly outstretched above others.

The novice-master was soon to be a prey to fresh doubts and scruples as to his own vocation, and to take a decision which set him upon an unexpected course. One day there arrived in the convent a young *indio* requesting admission as a novice. The term *indio* was used at this time in Spain to designate not only one of the indigenous population of the continent which Columbus had taken to be India but anyone born in "The Indies". We may thus take it that the new-comer was a Creole, a Spaniard born in America, or perhaps a *mestizo,* with some tincture of Indian blood, but hardly a full-blooded Indian, for it was then only in the rarest cases that such a one was accepted for the priesthood. Perhaps he was also an adventurer, for many were attracted to the Church, no less than to the bands of con-quistadores, by the prospect of making their fortune. Father Antist tells us that the papers which the *indio* presented at the monastery were later discovered to be forgeries and the *indio* a fraud. "He lived with us for more than a year," Father Antist relates, "and as he had never been a novice, nor brought up in the Order, he caused the novices no small trouble, and even the Father himself; but I believe that God permitted this deceit on the part of the *indio* in order to try the patience of the novices and their novice-master. When the Pro-vincial had a mind to punish the *indio* Father Bertrán fell on his knees and interceded for him saying 'If the *indio* has done wrong, I am the one to blame!' "

The culprit, it transpired, came from the Spanish Main, and how-ever shamelessly he deceived the friars about his own qualifications, he seems to have given them a truthful and moving account of the benighted conditions under which the people of his land lived. "Thanks to all the things which this *indio* related about the sufferings they endured," Antist writes, "Our Lord inspired him [Fray Bertrán] with a consuming thirst to suffer martyrdom on their behalf, and to this end he resolved to go to the Indies where he gathered that the Indians often killed those who preached to them, and sometimes even ate them. But he could not fulfil his desire until there came two Fathers from the West Indies who also spoke to him of the lack which there was there of preachers in the Kingdom of New Granada for the conversion of the heathen". Moved by the words of these two missionaries, Fray Luis presented himself before the Prior and declared that he felt the call to go to America. The Prior demurred, spoke of the harvest which still needed to be gathered in Spain, and seemed to have dissuaded him. Fray Luis returned crestfallen and confused to his novices. A companion who had volunteered to accompany him set off alone. But the call continued to obsess him; yes, it *was* God's will that he too should go! Again he appeared before the Prior, insisted with renewed eloquence, and finally won his Superior's permission and blessing. One of his younger brothers, who overtook him on the road to Seville and tried to induce him to turn back, was likewise forced to acquiesce and gave him money to buy a donkey, for Fray Luis was so frail that even the journey to Seville seemed likely to prove too much for him.

His brother friars were loth to see Fray Luis leave, for his poor health and known longing for martyrdom made it seem unlikely that they would set eyes on him again. Antist also assures us that he was much beloved, though the portrait which he paints of the novice-master turned missionary is somewhat forbidding. "From the time of his profession," he writes, "he was very austere, sparing in the use of food and drink, eager to afflict his body with scourges, hair-shirt and vigils, and he was ever diligent in prayer. In conversation he always spoke with a certain gravity. I never remember him making the slightest joke or relating any idle talk or indulging in laughter at other things." Though an eloquent preacher, he was excessively reserved and uncommunicative; "he never listened to news and was never heard to recount to others what he might have seen or heard himself." As a child he had been much given to tears and was noted for his *condición triste:* "his whole life, like Jeremiah's, was passed in sorrow and affliction for the sins of the world." His love of penance was extreme; not content with hair-shirt and discipline, he is said, when in the torrid forest of New Granada, to have spent many watches of the night with his body bared to the tormenting sting of the mosquitoes. In physical appearance he was tall and lean, with a long face and unusually bright eyes. Such was the man who, at the age of 36, stepped ashore at Cartagena, the chief port of New Granada on the Spanish Main, to begin his career as a missionary.

*   *   *   *

The Order of Preachers had done notable pioneering work in the evangelizing of the New World. Its voice had been the first to be raised in protest against the scandalous abuses to which the Spanish conquest soon gave rise. On the Sunday before Christmas of 1511—less than twenty years after Columbus had set out on his first voyage—a Dominican friar called Antonio de Montesinos preached a sermon passionately upbraiding the conquistadores and officials of Española, the first island to be settled by the Europeans in the Caribbean, for their heartless maltreatment of the Indians. "By what right," he thundered, "do you keep these Indians in such cruel and horrible servitude? Are they not men? Do they not possess rational souls? Are you not obliged to love them as yourselves?" The indignant Spaniards demanded that the friar should be silenced. But the little community of Dominicans, under their Superior Pedro de Córdoba, stood firm, and the next Sunday the attack from the pulpit was resumed. It was not until the following year, after strong representations had been made at Court, that the troublesome friar was recalled to Spain. His words did not stem the tide of Spanish conquest or mitigate its cruelties. But they troubled the conscience of some, including that of the young conquistador Bartolomé de las Casas who, three years later, was to undergo a radical conversion and to win fame—or notoriety in the view of many contemporaries—for a life-time spent in tireless denunciation of Spanish iniquities and in defence of the Indians.

Pedro de Córdoba and his friars believed—as did Las Casas after his conversion—that the Indians could and should be brought to a knowledge of the Catholic faith and civilized ways by peaceful means. Missionaries, armed only with the word of God and the example of virtuous living, would go amongst them and win them from paganism. But if they were to succeed in their labours, it was essential that the conquistadores, whose greed and violence would quickly undo their work, should be forbidden access to the territories set aside for the missionaries. The latter had already suffered at their hands and were to see their work constantly frustrated by the sins and follies of their compatriots. The Caribbean coast of the Isthmus and the adjoining Spanish Main or Tierra Firme, comprising the northern shores of what is now Venezuela and Colombia, had been explored by Columbus and the early Spanish navigators. The country was wild and the inhabitants fierce. Its chief wealth was in pearls which the Spaniards, operating mainly from a base established on the island of Cubagua, opposite Cumaná, obtained first by barter and then by kidnapping the natives and forcing them to dive for them. Further to the west, the Crown granted licences for exploration and settlement; one to Alonso de Ojeda, for what is now the north coast of Colombia, another to Diego de Nicuesa, along the Isthmus, in today's Panama, Costa Rica and Nicaragua.

In 1513, a handful of Dominican friars established a small monastery at Cumaná and began to win the confidence of the neighbouring tribes. But the slavers soon undid the work of the missionaries. Suspecting that the friars were secretly in league with their compatriots, the natives turned on them and martyred them. Pedro de Córdoba urged Las Casas, now back in Spain, to petition the Crown to grant the Dominicans a concession on Tierra Firme where they could work freely without interference from Spanish adventurers. A royal order was issued to this effect in 1516, and two years later the Dominicans and Franciscans established new outposts on the Spanish Main. The Indians seemed ready to forget their suspicions and some even came forward for baptism. But the following year, "either because of their natural wickedness, or because they were forced to labour in the pearl-fishing," as the historian Gómara observes, a fresh revolt broke out, the monasteries were burned down, and two Dominicans killed as they were preparing to celebrate mass. Survivors brought tales of the disaster to the Spanish authorities on Española, who seized on this pretext to prepare a major punitive expedition against the natives of Tierra Firme.

It was at this critical moment that Las Casas returned from Spain intent on putting into effect an entirely new type of pacific colonization. In place of the incursions for pearls and slaves, or attempts at permanent conquest and subjugation, he proposed to found settlements of peaceable farmers, dignified by the title of "Knights of the Golden Spur", and missionaries. But the territory granted by the Crown for this venture was precisely where the natives had already tasted and reacted against the traditional methods of Spanish conquest, and where Captain Ocampo was at that very moment preparing to teach them a dire lesson. Las Casas, pleading, threatening, invoking the royal authority, did his utmost to avert the punitive expedition and secure a free hand for his own enterprise. The conquistadores turned a deaf ear to his arguments whilst his own colonists melted away amongst the ranks of the armed adventurers. All he could achieve was a fatal compromise by which the few who remained with him were able to join forces with the mission outposts, now re-established by the Franciscans, whilst Ocampo's men pursued their work by fire and sword. The outcome was inevitable—another Indian rising against the missionaries and the complete collapse of this first venture in peaceable colonization. Las Casas, deeply disheartened, withdrew to a monastery and joined the Dominican Order. But his vision, though dimmed for a time by this set-back, never faded. Sixteen years later, with the help of his brother Dominicans, he embarked on a fresh

scheme of pacification by missionary work in the wild and still unsub-
dued province of Tuzutlán, today a part of Guatemala. The venture
at first gave promise of spectacular success and the friars seemed to be
accomplishing what the soldiers had failed to achieve, thereby justify-
ing the name of Vera Paz—True Peace—by which the once troubled
region was now known. But after little more than a dozen years disaster struck again. The Indians rose against the missionaries, killing
some thirty of them and driving the rest from the land. By 1550, those
who had always claimed that the Indians could only be reduced by
brute force seemed to have been amply vindicated.

Not all the friars shared Las Casas' unshakeable conviction that the
Indians had a fundamentally innocent nature which must in time
respond to Christian preaching and example. The famous Franciscan
missionary Motolinía, whose selfless labours for the Indians of Mexico
none could gainsay, often took vehement issue with him. Even
amongst his own Order of Preachers there were those who held very
different views. Fray Domingo de Betanzos, the founder of the
Dominican province of Mexico, though he was later to change his
opinions and retract them formally on his death-bed, presented a
memorial to the Council of the Indies declaring that the Indians were
no better than beasts and fully merited God's punishment. Fray Tomás
Ortiz, who had headed the earliest party of Dominicans to be sent to
Mexico and was later appointed to the see of Santa Marta, the first
port founded by the Spaniards on the coast of New Granada, was
even more categorical in his denunciations. "The men of Tierra
Firme," he wrote "eat human flesh. There is no justice amongst them;
they go naked and know neither honour nor shame. They are crazed
and impervious to reason, holding it of no account to kill or be killed.
They never keep faith, unless it be to their advantage. They glory in
drunkenness, for they make wine of different herbs, fruits, roots and
grains; they also intoxicate themselves with smoke and certain herbs
which make them lose their reason. The youths show no obedience or
courtesy to the old, neither sons to their fathers. They are treacherous
and vengeful. They are slothful and great enemies of religion. When
they forget things which they have learned appertaining to the Faith
they say that such matters are for Castille and not for themselves, and
that they have no wish to change their customs or their gods. They
show no compassion towards the sick, and even their neighbours and
relatives they leave alone when they are dying and take them out into
the forests and abandon them there with a little bread and water.
They keep neither faith nor order. The older they grow the worse
they become. Up to the age of ten or 12 they seem capable of some

education and virtues; but as they grow older, they become like brutes. We who have treated with them know this by experience, as can be certified by Fray Pedro de Córdoba, on whose behalf I am writing all this, and with whom this and other things which I pass over in silence have been discussed."

*   *   *   *

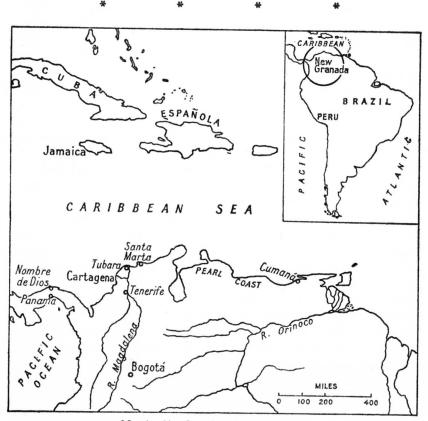

Map 1.   New Granada and the Caribbean

With some prelates so unenthusiastic about their barbarous flock and others grieved over the misdemeanours of their own compatriots —the Bishop excommunicated the Governor of Cartagena for persistent ill-treatment of the natives—missionary endeavour on the Spanish Main languished. Cartagena itself, founded less than 20 years before by Pedro de Heredia, had not yet grown into the great walled fortress of later years. It was still a modest settlement perched on the edge of a superb bay. But the Dominicans already had a small monastery, and there Fray Luis was able to rest a while to regain his strength after the fatigues of the voyage and to prepare for work in the *doctrina,* or missionary parish, to which he was shortly assigned. This was at Tubará, today a place of some 2,000 inhabitants in Colombia's Atlántico Department a few miles inland from the flourishing port of Baranquilla. There he remained for three years, reaping a rich harvest of converts in the surrounding region; his biographers speak of 10,000 or more, as recorded by entries made in the saint's handwriting in the baptismal register, and all, moreover, well instructed by him in the Christian faith. A well of drinking water, reputedly discovered by the saint, is pointed out today to any who visit Tubará, and also a chalice, but one clearly of a later date, said to have been used by him. We know that the centre for Fray Luis' later missionary activity was at Tenerife, a small town on a bluff overlooking the great Magdalena River, the main highway leading inland to the upland capital of Bogotá. Where else the saint laboured remains obscure, for the other places mentioned in Antist's narrative have since disappeared or changed their names. All we can say is that he seems to have travelled widely through the present departments of Atlántico, Bolívar and Magdalena, and perhaps through parts of Antioquia and Panama, the foothills of the Sierra Nevada above Santa Marta, and to some of the small off-shore Caribbean islands.

Of the seven years that Fray Luis spent in New Granada there remains tantalizingly little of which we can speak with any certainty. "Would that many other things done by this servant of God in the Indies had been recorded," Antist exclaims. "But hitherto we are ignorant of them, nor I fear shall we ever know them except in Heaven!" We may well share the hagiographer's pious regret whilst wondering why he failed to make better use of the opportunities afforded him of learning those things from the lips of the servant of God during the dozen years of life which remained to Fray Luis after his return from America. No doubt this can be explained in part by the saint's well-known modesty and reticence and by his habit of remarking ambiguously when asked whether some supernatural event attributed to him had really occurred, that miracles, in any case, were not necessarily a mark of sanctity since God may choose to work through the meanest instruments. Often, moreover, the saint had been alone in his adventures, or accompanied only by a few Indians or negroes, or by companions such as the almost equally heroic Father Vero (not so much as mentioned by Antist) who stayed on in America. Nor do any physical vestiges remain of Fray Luis' sojourn in those poor and untamed parts, and only the roughest idea can today be gained of the scene of his missionary labours and the itinerary of his journeys.

Where he succeeded in converting the wild Indians, Fray Luis, before passing on, "would leave the Creed and the Commandments of God in writing, saying that it was very necessary to do this so that if anyone should come that way who could read, they could repeat them to the Indians so that they should not forget." He seems to have been accompanied sometimes either by one or two converted Indians who served as best they could as interpreters, or by negroes, probably slaves who had been brought over to Cartagena from Africa and then assigned to the use of the friars. He also occasionally found some compatriot who was willing to accompany him for a time until discouraged by the dangers and rigours which the saint seemed to welcome rather than avoid. One of these volunteers, Antist tells us, was a certain Jerónimo Cardilla, a lad from Valencia, whose office it was to carry the saint's belongings—a small bag containing his bible and breviary. Fray Luis took literally the injunction which Christ had given to his disciples to carry neither scrip, money, nor bread, and subsisted only on what was given him or on the fruit plucked from time to time in the forest. When Jerónimo prudently stored some fruit away in his bag against the morrow, the inexorable saint soon discovered this indulgence and threw it away. This proved too much for Jerónimo who turned back at the next village, despite the saint's gloomy prediction that he would lead a wretched life and come to a bad end. Antist relates that Jerónimo returned to Spain, entered the service of a Spanish nobleman, and outlived his old master. The latter charitably forgave his desertion, and when Jerónimo was wounded in a brawl with a fellow servant, the saint appeared to him in a dream and healed his injured head.

As for the miracles ascribed to the saint, we read that he effected many marvellous cures and enjoyed supernatural protection from attack by wild beasts or Indians. The latter, moreover, understood his preaching by virtue of the gift of tongues bestowed upon him, as upon the Apostles at Pentecost, of whom we read in the Acts that they addressed the Jews gathered in Jerusalem from every part of the world, and that "every man heard them speak in his own language." So the Indians of New Granada, comprising men of many different tribes and dialects, are said to have been miraculously enabled to comprehend the preaching of the Spanish friar. "It would sometimes happen," writes Antist, "that the Indians understood him when he spoke to them in Spanish, and although he would preach to them through an interpreter they would tell him that they understood him direct without the need of any interpreter, which never happened when others preached. And when Fray Luis Bertrán was asked whether it was true that the Indians understood him in this way he replied that it was . . . The reason why Our Lord vouchsafed that he should be understood when he spoke Spanish was the following, as he once told a devoted follower of his. He had an interpreter who either from ignorance or malice misinterpreted what he preached to the Indians; and when he understood this (whether by revelation or in some other way) he prayed Our Lord to give him the grace to be understood by them, and this was granted."

But not all the Indians responded gladly to the Christian message. Many clung to their pagan ways and some attempted to rid themselves of the troublesome friar, especially when he exhorted them to make a bonfire of their idols. From all their attacks Fray Luis seemed miraculously protected. But his proselytes proved more vulnerable, and Antist has a sad story to tell of the fate which befell one of them. "He converted a boy," his biographer writes, "and baptized him with the name of Luis, who was virtuously brought up and helped him in the celebration of the mass. But as the Devil was sorely grieved at this, and one day when the Indians were praying to their idol to give them maize (which is their corn) the idol answered that he would give them nothing, neither make any reply, until they sacrificed the lad to him. So when Fray Luis was away, the Indians seized the boy and sacrificed him to the idol. When the Father returned and asked for him, they replied that the caymans (a sort of crocodile which often come out of the great rivers and boldly swallow up those who venture near the banks) had eaten him up. The Father was much grieved at this; still more when he discovered the wickedness of the Indians and of the Devil."

Fray Luis all but succumbed himself to a more subtle attack. The poisoned arrows of the Caribbean savages had been much dreaded by the *conquistadores;* a few drops smeared on an arrow tip were enough to bring its victim an agonizing death, and one chronicler has described how the Spaniards sought desperately for an antidote by wounding an Indian with one of his own arrows and then secretly watching him as he crawled off into the forest to look for the herbs which would salve his wound. The friar neither knew nor cared about any such remedy, for he was resigned, and even eager, to accept martyrdom. The story is told by Antist in the following words : "When he was preaching to the Indians in the lowlands beneath the Sierra of Santa Marta, he converted and baptized many of them. He then found a village where he could make no headway, even though he preached for some days. He learned that they venerated there the bones of an old priest who had lived in that place of yore and that the devil had put into their hearts the belief that if those bones were to be taken away the heavens would fall on them. So they took good care of them and did them great honour and celebrated their feasts and drunken orgies in front of them. The Father therefore entered the temple by stealth and stole the bones and carried them off for two or three leagues. When the pagans learned of this, or suspected it, they plotted with an evil old priest to put poison into his drink. In this way he was suddenly seized with a mortal fever and a burning of the bowels and he lay stricken at death's door. After five days he vomited up a snake and found some relief, although a like poison was once administerd to another Carmelite father, from which (after confessing to Father Bertrán) he very soon died, and they found his stomach full of worms. I remember the Father telling me that in those days when he was at death's door, the thing which most grieved him was the absence of any priest who might receive his confession and administer communion to him, for the only Christians who were with him were two negroes. But he found great consolation in a wooden crucifix which hung from his rosary, to which he tearfully commended his soul.

"When the Indians saw that he was recovering from the poison, more than three hundred pagans came together and made ready their arrows to kill him. One of the negroes loaded an arquebus to defend him, but the father would not let him. Instead, he summoned the Indian chiefs and began to preach with great zeal, being grieved at their perdition. He told them that they should now understand that the Devil had been lying to them, for the heavens had not fallen on them nor had any other great disaster come upon them as the Devil had threatened. But seeing that they would pay no heed or seek conversion, and holding that God does not force or compel men to be baptized, he permitted the bones to be returned to them." A later biographer, Alonso de Zamora, who wrote a history of the Dominican province in which the famous incident occurred, gives a rather different version at this point which seems more in keeping with the saint's unyielding spirit. In later years, according to Zamora, he was often heard to exclaim: "If I had been able to get up and stand on my feet to defend them, I would have died a thousand deaths in order to stop the pagans carrying off those bones!"

However this may have been, the Indians were dumbfounded to see that their poison had not killed the friar and their anger was suddenly turned to superstitious veneration, so that, as Antist relates, "they would have made gifts to him of many fowls and peacocks in exchange for their idol. But he refused to accept anything from them, and they again made to kill him, and would have done so had he not been rescued by a *cacique* whom he had previously converted. And so to save him from this danger, when the Indians had made off, the two negroes and some friendly natives carried him on their shoulders for five leagues, and then embarked him in a canoe and took him to a place where Pedro de Salazar, an *encomendero* of those parts, took him into his house, and there he lay sick with fever for many months." Zamora adds that in five days of agonizing pain he lost all his hair and his toe- and finger-nails. The ordeal seems to have left him permanently weakened and he continued to suffer fits of vertigo and severe stomach disorders to the end of his life.

Fray Luis' marvellous immunity from the mortal effects of the Indians' poison has become the most celebrated episode of the saint's life. Zurbarán painted a splendid picture of him holding the poisoned cup, from which a brilliantly coloured scarlet and green serpent rears its vicious head, whilst in the background the saint is seen preaching to the Indians and burning their idols (Plate 3). Round the undoubted fact of the attempted poisoning, hearsay and legend have added their accretions. The poisoned cup becomes a communion chalice in which the consecrated wine robs the venom of its sting, whilst the saint himself deliberately quaffs the potion to prove his God's miraculous power over the forces of nature. Antist himself, after giving the account quoted above, seems to refer to a second occasion when "in order to convert a *cacique*, Fray Luis drank a cup of poison and it did him no harm". Father Abiñón, another biographer, makes a similar claim. To drink poison as a challenge to God to perform a miracle seems scarcely in keeping with a saint's humility or the prudent fear of doing anything which might "tempt God". On the human level, to court a second poisoning after undergoing the atrocious agony of the first would suggest an almost masochistic pitch of foolhardy heroism. Certainly the saint was prepared for martyrdom and may even have sought it. Providence ordained that he should suffer its pangs without wearing its crown. Or perhaps, since his body was never thereafter wholly free from the effect of the Indians' poison, we can accept his biographer's assertion that his remaining days were one continual martyrdom.

Fray Luis Bertrán's life and character leave many questions unanswered. One strange episode amongst those recorded in the Process of Canonization suggests that, even in the midst of his missionary labours, when the hand of God was so manifestly outstretched to

protect him, Fray Luis continued to be assailed by "scruples". Was he
following his true vocation? Could the Prior, and the good brothers
who had striven to dissuade him from setting out for America, have
been right? Was he more suited, after all, to the contemplative life?
Once, when on his way to visit some Indian neophytes, Fray Luis fell
in with a stranger whom Antist describes as a "hermit"—a curious
personage to find amongst the forests of the Spanish Main. The hermit began to discourse piously of the celestial joys of the contemplative
life, and finally taxed the friar with having rejected his true calling
in order to undertake an unrewarding ministry amongst savages. Fray
Luis was shaken and half convinced by the hermit's words, but
suddenly recognized them as a temptation and the stranger as a manifestation of Lucifer himself. No sooner had the friar received this
enlightenment and made the sign of the cross over the false hermit
than the latter, "uttering fearful howls", disappeared into the woods.

Why then, may we ask, did the man of God, resisting all temptations to return to the peace of the cloister and still aflame with a desire
to win heathen souls for Christ, choose to go back to Spain after only
seven years in the mission-field? His biographers leave us in no doubt
that his recall came, at his own request, just after he had been
nominated to take charge of the Dominican monastery at Santa Fé,
the capital of New Granada. Why did the man who was to be
America's first canonized saint turn his back so readily on the New
World? The rather defeatist explanation offered in the Bull of Canonization cannot surely tell the whole story : "Seeing the oppression of
the natives by certain officials, who did not hesitate to wound and
even to kill them, and finding that he could not tolerate what he was
powerless to prevent, he obtained an obedience to return to Spain."
Antist bears this out but hints that there was something more—
"scruples", and perhaps an unwillingness to accept the intransigent
views of the most controversial figure of his Order and of his age in the
great dispute over the nature of the Indians and the ethics of Spanish
conquest, the now nonagenarian but still indomitable Bartolomé de
las Casas. "At the end of some years," Antist records, "Fray Luis
resolved to return to Spain, since he was much grieved to see the
cruelty of some *conquistadores* and *encomenderos* who not only often
killed the Indians for trifling reasons, but prevented any preaching.
And it might sometimes occur that when he had been preaching to a
great number of Indians, the *encomendero* would come in and drive
them out of the church shouting—'To work, curse you !' And as they
were not only unarmed but also quite unclothed (for there are parts
of that province where the Indians go stark naked) they would quickly

be gone and leave him alone in the pulpit. But—as he many times told me—what finally convinced him to return to Spain was a letter which he received from Fray Bartolomé de las Casas . . . The gist of this letter which the Bishop (las Casas) wrote him was that he should zealously attend to the conversion of the Indians and look well before he confessed or gave absolution to those *conquistadores* and *encomenderos* who, not content with the privileges they had received from the Crown, dealt tyrannically with the natives, against the express intent of His Majesty. As Father Bertrán greatly venerated the learning and goodness of the Bishop, he was filled with a mighty longing to return to Spain so as to free himself from scruples."

Fray Luis himself suffered at the hands of wicked *encomenderos*. One whom he had rebuked for his immoral life tried to get even by sending a loose woman to seduce him, but the fearsome penances which the saint inflicted on his flesh had made it proof against such temptation. Fray Luis had equally received kindness and respect from his compatriots in the New World. It was an *encomendero* who had taken him into his own home and cared for him whilst he was recovering from the Indians' poison. Perhaps Las Casas' sweeping condemnation of all *conquistadores* and *encomenderos* seemed to him excessive. Fray Luis would rebuke erring Spaniards and prophesy their doom if they persisted in their evil ways, but we do not read of him refusing them on principle the comfort of the sacraments. His own experience of the Indians was unlikely to lead him to share Las Casas' naïve belief in their universal goodness. He was a stern man, stern to himself, stern towards wickedness in high places, but stern too towards all who hardened their hearts against the Christian message, whether the Indians of the New World, or the nominally converted Moslems who still remained secretly attached to their old faith in Spain. Antist records an incident which occurred two years before the saint's death and which throws light on his attitude in this respect. The Viceroy of Valencia wrote to consult the holy man as to what should be done with those impenitent and untrustworthy Moriscos. The saint's reply was given in a letter dated 30 December, 1579. In it, he refers to "the great hardness of heart which they display, since nearly all (and God grant it may not be quite all!) are heretics and, what is worse, apostates . . . and clearly show hatred for the Christian religion and observe the ceremonies of Mahomet as far as they are able." Many of those ex-Moslems, or their forefathers, had been forcibly converted. "That was not well done," Fray Luis declares, for baptism should be accepted freely. But since Christians they were, yet for fifty years had made no progress in the faith though treated with "kindness and indulgence," it was now necessary "to compel them to adhere to the faith of Jesus Christ and renounce the sect of Mahomet by severity and punishment." Above all, they should be forbidden to speak Arabic. Their women should not be allowed to marry until they had learned the Christian catechism. Their children should not even be granted baptism so long as they remained in the care of their parents, as it was certain that they would become apostates. As for any further steps that needed to be taken, the King should place the whole problem before the Pope.

This letter of Fray Luis to the Viceroy of Valencia must give us pause. If this was the stern treatment recommended for the Moriscos of Spain—and thirty years later the King was to settle matters by driving all of them, men, women and children, from his domains—how did Fray Luis really look upon the Indians of America? How could he urge "severity and punishment" for the one, yet have been willing to lay down his own life in martyrdom for the others? Could the voice raised to urge that the use of Arabic should be forbidden be the same as had once preached to the natives through the gift of tongues? Much remains obscure and perplexing in the life of Fray Luis Bertrán. His declining years were passed uneventfully in Valencia, many of them in his former office of novice-master and later as Prior in his old monastery. Even in the evening of his life the old doubts and scruples never entirely left him. The temptation symbolized by his encounter with the false hermit in the forest of New Granada recurred in a different form. Fray Luis all but decided to leave the Dominican Order, in which he had spent his life, and join the Carthusians, strictest of the contemplative orders. Their monastery of Porta-Coeli stood ready to receive him, as it had once been ready to receive his vacillating father. But once again, just as his father had been prevented by the apparition of the saints from becoming a Carthusian monk, so Fray Luis was given to understand that this path was not for him and that he should remain with the Dominicans. "He did so for three reasons," Antist declares. "First, for the great love he bore St. Dominic and St. Vincent Ferrer, and all the saints of the Order and the many good religious who today live in it. Secondly, because he realized that even there [at Porta-Coeli] he would not escape from the many visitors who insisted on seeing him. Thirdly, because they persuaded him that it must be a temptation of the Devil in order to deprive the devout of the benefit they received from his conversation and sermons. Thus it was that he resolved to continue in his first calling, which was the Order of Preachers."

Spain was experiencing the full force of the great wave of mysticism then sweeping through her religious life. There was carried with it too a froth of pseudo-mystics, *alumbrados* and fraudulent or deluded ecstatics of every sort. Fray Luis sternly denounced such aberrations from the pulpit. But even here, in this twilight world of the spirit, was it always possible to distinguish the true from the false, the voice of God from the voice of the Devil? Only by the light vouchsafed from on high for the discernment of spirits. In Valencia there was living a devout Franciscan friar called Nicolás Factor, famous for his visions and revelations, which form the subject of many of Zurbarán's pictures. A close friendship sprang up between this Franciscan mystic and the austere Dominican who could never quite decide whether to follow the path of contemplation or that of apostolic militancy.

At all events, the seven years of labour amongst the Indians remained an interlude of heroic activity in the life of the Spanish monk. There is nothing to suggest that the great missionary enterprise of the Indies formed a particular object of his later thoughts or words; he took no part in its continuing controversies and left no writings about it. He died (1581), as he had been born, in Spain, and his whole character bears an indelibly Spanish stamp. Yet those seven years in the New World had left their mark of heroic sanctity. When, in 1671, Fray Luis was canonized by the Pope, America could claim its first saint. Nineteen years later he was proclaimed the patron of New Granada.

CHAPTER 3

El Arzobispo Santo —
San Toribio de Mogrovejo

IF the gospel word had fallen upon stony ground along the shores of
the Caribbean, it promised a far richer harvest in Peru. There the
Inca had ruled over a populous and well-ordered empire. It even
seemed possible that his people had been vouchsafed some foreknow-
ledge of the Christian faith. Though sun-worship had been the official
religion, Viracocha the Creator-God had also been adored, and prayers
addressed to him which breathed an almost Christian piety. The
Indians were acquainted with rites which seemed to foreshadow the
sacraments of baptism, confession, and even the Eucharist, and institutions such as the Virgins of the Sun which curiously resembled
Catholic convents. Some missionaries maintained that St. Thomas or
St. Bartholomew had undoubtedly found their way to the New World
and that the natives still preserved glimmerings of the faith preached
to them by an Apostle.

But no one could claim that the first proclamation of the Catholic
faith by a Spanish friar struck any spark of recognition in the breast
of the Inca and his suite who listened only with bewilderment and
mounting indignation. The scene is one of the most famous and
dramatic in all history. Atahualpa, borne on his gorgeous litter and
surrounded by his warriors in the great square at Cajamarca, is
addressed by Fray Vicente de Valverde whilst the Spaniards wait in
ambush. Valverde recites the Summons or *Requerimiento* summarizing
the Christians' creed and the reasons for their coming to claim
suzerainty for the King of Spain. The friar holds in his hand a breviary
which the Inca first examines curiously and then throws to the ground.
What next transpires has been variously recorded. The version commonly accepted is that the friar, moved to righteous indignation, calls
out to the waiting Spaniards to avenge the insult to the word of God.
At all events, they rush out, seize the person of the Inca, and massacre
a great number of his attendants. Within a few minutes, the soldiers
of Santiago have triumphed over the children of the Sun.

Tradition may have done less than justice to the memory of the Dominican friar. We see him only at this fateful hour in Cajamarca, urging on the Spaniards to their work of bloodshed. But later, named Bishop of Cuzco and vested with powers as Defender of the Indians, he is on record as repeatedly intervening to mitigate the *conquistadores'* harsh treatment of the natives. But it was then almost too late; the harvest was already spoiled, not so much through any failure or fanaticism on the part of the missionaries, but because the *conquistadores,* falling out amongst themselves and plunging the country into civil war, prevented the Church from carrying out its task. The institutional framework, it is true, was slowly taking shape, *doctrinas* and dioceses were being mapped out, churches built, and the ecclesiastical structure gradually established. But the spirit which should animate it all still languished. The first Archbishop of Lima, don Jerónimo de Loaysa, died exhausted by these labours and by endeavours to reconcile his compatriots, and the new see was left without a shepherd.

*   *   *   *

On the morning of 11 May, 1581, whilst Fray Luis Bertrán lay stricken with his last illness in Valencia, Lima made ready to welcome its new archbishop. Rugs and embroideries hung from the windows, music and fireworks enlivened the streets, and bands of gaily attired dancing-boys paraded beneath triumphal arches, one of which bore the prelate's coat of arms. Only a week before a new Viceroy, don Enrique Martínez, had made his solemn entry. Now the church bells were pealing in glad expectation that the archiepiscopal palace, empty since the death of don Jerónimo six years before, would have a new incumbent. Curiosity was heightened too by reports that the latter was 43 years old, with no experience of the Indies or even of the pastoral work of the Church, since he had taken major orders only on being chosen for South America's highest ecclesiastical office. Some may have felt misgiving on learning that Licenciado Mogrovejo had been an Inquisitor in Spain. Others, more hopefully, repeated the rumours that he was a man of quite exceptional piety and virtue.

The appointment was indeed an unusual one. Born in Mayorga, Castille, in 1538, when the *conquistadores* were fighting amongst themselves for the heritage of the Incas, Toribio de Mogrovejo had been quietly brought up in Spain by noble and devout parents and seemed destined, like one of his uncles, for the academic life. His bent was for canon law, but his leisurely progress through the universities of Valladolid, Salamanca, Coimbra and Santiago de Compostela had

been interrupted, before he had completed his doctorate, by an unexpected summons. He had been nominated, at the age of 32, to the
Holy Office in Granada. We know little of his activities there; certainly nothing to suggest the proverbial harshness and bigotry of the
Inquisitor. The records tell of enquiries into loose talk and loose
morals; of penances imposed on foolish women who claimed to have
received revelations or had gossiped in favour of bigamy and licensed
prostitution, on another who had declared that an infant was only
properly baptized if well soused with holy water, or a labourer who
had angrily refused alms on the grounds that "there was no need for
friars". There had been disputes of jurisdiction too between the civil
and the inquisitorial authorities in which the young inquisitor had
survived the discomfiture of his seniors, thanks to his conciliatory and
prudent temper. Such qualities, coupled with an impeccable orthodoxy
of belief and rectitude of conduct, and the hint of steel behind the
modest courtesy of his manners, had brought him to the favourable
notice of the Council of the Indies. The latter had sent the great Viceroy, don Francisco de Toledo, to impose order and administrative reform. His work now needed to be completed, for State and Church
were closely interlocked, by a corresponding reorganization of the even
vaster metropolitan see of Lima. The Indians had lost their old gods
but understood little or nothing about the new faith which they
nominally professed. An upsurge of missionary endeavour, reform of
the clergy, and the consolidation of the still fragile structure of the
Church throughout the King of Spain's domains south of Panama—
such would be the main tasks confronting the new archbishop.

Toribio de Mogrovejo was not yet forty when the offer of the
metropolitan see was made to him. His first impulse had been to
decline it. The Council of the Indies pressed him to accept; so did his
sister Grimanesa who was married to his friend and cousin Francisco
de Quiñones and was to share devotedly in his new destinies. Worldly
pomp held no attractions for don Toribio and when he finally decided
to accept, the dignity of his new office filled him with confusion.
Sancho Dávila, who had been his page in Granada and was to remain
in his service until his master's death, relates that, whilst journeying
to take leave of his mother in Mayorga and to be received by the King
and Council of the Indies, "he would not reveal it himself or suffer
his servants to make it known", and that to avoid the deference paid
him by fellow guests in the inns, "he would sit down on the ground on
the cloaks which his servants spread for him, and eat there with them,
in all humility." In September, 1580, the fleet set sail. Six months
later, after crossing the isthmus of Panama and taking ship again to

the south, the Archbishop landed at Paita, in the north of Peru. The three months' journey overland to Lima was his introduction to the country where he was to spend the rest of his life.

The metropolitan see, vaster in area than the great Viceroyalty of Peru itself, covered the territory made up today by the republics of Nicaragua, Panama, parts of Colombia and Bolivia, all Ecuador, Peru, Chile and Paraguay, and the northern area of Argentina. The Archbishop's own diocese stretched for a thousand kilometres from the present Department of Ica, south of Lima, to the confines of Ecuador in the north. Its three hundred kilometres of width ranged from the coastal zone of desert and fertile valley across the ranges of the Andean cordillera, to the steaming eastern lowlands drained by the Amazon. No bishop had a flock scattered over a more varied or challenging landscape, and none showed greater determination to visit it in person. The Indies had never lacked painstaking and well-intentioned laws. The problem was to enforce their observance throughout the far-flung empire, to test them constantly against the unfamiliar realities of America, and to discover and root out local abuses. This, the Archbishop at once realized, could only be done through the diocesan visitation. Of the 25 years he was to spend in the Indies, half at least were taken up by these exacting labours. Much of his metropolitan and diocesan business had to be transacted during his incessant travels, as Viceroy Toledo had transacted his, and as the monarchs, with their peripatetic court, had governed Spain until Philip had made the Escurial the hub of empire.

But first the Archbishop had to set in train an important matter in Lima. The Council of Trent had enjoined the metropolitans to summon provincial councils which should implement locally the Council's directives for the reform of the Church. Don Toribio was himself deeply imbued with the austere spirit of the Tridentine reforms and so assiduous in studying them that he is said by his contemporaries to have known the text of most of them by heart. Few of his bishops showed like zeal. Archbishop Loaysa had summoned a council in 1551, but no bishops troubled to attend, though some sent their deputies. A second council, held in 1567, fared somewhat better and did useful work which Loaysa's successor was later to carry to fruition. But neither King nor Pope gave formal endorsement to the resolutions reached by these earlier councils, which thus lacked legal validity and left the state of affairs in Peru much as they were. A new call to effective reform, as the young Archbishop was to discover, was likely to meet with the most tenacious opposition.

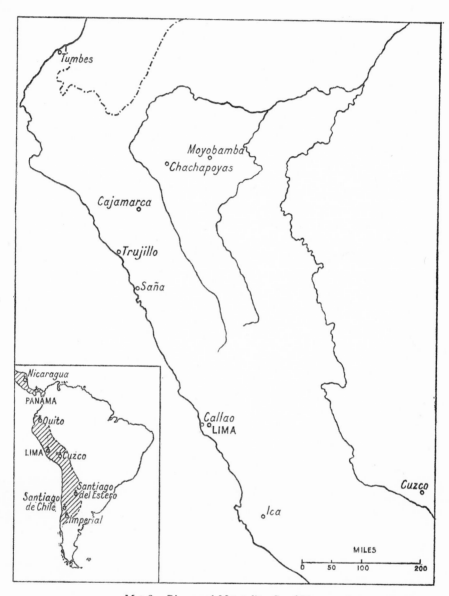

Map 2.   Diocese and Metropolitan See of Lima

The third Council of Lima, which met under the aegis of Archbishop and Viceroy in 1583, can best be considered under a double aspect. One facet was that of unseemly and sometimes scandalous dispute; another revealed a remarkable consensus regarding the fundamental problems facing the Church in South America and the lines on which they could best be solved. A cynic might have observed that the bishops were so absorbed in their own contentious affairs that they were content merely to endorse the labours of those churchmen who had weightier matters at heart. The Archbishop, for his part, was resigned to rebuffs and humiliations on a personal level so long as the deeper purposes of the Council could be served.

The storm broke over the head of the bishop of Cuzco. The ancient city of the Incas had been the site of the first bishopric to be established after the Spanish conquest, but for 15 years it had been left without an incumbent and the cathedral chapter and city *cabildo* had grown used to having things their own way. A bishop had at last been appointed and attempted to recover the prerogatives of his see. Allegations of the prelate's high-handed actions soon began to reach Lima. Archbishop Loaysa had played for time and deferred a consideration of the complaints until the next council. The feud, deepening with the years, outlived the old archbishop and cast a blight over the labours of his successor. Don Toribio, finding it impossible to achieve any local reconciliation between the parties and anxious to turn to the real business of the council, proposed to submit the dispute to Rome.

But two fresh contestants now entered the fray and gave a sinister turn to the conflict. The Bishops of Tucumán and Charcas had originally excused themselves from attending the Council, the first on the grounds that the journey was too long, the second on the plea of illness. Seven months after the opening of the Council the two bishops made an unexpected appearance. "Their absence," don Toribio was later to write wryly to the King, "would have been of more service to God than their presence." Fray Francisco de Vitoria, Bishop of Tucumán, was a corrupt and turbulent prelate with a marked preference for the flesh-pots of Potosí over his own poverty-stricken see. If the Bishop of Cuzco was to be indicted—and their Metropolitan was seemingly prepared to secure a hearing for the charges—might not his brother of Tucumán be called upon to give an account of his stewardship? The new-comers determined to frustrate the Archbishop's plans by forcibly seizing the dossier which he was preparing to send to Rome. Don Toribio appealed to the civil power to order the papers to be returned. But the Viceroy, on whose support he could have relied, had died, and power now rested solely with the *Audiencia,* the supreme tribunal, two of whose judges happened to be Basques, as was the accused Bishop of Cuzco. The Audiencia demurred; as for the papers themselves, don Toribio's first biographer records that it was commonly related in Lima that the Bishop of Tucumán "when passing by a pastry-shop, went in and threw them into the oven there, remarking that this was the way to deal with complaints against a Bishop."

Emboldened by their impunity, the rebel bishops next prepared to oust the Archbishop from the presidency of the Council and to continue its sessions under their own auspices. Faced with such open defiance, don Toribio found himself forced to take extreme measures. The dissidents were suspended from office and pronounced excommunicated. The Bishop of Tucumán remained defiant. "The Archbishop of this city, usurping the apostolic authority to which he has no right, has, with diabolical intent, thrown the whole realm into confusion . . . and pronounced excommunication against me," he declared in a diatribe which the Audiencia forwarded to the King. In due course it drew upon its author a royal rebuke "for its lack of substance, and the duty laid upon you to uphold the authority of your Metropolitan, whose life and person you so mistreat". The Archbishop, deprived of the full dossier, had to content himself with sending to the King a transcript of the original charges levelled by the chapter and *cabildo* of Cuzco—a mere trifle of 23 items—against their bishop. The latter, worn out by the acrimony of which he had so long been the centre, fell ill, withdrew from the Council, and died. The indictment was allowed to lapse. But the Archbishop had already bowed to the storm. On the insistence of the Audiencia he had revoked the sentence of excommunication and the Council had resumed its sessions. Don Toribio's humiliation was the price to be paid for the triumph of the measures which his collaborators had been quietly preparing whilst the bishops wrangled, and which were now submitted for the endorsement of the Council.

The Archbishop's staunchest allies—though he was later to have his differences with them too—were the representatives of the five great Orders in Peru—Dominicans, Franciscans, Augustinians, Mercedarians and Jesuits. Amongst the latter was his right-hand man— Father José de Acosta, the famous author of the *History of the Indies* and of a study of the problems of missionary work amongst the Indians, *De procuranda Indorum salute,* which was to serve as an invaluable frame of reference for the Council's labours. One year younger than the Archbishop, Acosta had already had ten years' experience there when the former set foot in the Indies. His tact and persuasiveness proved as valuable in the Council as his missionary experience, wide knowledge, mastery of theology and canon law and his skill in drafting. Once the Council had completed its work, Acosta was chosen as the emissary who was to secure its formal approbation by the Holy See and the Spanish Court.

The Third Council of Lima lasted for 14 months and produced 118 decrees. The latter were mainly concerned with two broad issues —the discipline and quality of the clergy and the evangelization of the Indians. The fabled wealth of Peru had attracted many tonsured adventurers who cared less for the spiritual needs of their flock than for making a rapid fortune by exploiting its labour in mine, workshop or agriculture, and by selling European goods at inflated prices. All such transactions were strictly forbidden by the Council on pain of fines and excommunication. The commercially-minded clergy carried their protests to the Spanish Court but the Council's prohibition of the *mercadura del clero* became law when Philip II approved the Council's decrees in July, 1585, and it was rigorously enforced by the Archbishop in the course of his diocesan visitations. Though the abuse was never fully extirpated, given the frailty of human nature, so long as the colonial period lasted, the firm stand taken by the Council did much to raise the calibre of the clergy and purge its ranks of fortune-hunters. Other measures tending to the same end were the requirements that a priest should remain for at least six years in the same parish and should learn the language of his flock. A standard catechism in three languages—Spanish, Quechua and Aymará—was drawn up and became widely used by missionaries in South America. The decision was also taken to found a Seminary so that Creoles, and not only European-born Spaniards, could be prepared for the priesthood. This institution was to pass through many vicissitudes and to give rise, as we shall see, to one of the stormiest episodes in the Archbishop's career.

The scene of the priest's labours was the *doctrina* or missionary parish. In the early days of the Conquista, when missionaries were in short supply, the *encomendero* himself was supposed to perform the work of evangelization in return for the privilege of benefiting from the Indians' labour. This arrangement gave rise to abuses which the Crown sought to remedy by abolishing the *encomiendas,* and when that proved impossible, by limiting their scope. The personal service which the Indians were obliged to render their *encomendero* was to a large extent commuted to an annual payment—the tribute due to the King from his vassals but made over on certain conditions to the *encomendero.* Out of this tribute, the amount of which was assessed by royal officials, the *encomendero* was expected to pay the stipend of a priest. The latter, charged with instructing the Indians in Christian doctrine, became known as a *doctrinero* and his flock a *doctrina.* The policy of the Crown was to promote the settlement of the Indians into *reducciones* or *pueblos de Indios,* of which the *doctrinas* served as missionary parishes. They thus became the basic units of church organization in Peru and the abiding object of the Archbishop's pastoral care. He found some 200 of them when he arrived in his diocese, some too large for the *doctrinero* to cope with. The third Council of Lima fixed the maximum size of each *doctrina* at a thousand Indians. By the end of the century their number had risen to nearly 250.

Mass conversions had at first been frequent amongst the Indians. The old gods had failed. The white man's must be mightier, since they had given him the victory, and to accept the new faith assured the Indians a place, however lowly, in their masters' temporal and spiritual order. If a *cacique* was converted, his people generally followed suit. Some Indians embraced Christianity, it had been reported to an earlier Council, merely for the novelty of being given a Christian name—"just that they might be called Pedro or Juan". From the superficial nature of this evangelization many problems stemmed. The Indians were quick to venerate the Christian saints; but why should they not continue too to worship their own local deities in secret? Survivors of the priestly caste encouraged such surreptitious practices. Archbishop Loaysa had tried without much success to root out the malign influence of these men. The Third Council ordered that they should be unmasked, removed from the *doctrinas* and confined to some correction centre or monastery.

Amongst the most momentous decisions reached by the Council were those relating to the use of the native languages for the propagation of the faith. The first missionaries had been forced to work through native interpreters who neither understood what they were required to translate nor could find terms in their native tongue for such words as *Church, Grace, Trinity* and many other Christian concepts. Some missionaries held that the Indians must first be taught Spanish, and their neophytes were made to reel off passages of the catechism in that language, or even in Latin, parrot-fashion. The Council of the Indies, after some uncertainty, saw advantage, doctrinal and other, in urging the Indians to learn Spanish. But the Church became convinced that the Indians could only be well grounded in the faith if instructed in their own tongue. The Archbishop was firmly of this conviction and acted with great energy. An exposition of basic Christian doctrine, in the form of question and answer, was drawn up and translated into the two main native languages. Its composition was entrusted to the Jesuits, and the work was published, by royal permission, in 1584—the first book to be printed in South America. It was followed in the next two years by a Quechuan handbook for the use of preachers and confessors and an *Arte y Vocabulario* of the same language. Don Toribio himself set about the study of Quechua with great diligence and preached regularly in that difficult language. The Council laid down that all *doctrineros* would be required to show proficiency in the language of their flock. Diocesan commissions were set up to undertake the translation of the Catechism into the lesser known local native tongues. The result was that for three centuries the "Catechism of St. Toribio" remained in constant use throughout the greater part of Spanish South America and helped not only to preserve the lingua franca of the Incas, but to extend its use to regions which the tide of Inca conquest had never reached.

Versed in the language of his flock and obliged to stay with them for not less than six years, the *doctrinero* was expected to set an example in Christian living and provide regular instruction in the Catholic faith. The children were placed under his special care until the age of 12. He was also required to assemble all adult Indians for an hour's religious instruction every Wednesday and Friday, besides seeing that they brought their infants to be baptized, confessed once a year, and attended mass on Sundays and Saints' Days. Twelve of the latter were prescribed every year as obligatory for the Indians, though the Spaniards observed three times that number. Those who lived on the Indians' labour resented the time set aside for religious practices, but the Archbishop insisted that "no Spaniard or Indian or Negro or other person whatsoever, on the pretext of contracting Indians for labour in the fields, shall impede or interfere with them or remove them from their *doctrina* once they are there". In addition to a school for the children, each *doctrina* was to have its own choir and band, for the Indians were fond of music and of playing their part in the celebration of the church services. Viceroy Toledo had decreed that the four Indians chosen to lead the singing could claim exemption from the payment of tribute. The Archbishop was shocked to discover that the *encomenderos,* in order to avoid this loss to their revenue, saw to it that only the old Indians, who were in any case no longer liable to tribute, were chosen for this privilege, though "they are old and cannot sing and are quite unable to learn". He urged that the Viceroy's instructions should be observed and the Indians encouraged to sing to the accompaniment of "flageolets and flutes and other instruments, to increase the delight which they take in divine worship".

There were weightier matters which brought the Archbishop into conflict with the *encomenderos* and, still more, with the *corregidores,* the officials who ruled, often tyrannically and corruptly, over the *pueblos de Indios.* The *doctrinero* was strictly forbidden to levy charges for the administration of the sacraments or demean his office by buying and selling. He was thus left entirely dependent on his stipend, which was to be met, as were the general church expenses, out of the tribute paid by the Indians to the *encomendero.* The latter was tempted to evade, or at least to minimize, these obligations. He resented the loss of labour caused by the Indians' attendance at religious instruction and festivals, opposed the creation of new *doctrinas,* and stopped paying the *doctrinero's* stipend when the Indian population declined, as it did drastically through the ravages of smallpox at the end of the 16th Century. The Archbishop fought hard to defend the *doctrinero's* rights and in 1596 secured a ruling from the Crown that "when the fruits and proceeds from an *encomienda* are insufficient for both the *doctrina* and the *encomendero,* priority should be given to the former, even if nothing is left over for the *encomendero".*

To protect the Indians from exploitation was a still harder task. Viceroy Toledo had decreed that they were to pay tribute not in kind but in cash. This meant that the Indians had to leave their homes and seek work in mines or in the textile workshops known as *obrajes.* The sight of the inhuman conditions under which they were forced to work left the good Archbishop appalled. His brother-in-law, Francisco de Quiñones, who accompanied him and reported on their visit to the King, wrote that "the Archbishop determined that all the Indians should be sent home". But this was something that lay quite outside his province, and the realization that he could do little or nothing to relieve their misery filled him with such distress that he thought seriously of resigning office and retiring to a monastery. But there were other ills which he could help to put right. One was the matter of the hospitals for sick and needy Indians which Toledo had ordered to be established in each *doctrina.* The money had been raised through a special levy and paid into the community chests controlled by the *corregidores,* but the hospitals had not been built. Don Toribio, "being moved by the wretchedness, poverty and calamitous state of the poor folk which those who have not seen for themselves cannot possibly imagine", took energetic action in person to see that a start was made on acquiring and equipping suitable buildings. Some *corregidores* also refused to disburse money for the upkeep of the churches and the celebration of the services. Against one such obdurate official, the *corregidor* of Cajatambo, the Archbishop pronounced an edict of excommunication, and refused to lift it even when required to do so by the Audiencia.

*   *   *   *

To draw up decrees for administrative and spiritual reform was indeed one thing; to ensure that they were faithfully carried out clearly another. Hence the importance of the diocesan synod and the episcopal Visitation. The first brought together *doctrineros* from the *pueblos de indios* and parish priests serving the Spaniards and mestizos to consider the implementation of the measures proposed by the Council. Thirteen such synods were convened by don Toribio and held wherever his duties might take him; a few in Lima, the rest in the provincial towns on the route of his Visitations. The latter, and his lesser travels in the environs of the capital, claimed the greater part of the Archbishop's time. The first Visitation lasted no less than seven years (1584-90), the second four (1593-7), the third (1605-6) was cut short by his death. The Archbishop was to be found in his capital, in short, only for the Provincial Councils which he was required to hold every seven years, and for the transaction of other essential business. The rest of his time was dedicated to the unremitting and arduous pastoral round.

No diocese offered greater natural obstacles. Peru is not one land but three; the arid coastal belt, intersected by valley oases, the towering ranges and plateau of the Andes where the bulk of the Indian population lived, and the Eastern jungle lowlands sloping away to the Amazon. To traverse these remote regions the traveller still had recourse to the old Inca highways, now often fallen into decay. The Archbishop journeyed on mule-back or, where the way was particularly rough, on foot, with his chaplains and secretaries and the Indian servants bearing the portable altar, the robes, vessels and other things needed for the celebration of the mass. To the fatigues of the journey were added the sudden changes of climate and altitude, the hazards of storm, flood and landslide, and the threat of contagion which, even when the smallpox epidemic was at its height, never deterred the Archbishop from entering the Indian huts to minister to the sick and dying. "Being of such a weak and delicate constitution," wrote Sancho Dávila, "it seems an impossible and incredible thing that the Archbishop could have survived all the misadventures which befell him." But don Toribio's slight frame concealed a constitution, as well as a

will, of iron. Towards the end of his life he was able to write that "he
felt as young as when he left college at Salamanca, with no trace of
illness or other disability". On completing his first Visitation, the Archbishop reported to the Pope that he had covered "more than two
thousand leagues of my District"; eight years later, he was able to
speak of five thousand two hundred leagues, by the end of the century,
of more than six thousand. A rough calculation of all the distance
covered, on mule-back or on foot, in the course of the three Visitations,
suggests a total of around 25,000 miles.

The first Visitation took the Archbishop to the far north of his
diocese, its course tracing a rough T, the arms of which extended
from Trujillo on the coast to Chachapoyas, on the eastern slopes of
the Andes. It was interrupted by an urgent summons to return to
Lima. Philip II, in his exertions to equip the Invincible Armada which
was to bring England to heel, called on all prelates throughout his
realms to organize a special fund-raising campaign. The Indians had
little left to give, but there was money in plenty in the pockets of their
Spanish masters. Don Toribio did the duty required of him, "being
grieved at the trouble and wars which Your Majesty has with these
enemies of ours, the English heretics". By 1589, when the sea had
already consumed the bulk of Philip's treasure and the pride of his
armada, the Archbishop was back amongst his Indians. He even
penetrated to the distant province of Moyobamba, on the forest confines of the old Inca empire, which the *conquistadores* had sought to
explore in their quest for El Dorado more than half a century before.
"This land of Moyobamba is unhealthy, and it rains most of the
year," Alonso de Alvarado had then written. "It is full of foul places,
of great mountains and rough forests and rivers great and small." The
wildness of the land and of the tribes who lurked in its rain-drenched
forests caused the Archbishop's party to melt away. Sancho Dávila
and another faithful attendant who stayed with him have left vivid
accounts of their ordeals—the floundering through swamps, in which
the Archbishop lost his boots and his cassock and then consciousness
itself, recovering some hours later as if by miracle to celebrate mass
and preach to the Indians in their own tongue "just as if nothing at
all had happened".

Danger sometimes threatened from the Indians themselves. Some
were still quite wild, and one witness has described how, in one remote
spot, his party was beset by "a great company of them, all armed, but
after His Lordship had spoken to them, they threw themselves at his
feet and kissed his garments". The Archbishop's party penetrated into
regions where the lingua franca of the Incas was unknown. But when

the natives spoke to them, he assured the baffled interpreters that he understood perfectly what they were saying, and the savages seemed equally to understand what the Archbishop replied. Like Fray Luis Bertrán, he appeared to have been given the gift of tongues. Nor was the Archbishop satisfied with mere preaching and exhortation. His purpose was the incorporation of each adult member of his flock into the full life of the Catholic Church. Hence the Archbishop's incessant labours to see that they were properly instructed, or to instruct them himself, so that he could confirm them and admit them to partake of Holy Communion. Some maintained that the Indians were by nature too rude or inferior to have access to the Sacrament. The Archbishop never faltered in his belief that, though children of nature, they were no less the children of God and should enjoy the same rights as other men and other Christians.

Don Toribio's fatherly concern for the Indians and his prolonged sojourns amongst them gave offence to some of his proud compatriots. Prominent amongst them was the Viceroy, García Hurtado de Mendoza, Marquis of Cañete, who made his entry into Lima at the beginning of 1590, when the Archbishop was absent on his first Visitation. Irritable and overbearing, don García was the son of a former viceroy who had sent him, whilst still a headstrong youth, to govern and subdue the fierce Araucanians. He had failed, but sycophantic poetasters had nevertheless done their best to build up the legend of don García de Mendoza as one of the great military and administrative figures of the Indies. The passage of time had done nothing to diminish the vanity, violence and intolerance of his temperament. He seems scarcely to have set foot in Peru before conceiving a passionate antipathy for the Archbishop. Perhaps it was the latter's rank, second only to that of the Viceroy himself, or his already widespread reputation for sanctity, to which he took exception. The flames of resentment were fed by a Memorial, full of unjust accusations and personal spleen, drawn up against don Toribio by one of the *oidores,* Ramírez de Cartagena, who had similarly attempted to discredit don García's great predecessor, Francisco de Toledo. The Archbishop sent the new Viceroy letters of deferential greeting explaining that his pastoral duties prevented him from conveying them in person. The Viceroy left the letters unanswered and was soon writing irritably to the King: "I have not yet seen the Archbishop of this city, and indeed he is never here. He excuses himself on the plea that he is making a Visitation of his diocese which is most unwarranted, for he and his attendants are for ever travelling amongst the Indians, eating up what wretched pittance they have, and doing even worse things for all I know . . . Everyone considers him to be quite unfitted for this arch-bishopric".

By the time the Archbishop returned to Lima at the end of 1590, the Viceroy had given practical effect to his hostility. Just outside the city, round the church and hospital of San Lázaro on the banks of the river Rimac, there had grown up a community of Indian fishermen. Don Toribio had taken a special interest in these Indians, who came directly under the care of the cathedral, and would go out to visit and preach to them every Sunday when he was in Lima. The Viceroy decided to transfer the Indians of San Lázaro to a *doctrina* under the charge of the Jesuits, one of whom was his brother. When don Toribio's Vicar-General attempted to protest against this arbitrary arrangement and defend the frightened Indians, who had sought sanctuary in the church of San Lázaro, he was clapped under arrest and incarcerated in a galley.

More serious clashes were soon to follow. They hinged primarily on the delicate issue of the *Patronato Real* which governed the relation-ship between Church and State throughout His Most Catholic Majesty's domains. By virtue of the Patronato the King exercised the right of presenting candidates for appointment to episcopal and other major benefices; in matters of less importance, particularly in respect of appointments to the Indian *doctrinas,* similar rights were exercised on the King's behalf by his Viceroy. The line between the civil and the ecclesiastical jurisdiction was finely drawn and gave rise to constant disputes. The Archbishop, the least self-seeking or quarrelsome of men, could nevertheless be diamond-hard in defence of what he deemed to be the prerogatives and authority of the Church; he was also expert in all questions of canon law. The Viceroy, domineering and intran-sigent, cared little for legal niceties and was intent only on imposing his will. As the test-case for his confrontation with the Archbishop he chose one of the most important decisions reached by the Third Coun-cil of Lima—the establishment of the *Seminario.*

The Council of Trent had laid down that seminaries should be founded in all the provinces of the Catholic Church where candidates could be given sound training for the ministry. The quality of the priesthood was basic to the effectiveness of the whole Counter-Reformation, and the selection and training of those destined for it was therefore of cardinal importance. In the Indies the question assumed particular significance, since hitherto all clergy had received their training in Spain. Creoles were not excluded from Holy Orders, but they had first to make the long and costly journey to Europe before qualifying for ordination. The establishment of seminaries in the

Indies was the pre-requisite for an adequate supply of locally-recruited and trained clergy, familiar with the environment and languages of the New World, through whom the Christian faith might extend its roots more deeply into the lives of the indigenous population. The Archbishop's *Seminario,* with its 30 pupils carefully selected from local applicants and educated in accordance with a specially drawn-up curriculum, was not only the first post-Tridentine theological college to be established in the Indies, or indeed anywhere else in the world; it could also lay claim to be one of the first of Latin America's own autochthonous institutions.

Such an achievement could hardly fail to arouse the jealous resentment of Mendoza who determined to take this important new field of patronage into his own hands. He claimed that the selection of the seminarians and the control of their college was a matter for the Viceroy under the terms of the Patronato Real and wrote to the King urging that it should be reserved for "the sons of Your Majesty's servants, of discoverers, and of other deserving persons" as recommended by the Viceroy. Without awaiting any reply from Spain, don García issued peremptory orders that its management should be promptly surrendered into his charge. When the Archbishop objected that the control of its seminaries had always been regarded as a matter for the Church alone, Mendoza sent a gang of masons, escorted by his personal guard, to hack down the archiepiscopal coat-of-arms carved over its entrance and substitute his own. Don Toribio retorted by placing the perpetrators of this indignity under excommunication. Not daring to strike against the person of the Archbishop himself, Mendoza ordered that his brother-in-law, Quiñones, who had served with distinction as Commander of the Fleet and *corregidor* of Lima, should be arrested and sent down to the galleys at Callao. He even threatened the Archbishop's sister, doña Grimanesa, with a like fate. Faced with this show of force, don Toribio's only option was to declare the Seminario closed until the Crown, to whom he promptly appealed, should give its ruling on the question of jurisdiction. The Viceroy, meanwhile, accused his enemy of keeping the seminary shut so that he could pocket its revenues. When the royal decision reached Lima it was wholly in favour of the Archbishop. The Seminario was re-opened; but as a sop to the Viceroy's vanity and in token of reconciliation between Church and State, his coat-of-arms was allowed to stand, together with the Archbishop's restored insignia, above its portals.

Whilst the dispute over the Seminario was dragging on, another and more serious storm broke over the Archbishop's head. How far Mendoza's hand was behind the affair remains unclear. He had worked assiduously to persuade the King that don Toribio was attempting to undermine the authority of the Patronato Real, and he must have derived enormous satisfaction from the sudden reversal of royal favour his efforts at last brought against his enemy. On 29 January, 1593, Philip II's ambassador in Rome, the Duke of Sessa, reported to the Council that Cardinal Matei, on behalf of the Pope, had received a memorial from the Archbishop of Lima listing a long series of complaints against the civil authorities and impugning the whole concept of the Patronato Real. The Crown took a serious view of this report. The Viceroy was immediately instructed to summon don Toribio "and in the presence of the Audiencia and its ministers, to give him to understand how unbefitting his state and profession it had been to write such things to Rome; for it is untrue that in the Indies the Bishops take possession of their churches without papal bulls, as the Memorial declares; it is likewise untrue that my Council of the Indies prevents him from visiting the hospitals and workshops in his Archdiocese. Nor is it true what he says about the Seminario being deprived of funds . . . And when this has been made clear to him, you shall likewise tell him that it were proper for him to be recalled to my Court that this business might be more fully gone into, and a public example made as befits the enormity of the case, but that I have forborne lest his church and flock should suffer from so long an absence of their prelate".

When the King's letter reached Lima, don Toribio was away in the north of the country on his second Visitation—"at great cost and trouble to the people", Mendoza maliciously commented, though "here we are very quiet without him". His absence deprived the Viceroy of the satisfaction of publicly administering the royal reprimand. "The words which Your Majesty commands me to address to him would suffice to strike others with great consternation and distress", he peevishly observed, "but he is quite unmoved". Such apparent indifference was quite unaccountable in a Spaniard, and "I can only imagine he must have been born in London or Constantinople". Don Toribio, in reality, was deeply affected by the royal displeasure and immediately wrote back disclaiming authorship of the Memorial attributed to him. But the King's suspicions were not to be easily dispelled. Two years later we find Philip writing irritably to the Archbishop blaming him for "the long absence from your Church, on which plea you have not complied with my commands to the Viceroy, as you ought to have done, so without further excuse you must forthwith return to the city and report to the Viceroy". Don Toribio faced the humiliating ordeal which awaited him after the four arduous years of his second Visitation with his customary fortitude, listening meekly to the reading of the *cédula* in the presence of the *oidores*. One consolation at least was his; the official who administered the royal reprimand was not his enemy Mendoza but a new and fair-minded Viceroy, don Luis de Velasco. In his defence, the Archbishop declared that he had already written to Spain to protest that he was innocent of the charges made against him, and that if any such Memorial had been sent to the Pope he was not the author of it, and that whenever he had occasion to correspond with Rome he sent his letters under flying seal to the King and Council with the request that they should forward them to His Holiness. As for the Patronato Real, he had always scrupulously observed its provisions, and he and his bishops had passed a solemn resolution pledging full respect for it at the Third Council of Lima.

The Lima Councils had nevertheless been themselves seized upon by Mendoza as ammunition in his campaign to show up the Archbishop as an enemy of the Patronato. Delays in correspondence with the Council of the Indies, and an apparent confusion of views within that body, played into his hands. The Council of Trent had laid down that provincial councils should be held every three years. The difficulty of gathering together the bishops scattered over such a vast metropolitan see as that of Lima clearly made frequent assemblies impracticable. Don Toribio solicited and obtained permission from Rome to modify the Tridentine ruling and to hold them every seven years. The Council of the Indies also favoured longer intervals between councils but expected to be consulted over the specific dates proposed. Don Toribio considered that this was a matter which could justly be decided locally and he prepared to hold his next council during 1590, seven years after its predecessor. The Bishops were summoned to Lima and arrived there before their Metropolitan was back from his second Visitation. Mendoza, finding no *cédula* from the King expressly authorising the convening of the Fourth Council of Lima, claimed that the Archbishop was infringing the Patronato, and promptly ordered the Bishops back to their dioceses. Don Toribio reached Lima to find his episcopal colleagues dispersed, but determined nevertheless to proceed with the assistance of the Bishop of Cuzco, who had once more to make the long journey down from the Sierra, and of the leading church dignitaries of Lima. Held under such inauspicious circumstances, the Fourth Council had little to show for its labours. Its deliberations centred round two main administrative issues; the right of the religious Orders to run parishes, in place of secular priests, and to enjoy exemption from disciplinary supervision by the Bishop, and the control of church finances and the *hospitales de indios*. These were delicate matters which threatened, on the one hand, to sow discord between the Archbishop and the Orders, and on the other, to incur the enmity of those *corregidores* who frequently abused their powers, to the detriment of Church and charitable institutions, on the familiar plea of acting within the privileges of the Patronato. Victory on such issues was not to be lightly won in any council chamber. Nor did the Fourth Council of Lima find the ready endorsement for its resolutions which King and Pope had given to those of its predecessor.

The obligation to convene provincial councils every seven years was one of the heaviest crosses which don Toribio had to bear. "It would be a relief indeed to me not to concern myself with such assemblies", he wrote to the Viceroy, "with all the difficulties and trouble of calling the bishops together and offering those of them who lack means the hospitality of my own hearth and home". The Archbishop found himself caught between Rome and the Spanish Court. His duty to convene the councils was inescapable; but the Court remained strangely deaf to his proposals for doing so. No answer came to his letters. The Archbishop waited for a further three years beyond the prescribed seven, but his conscience allowed him to delay no further. The Fifth Council of Lima opened in 1601. Luis de Velasco was prudent and well-disposed, but without the royal *cédula* authorizing it to be held, the Viceroy could not honour its sessions with his presence. The Council lasted no more than a week and passed only five resolutions, the chief of which was a renewal of the earlier regulations forbidding the clergy to engage in any sort of trading.

*   *   *   *

Much of the Archbishop's time in Lima was claimed by such difficult, and often stormily controversial, administrative matters. Diego de Morales, who served him as secretary for many years, assures us that "in all adversities, persecutions and affronts, he showed great fortitude and patience, and was never seen complaining against anyone or giving way to anger, but rather commending all things to God and asking His pardon for them". In the matter of the royal reprimand, which Viceroy Mendoza was piqued to find left the Archbishop so unmoved, Morales justly comments that "others would have been greatly troubled, but he was neither cast down, angered, nor abashed, for as he lived and acted without passion or personal interest, but thought only to serve God, nothing could disturb his peace of mind". Morales, and other witnesses later called to give evidence for the Process of the Archbishop's beatification, have given us many vivid glimpses of the austere piety of don Toribio's personal life; his assiduity in attending mass and the other canonical offices, and his long hours of study and prayer, when he remained "suspended in the heavenly contemplation of the divine goodness"; his severely rationed hours of sleep, "on a trestle instead of a bed, with his head resting on a wooden hat-box for a pillow"; the mortifications inflicted on himself in the solitude of his chamber, and the bloodstained discipline found by his valet; the extreme simplicity of his table, "so frugal, that saying grace took longer than eating the meal", accompanied by the reading of passages from the breviary, the lives of the saints, or the decrees of the Council of Trent; the great windows of the palace barred and shuttered to mark the Archbishop's distaste for the jousts and bull-fights given in the plaza outside, or his grief when some poor wretch was led away to execution, when he would retire to the chapel and pray earnestly for the victim's soul.

If such scenes give us an unduly gloomy picture of life in the Archbishop's palace, there is no lack of lighter touches; the informal atmosphere of the great building, without anterooms or ushers, where the Archbishop, dressed plainly, "sin curiosidades, or anything smacking of vanity", was readily mistaken for one of his chaplains; his affability and courtesy to great and small, not excluding the negroes and Indians for whom he showed special affection—"he knew almost all the Indians in his diocese and called each by his name". One characteristic which struck his acquisitive and often venal contemporaries with special force was his unwillingness to accept hospitality or gifts of any sort for himself, yet to decline them with such grace and unaffected pleasure that the refusal never gave offence. Bartolomé de Menacho, another of his secretaries, has given us a charming picture of a friar presenting him with a basket of fresh fruit, and the Archbishop taking out a rosy apple and exclaiming with delight—"What a lovely sight, what a lovely sight!" and then carefully replacing the vineleaves which covered the fruit and setting it aside for the use of the invalids of his household. Or the other scene described by Morales when the Archbishop took a fancy to go picnicking, and when the meal had been spread sent for all the Indians around and had the food distributed amongst them, "with great mirth and contentment, but without touching a mouthful himself".

Don Toribio's charity was the object of general amazement and sometimes an occasion for abuse. He was not only totally detached from personal possessions but constantly prone to give away whatever came to hand, even literally, to the shirt off his back, or the cassock he was wearing, to some threadbare but startled priest. To a widow who lacked a dowry for her daughter he presented the mule which was waiting, fully saddled, to carry him on his pastoral rounds. To hungry Indians who came to the palace begging for food he had been known to give not only the food from his table but the silver dish on which it was served, to the great scandal of doña Grimanesa who would send secretly after the Indian to buy it back. Poor doña Grimanesa! It is no light matter to be sister to a saint; she was for ever sending him messages enjoining him to eat properly, wear warm clothes and look after himself. Her brother was sometimes obliged to do his good deeds by stealth. "Take them quickly—before doña Grimanesa sees you!" he is reputed to have exclaimed to a beggar whom he had presented with a pair of mules. If there was nothing else to hand, he would give a chair from his study or strip a tapestry from the wall. In times of communal need, when a ship arrived at Callao and the master had no money to pay off his crew, or to relieve the Spaniards who had lost their all in the Chilean wars, or the flock of his own diocese decimated by an epidemic, he would mortgage the whole revenue of his see.

Zealous defender though he was of the patrimony of the Church and the right of his *doctrineros* to draw the full stipend due to them, or of the *hospitales de indios* to regain the funds misappropriated by dishonest *corregidores,* don Toribio showed a more than childish naiveté in the personal handling of money. An early biographer assures us that, since he habitually left all such matter to his brother-in-law and majordomo Francisco de Quiñones, the Archbishop was incapable of distinguishing between coins of different value and was even unable to count beyond ten! Some of his less unworldly clergy were not above exploiting their prelate's foibles. One, fined 400 pesos for some misdemeanour, brought the money in a bag and poured it out before the startled Archbishop who had never set eyes on such a quantity of money. "No, No! It can't be as much as all that!", he exclaimed, "This is what was meant for your fine"—pushing a few coins to one side with his hand—"the rest you must take back and give to your poor relations!"

Four years after the abortive Fifth Council of Lima, don Toribio prepared to set out on his third, and his last, Visitation. He was now in his sixties, and although, as a contemporary observed, "even in his old age, the complexion of his face was that of a youth", the arduous years were taking their toll. The Archbishop had a premonition that he would never return to the capital. "God be with you, sister", he exclaimed on taking leave of doña Grimanesa, "We shall see each other no more." A year later, on reaching the little town of Saña, his strength failed him and he was put to bed in the house of the parish priest. The report quickly spread that *el arzobispo santo* lay dying. On

23 March, 1606, don Toribio Mogrovejo, Archbishop of Lima, breathed his last, "his death being bitterly lamented", his secretary Menacho records, "by whites, negroes and Indians, as by men who had lost their father and prelate . . . The people of this city commonly spoke of him as Saint Toribio, as they still do to this day".

CHAPTER 4

St. Francis of the Indies—
San Francisco Solano

THE Order of Friars Minor, founded by St. Francis of Assisi in 1209, played a notable part in bringing the Gospel to the New World. The Spanish branch of the Order had been reformed by the great Cardinal Ximénez de Cisneros, himself a Franciscan noted for his pious austerities, just as the *conquistadores* were beginning their great venture. Cortés sent for friars to implant the faith in the lands which his men were wresting from the Aztecs. The first contingent of Franciscans—the "Twelve Apostles"—reached Mexico in 1524 and they were soon followed by others. They included many who were to win fame in the spiritual conquest of America; Toribio de Benavente, known amongst the Indians as Motolinía, or "little poor man", on account of his austerities, Zumárraga, the first Bishop of Mexico, social pioneers like Peter of Ghent, and scholars like Bernardino de Sahagún, whose work was to become the corner-stone of ethnological studies.

In Peru, though they never produced such outstanding figures as in Mexico, the Franciscans did signal service in carrying the faith through the former realms of the Inca. They, together with the other Orders, formed the shock-troops of the Church, behind whom the secular clergy, deployed under the customary episcopal hierarchy, moved in to consolidate the ground freshly won from paganism. Some of the remote dioceses long remained primarily mission-zones, in which the work of the friars was all-important. One such region was Tucumán, to the east of the Andean cordillera, in what is now the republic of Argentina. Amongst those assigned to this wild and sparsely settled province was a Franciscan friar who had arrived in the fleet which had sailed from Spain in 1588 with the new Viceroy, don García de Mendoza. He was called Fray Francisco Solano.

The name of the man who was to become the St. Francis of the Indies is little remembered today, even in Argentina, the main scene of his missionary labours, or in Peru, where it once inspired veneration and awe. He was born in the little Andalusian town of Montilla in 1549 and sent by his parents to study in a Jesuit college, but his temperament was Franciscan and his vocation clearly that of following in the footsteps of the poor man of Assisi. Until the age of nearly 40, when the call to missionary work in the Indies came to him, he lived the humble life of a friar in the monastery of Our Lady of Loreto near Seville, as a novice-master in Córdoba, or at San Francisco del Monte, in the Sierra Morena, from whose welcome solitude he emerged with ardour to devote himself to the care of victims stricken by the plague. In the 1580's we find him living in Granada.

Spain has been called *tierra de cantos y santos*—land of stones and saints. Fray Francisco was clearly of that company of sometimes eccentric saints who had flourished but recently in his native Andalusia. In Granada, he can scarcely have escaped the impact of San Juan de Dios, the ex-soldier and hawker of pious broadsheets, who had died one year before Francisco's birth. The saint had commonly been accounted mad until his madness was seen to take the form of an obsessive compassion for the sick and suffering. From the apostolic charity of Juan de Dios there stemmed a great hospital—still flourishing in the Granada of today—and a new Order dedicated to the mission of healing throughout the world. One who knew him describes the unconventional saint as "very merry", and much given to singing, dancing and the clapping of hands, sometimes in the very presence of the Holy Sacrament exposed upon the altar. Of the saint's chief aid in the hospital, another ex-soldier known as Pedro Pecador, or Peter the Sinner, it is related that he would spend much of the night in the chapel alternately praying and dancing, or reciting pious couplets composed to suit each festival of the church; even on his deathbed, Peter continued to sing snatches of sacred song, snapping his fingers in Andalusian fashion, to give vent to the delirium of his holy joy.

More recent still was the memory of a Franciscan friar who died when Francisco was thirteen and was canonized seven years later. St. Peter of Alcántara was already famous for his asceticism and deep fervour when St. Teresa of Avila decided to seek guidance from him in the problems of her own spiritual life and the difficulties she was encountering as a reformer and foundress. She has given us an unforgettable picture of the old friar, whose austerities had left his body emaciated and gnarled "so that he seemed made out of the roots of trees". "However strong the sun or the rain", she continues, "he never put up his hood, nor did he wear anything on his feet, nor clothes other than a habit of coarse serge, as tight as he could bear it, with nothing else over his bare flesh, and above it a mantle of the same stuff". He took food normally once in three days and slept in a sitting position in a cell no more than four and a half feet wide. The mystical experiences to which he was prone could take the oddest and most disturbing forms. When the spirit was upon him, he would become strangely animated and his movements abnormally rapid, though usually they were measured and grave. Or else he would fall into ecstasy, sometimes to the accompaniment of sensational feats of levitation, which might leave him suspended in prayer several feet above the ground or even sweep him bodily through the air from the chancel steps to the cross which he was adoring. Sometimes he would utter involuntary cries, so piercing and impassioned that his brothers would come rushing into his cell in alarm. The fervour of his preaching was such that the most hardened sinners would be left conscience-stricken and penitent.

Fray Francisco Solano was of the same breed as these eccentric Spanish saints, and was to carry the contagion of their divine folly to the wilds of America and the intimacy of Andean convent cells. The aura of the supernatural invests him even before he reached the scene of his missionary labours. The party of 11 friars which set out from Spain was quickly reduced to eight, two having died in Panama, and a third in a shipwreck. For more than two months the travellers were marooned on an island where they survived, it was rumoured, thanks largely to the miraculous skill of Friar Francisco in catching fish. When at last, after travelling overland across Peru and what is now Bolivia, he had made his way across the great Andean plateau and down to Santiago del Estero, the chief town of the province in the foothills beyond, hearsay magnified the supernatural powers attributed to him still further. He had only, men said, to put his hands in the waters of the rivers which traverse the wilds of north-eastern Argentina for fish to swim into them, and for eels to wriggle trustingly up the sleeve of his habit, ready to offer themselves for the sustenance of the holy man.

But evil, no less than holiness, could weave its spell in those savage parts. How else can we explain the fall from grace of Francisco de Vitoria, once the most zealous of friars, whose merits had raised him to become Provincial of his Order and the first occupant there of an episcopal see? We have already met the right reverend Bishop of Tucumán; he was none other than the boisterous prelate who had flouted the good archbishop of Lima and raised such dissension in the Third Council. Tucumán had quickly grown too narrow for the scale of his ambitions, and he had abandoned his diocese to leave a train of scandal in Potosí, Lima, Buenos Aires, Bahia and elsewhere. At about the time that Fray Francisco was beginning his labours in Tucumán, King Philip addressed a stern letter of reproof to the errant bishop :—

"Whereas I have heard that, with scandal, notoriety and ill example, you have been publicly dealing and engaging in trade, taking merchandise in person to be sold in Potosí; and deeming that you cannot but be failing in your duties by busying yourself in such matters for gain, which is a thing unbefitting your state and profession and also unlawful; I am therefore writing to the Viceroy don García de Mendoza to send for you and to tell you on my behalf what you will hear from him. I command you to hear and do what he says, conducting yourself to the end that those who have been scandalized by your excesses may be edified by your amended life, for the contrary will in no wise be permitted."

With such a sorry example in high places it is not surprising to learn that the Spanish settlers of Tucumán were given to turbulence and feuding. Fray Francisco soon won fame amongst them, as amongst the savage tribes through whom he fearlessly moved, as a peace-maker. Yet of the next dozen years, during which period he served first as a *doctrinero* and then as Custodian and Vice-Provincial for all the small Franciscan outposts throughout Tucumán and Paraguay, we know little. Certainly it was a hard life, lonely, sometimes dangerous, and full of privations, all of which, his first biographer Diego de Córdoba assures us, "not only did he endure with patience, but with demonstrations of great joy, in the place or wilderness wherever he might be, celebrating it by dancing and singing canticles to the praise and glory of Christ and to the Most Pure Virgin Our Lady". Pictures of the saint often depict him carrying a *rabel,* or small three-stringed rebeck, with which he was wont to solace himself and probably to attract the Indians, great lovers of music, whom he wished to instruct in the faith. Of his actual doings in Tucumán the records are strangely silent. The witnesses in his subsequent Process of beatification, speak mainly of the friar they recall in Lima and Trujillo. The years of his strenuous apostolate amongst the Indians have been left largely to legend. One Spanish captain, Andrés García de Valdés, bears witness to his phenomenal gifts as a linguist; the barbarous *tonocote* tongue, he declares, was mastered by the friar in less than two weeks. From the parish priest of Nueva Rioja we learn that no less than 9,000 Indians, attracted to the little town by the Holy Week festivities, remained spell-bound by Fray Francisco's preaching and sought baptism. There are stories of plagues of ants and locusts averted by the holy man's intercession, of wild bulls tamed by the touch of his girdle. Springs gush forth at the touch of his staff, and less than a score of years after the friar's departure, "Father Solano's spring" was being pointed out to the episcopal Visitor. Nor was popular piety to be satisfied by such feats of general beneficence. We have the assurance of one Sánchez de Feria that "once when the saint was on a journey, he came to a very mighty river which it was impossible to wade. Taking off his cloak and raising his eyes to heaven, he placed himself on it and in this way passed over to the other bank".

In 1602 Fray Francisco left Tucumán and began the long journey back to Lima. The remainder of his life was to be spent between Santa María de los Angeles, a small and peaceful monastery in the Rimac valley, and the Franciscan house in Trujillo, where he was elected Guardian. During these last eight years of his life Fray Francisco was able to give himself more completely to his vocation for contemplation and intercession. "He was for ever at prayer, day and night, at all hours and in all places," Diego de Córdoba tells us. One of the prayers most frequently on the lips of the saint has been preserved and reads as follows :

Good Jesus, my Redeemer and Friend—
What do I have which Thou hast not given me?
What do I know that Thou hast not taught me?
What have I, if I lack Thee?
What can I, if Thou art not with me?
Much hast Thou done for me in creating and redeeming me.
Do this much more, I pray Thee, and forgive that which Thou has created,
Look upon me,
For I am poor and alone. Amen.

Fray Francisco's prayers were often accompanied by deep raptures, from which the friars could not rouse him even when they spoke or touched him. His face, they declared, was then suffused with an unearthly light. Some even vowed that they had seen him borne along through the air from the chancel steps to the high altar. At times, even when weak with lack of sleep or food, he would seem endowed with superhuman strength and would almost crush his brothers with the fervour of his loving embrace. More than once a novice had been startled to find the old friar standing before him, book in hand and face aflame, crying "Read this!" Then, transported by the gospel message of God's love, he would be swept into ecstasy and regain the solitude of his cell "with extraordinary fleetness". Sometimes the awareness of the divine presence would overwhelm him whilst he spoke of holy things. This happened once when he was in

1. The Cult of the Hero-saint
—Santiago intervenes at the
battle of Cuzco

2. The Cult of the Pseudo-saint
—Homage to the memory of
Eva Perón

3. San Luis Bertrán

converse with a doctor, the Licenciado Mondragón, much to the consternation of the good man, who could only think, until the friars
reassured him, that it was the enormity of his sins which had caused
the saint to take flight. "The holy man was wont," Diego de Córdoba
explains, "when treating of the love of God, and of His divine perfections and attributes, to become so inflamed that, without being able
to do otherwise, he was carried out of himself by the force and fervour
of his spirit, and fled from the place where he was, and they would
afterwards find him in adoration of a cross and fervently embracing
it."

Music Fray Francisco continued to love until the end of his life.
We read of him, *rabel* in hand, visiting his fellow friars to cheer them
when sick or dejected, or singing, and even dancing, in secret before
the altar to celebrate the feasts of the church. Córdoba tells us that
the friar had once spent all Christmas Eve "praying and singing
merry motets to the Infant Jesus", and in Lima he is described as
celebrating another Christmastide by "singing, dancing, and ringing
a little bell". These unconventional performances must have aroused
the curiosity of his brethren, and to one of them who caught sight of
him hurrying along, *rabel* in hand, he is said to have explained: "I
am going to play some music to a most lovely Maiden who is there
waiting for me!"

Fray Francisco was a saint with a sense of humour—black humour
it would seem at times. Córdoba relates a long story of how he taught
an edifying lesson to a covetous friar in the wilds of Tucumán. The
friar found him carrying a wooden box, which Fray Francisco mysteriously referred to as his "treasure", and eagerly offered him a hand
in carrying it to the church. Friar Francisco would say nothing further
but continued singing psalms until they reached their destination
whilst his companion grew more and more curious. When at length
they put down the box and opened the "treasure" it was found to
contain the body of a small child to whom Friar Francisco proceeded
to give Christian burial. Years later, when the saint was nearing the
end of his life in Lima, one of the brothers met him hurrying from
the monastery, "his sleeves full of presents", and asked him where he
was going. "To visit my *enamorada*," the old man replied. Friar
Francisco's *enamorada* proved to be a poor old bed-ridden hag, covered
with sores and abandoned by her family. She was one of the many
sick and destitute whom the friar had taken under his care.

Córdoba paints his portrait with many an expected Franciscan
touch. We are shown the saint playing his *rabel* to the birds in the
monastery garden and sharing his modest meal with them. But there

E

is also a hint of harsh puritanism behind these idyllic scenes which surprises us. During his term of office as Guardian of the monastery of Santa María de los Angeles, Fray Francisco had a mind to uproot the trees lest his monks spend too long away from their prayers in enjoyment of their tempting fruits and leafy shade. In Trujillo he became famous for his stern calls to repentance; when, eight years after his death, a great earthquake devastated Trujillo, the survivors superstitiously recalled how the friar had prophesied just such a fate should men persist in their wickedness. The startled citizens of Lima would sometimes see a very different Fray Francisco from the man of "peaceable and gentle disposition" described by Córdoba. At such times he would stride out, like one possessed, almost flying over the ground, so that the friar who accompanied him was unable to keep up and tried to hold him back by the girdle, the saint the while "crying out in a terrible voice, as he drew a crucifix from his breast : 'Sinners, grieve no more this Lord who, for the great love he bore you, died upon a cross. Adore Him, who is supreme Goodness. Do not crucify Him anew, I beseech you, with your sins!' " Then "he would enter into the houses where they were making merry and dancing, and there preach with incredible spirit and zeal for God, or at other times standing at the street-corners". Sometimes, too, the Friar would come rushing into one of the two theatres which Lima then possessed, and leaping onto the stage would start to harangue the audience waiting for the play to begin. Some, their conscience troubled, would leave the theatre, but others would murmur that no friar had a right to interfere with their lawful enjoyment, for the play was no offence to good morals. Still more terrible was the friar's wrath when he burst into the gaming houses and confronted the gamblers, "drowning their blasphemies and oaths with the great cries which he raised most terribly against them, so that they were reduced to silence and confusion".

One December night in the year 1604, the whole life of the pleasure-loving capital was paralysed by the friar's denunciations. In a land where earthquakes and volcanic eruptions can at any time bring sudden destruction, the prophet of doom can always find a ready hearing. The town of Arica had been all but wiped out by a tidal wave scarcely a month before. Four years earlier, Arequipa had been wrecked by a volcanic eruption. Trujillo was later to suffer a still more terrible destruction by earthquake. The superstitious and fickle crowds of the capital could thus be readily panicked into believing that their sins might draw down upon them a like fate. Córdoba describes how, on that December evening, Friar Francisco sallied forth from Santa María de los Angeles, "all aflame for God, and set off for the city, saying to the porter: 'Commend me to God, for I am going to do His Divine Majesty notable service!' " When he reached the main square and the people gathered round him, he began his sermon. Friar Francisco spoke of the wrath of God, "and in a voice louder than a trumpet he called them to repentance. Then forthwith a rumour began to run through the city. . . . Men rushed through the streets in amazement and terror, saying that the holy father Solano was preaching that the city was to be swallowed up that night. . . . The city was filled with tears, and all manner of folk—men, women, old people and children—all crying out to God, striking their breasts, and beseeching mercy. They ran to the churches, which were open almost the whole night through, and in all of them the Holy Sacrament was displayed. Although there are many confessors in the city, so great was the number of penitents crying out for confession that it was scarcely possible to give them all consolation. . . . Many went through the street flogging themselves. Others visited the churches carrying heavy crosses on their shoulders".

The tumult alarmed Viceroy Velasco who immediately conferred with the Archbishop; both were pious and prudent men to whom this spectacle of religious hysteria must have been highly distasteful. The Superior of the Franciscans was instructed to send at once for Fray Francisco and enquire into the origins of the commotion. The friar, unabashed, explained that he had done no more than call the people to repentance, and he proceeded there and then to repeat the burden of his preaching to such effect that "the hair of many of those present stood on end with fear and terror". If Fray Francisco was admonished by his superiors to show greater discretion his biographer makes no mention of it. Córdoba declares rather that the Viceroy was himself so moved as to exclaim: "This is God's work and the action of His divine spirit which has chosen this way to soften the hearts of sinners and reduce them to His grace!"

Fray Francisco lived on in Lima after the city's night of panic for another six years. His health was now failing, and we see him in a more human light writing to his married sister Inés back in Spain: "Gold and silver have I none to send you, only words—and those no words of my own, but of Jesus Christ, and that is why I venture to write to you. . . . Here I am still in this city of Lima, very weak and ill, awaiting the hour of my recall from this exile".The hour of recall struck on 14 July, 1610.

*   *   *   *

This is as much as the biographer can find to record with any certainty of the life of Fray Francisco Solano. But is it one life we have been tracing, or two? Sometimes it has seemed that the mild Franciscan tending his aged *enamorada* or solacing himself with his *rabel* has nothing in common with the prophet of doom thundering forth his denunciations from theatre-stage or street corner. At one moment, the friar is deep in contemplation, his faculties suspended in rapture; at another, he is galvanized into frenzied action, his limbs endowed with superhuman strength, so that he nearly crushes his brothers in his embrace, or leaves them behind as he speeds through the streets on his preaching errands. Are we in the presence of a schizophrenic or of a saint? To his contemporaries, the answer seemed quite clear. "So fervently did he love God that he could not endure that men should grieve Him," explains Córdoba. "Whatever he heard or treated of brought to his mind God's providence, His omnipotence, His goodness and His charity. Hence it followed that everything he heard or saw spoke to him of his Beloved, so that he was powerless to contain himself. His heart, aflame with love, seemed struggling to burst free of the flesh, and at times he would utter great cries and without being able to restrain himself (although his body was so thin that his very bones could be counted) he would run like the wind, swept along by the force of the spirit, crying aloud to all men that they should love God and grieve Him no more." The water, steadily heated over the flame of his love, is suddenly converted into steam and breaks forth into terrifying explosions of prophetic indignation. It was those apocalyptic outbursts which won such fame for Fray Francisco amongst his contemporaries as a man of God. Yet perhaps a juster measure of his sanctity is to be found in the unsung record of his labours amongst the Indians of Tucumán, in the seamless garment of his prayer life, and in the sweet songs with which he would sooth the cares and sufferings of his fellows.

CHAPTER 5

The Humble Healer—
San Martín de Porres

It is curious to reflect that, around the beginning of the 17th Century, there should have been living in the same city—and one, moreover, noted in colonial times for its flamboyant worldliness—four persons, scarcely acquainted with each other, leading lives of such singular sanctity as to merit canonization. *El Arzobispo santo* seems to have had some slight contact with San Francisco Solano and he confirmed Santa Rosa when she was a young girl. Rosa had heard and been moved by the fervent preaching of the old friar, and also had some acquaintance, we learn from his Process, with Martín de Porres. The latter had been born seven years before Rosa, only a few hundred yards away from her parents' home, and spent his life in the Dominican monastery in whose church she too came to worship. If this acquaintance never ripened, as far as we know, into a closer friendship, the reason is not far to seek; Providence had placed each in very different walks of life and assigned to Martín a place in the lowliest strata of a very rank-conscious society.

Martín de Porres was born in Lima in 1579. The baptismal register records him as being the child of Ana Velásquez, a coloured woman from Panama, and of a "father unknown". His father was, in fact, a Spaniard of distinction, don Juan de Porres, a native of Burgos and Knight of Alcántara, who later became Governor of Panama. The boy was thus illegitimate and a mulatto, born into the ambiguous no-man's-land between the Spanish conquerors and their negro slaves.

When he was a few years old, Martín and his younger sister Juana were taken by their father to the home of his uncle, Captain Diego de Miranda, in Guayaquil. In that sweltering tropical port they lived for a while, don Diego growing fond of the little girl and keeping her in his house until she was old enough to have a husband found for her. Martín, after being taught to read and write, was taken back to Lima to rejoin his mother. Ana Velásquez, not herself a slave but a poor negress, worked as a washerwoman. She could hardly expect a very bright future for her son. The more able and fortunate of the mulattoes might, with luck, make their living in some craft or trade. Martín was apprenticed to a barber and soon learned from his master the crude surgical practices which were then part of that calling. He also worked for a time in an apothecary's shop and became familiar with the uses of medicinal herbs. He seems to have given early signs of his vocation as a healer and friend of the poor Indian, negro and half-caste masses to which, by virtue of his own lowly station, he himself belonged. The patience of his hard-working mother was no doubt taxed by the readiness with which her son would give away to needier folk the hard-earned money intended to meet the family's own needs. The boy also gave early evidence of that love of plants and animals which was to impress his contemporaries. Years after his death, they would point to "Fray Martín's lemon-tree" which he had planted in the courtyard of the house where his mother lodged, and which was credited with the virtue of bearing its fruit all the year round.

Before leaving to take up his appointment in Panama, don Juan de Porres arranged for his son to be attached to the Priory of the Holy Rosary, one of the greatest Dominican houses in the New World. Its inmates numbered some 300 monks and lay brothers, together with a full complement of novices, servants and negro slaves. The Dominicans attended to the spiritual, intellectual and even to many of the material needs of the capital. They cared for the sick and for orphans, taught in the university, trained their own novices and missionaries for work amongst the Indians, and ran their own farms outside Lima for the support of the community. The Order was powerful enough to challenge, on occasion, the civil authorities in defence of its privileges or principles. When Martín was five or six years old, a posse of monks had rushed out from the Priory and seized two negroes who were being led off to execution, and had then attempted to give them sanctuary. But the Viceroy's men broke into the church and regained possession of the prisoners. The prior, together with the Provincial, Father Salvador de Rivera, were sent back to Spain in punishment for their part in this episode. Father Rivera, later allowed back on the intercession of his friend and pro-tector, the saintly don Toribio, became prior of the Order's *casa grande* and proved zealous in furthering the construction of its great church.

Martín was not destined to move in these exalted circles and aspired to no part in public affairs. His only desire was to serve, and that in the lowly capacity of a *donado,* "one given to God", whose menial status was one degree above that of a slave. Don Juan de Porres was

irritated that a son of his should be content with such a servile station
and threatened, unless he were admitted to the priesthood, that he
would not allow him to enter the Order at all. The Dominicans' rule,
as formulated a few years after Martín's death, affirmed that "we
ordain, as has been often ordained most severely in the past, and do
mostly strictly command, that nowhere in the Provinces of the Indies
may there ever be received into the holy habit and profession of our
Order those known as *mestizos* or those who are begotten on either
side of their parents of Indian or African blood". Some of Martín's
biographers maintain that, in view of his father's influence and office,
the Dominicans were prepared to waive their general objection to
taking a mulatto into their ranks, and that although Martín's humility
precluded him from aspiring to the priesthood, he was at length given
the habit of a lay-brother. The point is obscure, and it seems probable
that Martín in fact remained no more than a *donado* to the end of his
life. All we can say with certainty is that when he reached the age
of 24, after serving the Order loyally for nine years, he was allowed
the privilege of taking vows of some kind, though not necessarily
those which would give him full status as a lay-brother.

The Priory and its surroundings were to remain the scene of Fray
Martín's activities for the rest of his days. He never travelled more
than the few leagues which separated it from the monastery's farm
at Limatambo or the port of Callao, where he had taken a broken-
down and destitute old soldier under his care. No man ever crammed
a more astonishingly full round of lowly tasks into his life, whether
it was "cleansing the filthy places of the monastery", collecting and
distributing food to the poor, making new shirts for the monks, planting trees and medicinal herbs on some plot of waste ground, patching
up family quarrels or broken limbs, or looking after some stray cat
or dog, so that it could be said of him that "he would devote the
whole day and night to ardent charity, ceaselessly healing, bleeding,
and tending the patients and performing at one and the same time the
offices of barber, surgeon, wardrobe-keeper and infirmarian". Above
all, it was for his unfailing and universal compassion and his marvellous gifts of healing that Fray Martín's name became a household
word.

Only those who lived closest to him saw something of the intense
life of spiritual devotion and penance which nurtured this tireless
activity. Fray Martín left no writings of his own, nor, regrettably, do
we know anything from those who were his spiritual directors as to
his inner struggles and the graces which crowned them. Some ill-
natured contemporaries looked down on him as a "mulatto dog" who

"should be set to work in a galley rather than a monastery" (to which Fray Martín would humbly reply—"You know me only too well!") and refused to believe that a menial half-breed could be the instrument chosen for such singular favours. But there is a mass of testimony to Martín's personality and apostolic mode of life from the simple folk amongst whom he lived which furnished the matter for his beatification and the biography devoted to him by a fellow member of the Order.

First, there was his extraordinary gift of healing, the virtue which enabled him to relieve pain by a mere touch of the hand, the intuitive awareness of his patients' needs, which seemed to them something quite miraculous. "He was tireless in tending the sick, both day and night", writes his biographer, Bernardo de Medina, "serving them on his knees as if he saw Jesus Christ in each one of them. And there happened a strange thing. When the servant of God was away from the infirmary busy with other things, the sick had only to call him by name and he would immediately be at their side, although he could not have heard them calling. . . . Nor did they often need so much as to call him, for whenever he was needed Our Lord revealed it to him, and he would forthwith hurry to their help. . . . When the sick [monks] were in great pain and required his help, it was astounding to see that they had only to desire his presence and call for him inwardly, though it might be at dead of night, and he would come into their cells with the praises of God on his lips, and would soothe, tend and nurse them and then go back to his prayers, which he had broken off from the sweet office of Mary in exchange for the zealous labours of Martha."

Fray Martín ministrations were not confined to the brethren of the priory. He would go through the city visiting the sick, and would often bring them back to nurse them in his cell. As the fame of his compassion and healing powers spread, the number of diseased and injured who came in search of Fray Martín grew to such an extent that the monastery seemed in danger of becoming one huge hospital. The monks grew alarmed and decided that something must be done. "Fearing that infection or contagion might spread throughout the monastery, the prelates commanded him to have the patients moved. This greatly grieved the man of God, and he besought them with tears in his eyes and good reasons on his lips to give him leave to nurse them. But seeing that his Superior would not consent, he put obedience before piety." Providence soon provided a solution. Martín's sister Juana had married and was living in Lima, so "he asked his sister to put aside a room in her house where he might house the patients, and there he looked after them, bringing doctors, medicines and other things to them there".

But those in dire need still sometimes came to the monastery in search of the good friar, and, despite the Prior's prohibition, Fray Martín had not the heart to turn them away. One day a poor Indian, almost lifeless from a gaping wound, dragged himself to the door of the monastery and Fray Martín took him in and tended him in his cell until he was well enough to join the other patients in his sister's house. In due course the Indian returned, perfectly restored to health, to show his benefactor the scar which was all that remained of the wound. The affair, in the meantime, had come to the ears of the Prior who chided his infirmarian for breaking the monastery rules. "But Father," was Fray Martín's meek reply, "Charity knows no rules." It was impossible to be angry with Fray Martín, whatever inconvenience might be caused by the unorthodox forms which his extraordinary compassion and self-denial would sometimes take. On one occasion, when the monastery was short of money badly needed for the infirmary, Fray Martín came to the Prior and proposed a simple solution; the money could be raised by selling him as a slave. Fortunately, the Priory of the Rosary had the good sense not to part with their unique *donado*.

Another facet of Fray Martín's personality which gave rise to much puzzled comment was his love of animals. Peru, which had only known the llama and the guinea-pig as domestic animals before the coming of the Spaniards, was not a country of pet-lovers. Even the good monks could be surprisingly callous, as the following incident narrated by Fray Martín's biographer shows. There was an old dog in the Priory which had belonged for many years to the Procurator or Bursar who finally decided that the beast was too old to be of any further use and turned him out into the street. The dog kept coming back and being shooed away again until his master angrily told the negro slaves to make an end of him. Fray Martín came up just when they had carried out their orders and gave them a piece of his mind. Then he took the dog's apparently lifeless body back to his cell and went straight off to see the Procurator, and upbraided him, his biographer tells us, in the following words: " 'How could you treat so heartlessly someone who served you so truly and so long? Is this the reward you give him for his service?' And taking leave of him he went back to the wardrobe, which was his cell, and shut himself up there with the dead dog, and it can be presumed that he prayed God to restore the animal to life, which favour the Lord vouchsafed for him. The next morning he came out of the cell with the dog not only alive but healed of all the injuries they had done him. He then took him along to the infirmary kitchen and said, 'Do not go back, my brother, to the office where your ungrateful master is, as you know what sort of payment you can expect at his hands'. And the beast did so obediently what he had been told that, in the many years of life which still remained to him, he never went near the Procurator, but if he even so much as caught sight of him, the dog would make off as if he would not have anything more to do with such an ungrateful master."

Many are the stories related of Fray Martín's care and love for animals. We read of the innumerable stray cats and dogs taken in from the street and looked after until they were cured, the old mule left to die by the roadside which struggled to its feet at a word from the friar and followed him back to the monastery where it gave many more years of good service, the calves which had been left without food and water by careless servants and were saved by Fray Martín's attentions, the wounded deer which he nursed back to health in his cell and which for many years after would come down from the hills to be fed and caressed at his hands, the loathsome vulture even whose broken wing he mended, so that "dogs, cats, hens, birds, rats, even the most ferocious bulls, in short, each showed their gratitude after their own fashion towards the servant of God and recognized in him their benefactor".

The strange power which the friar exercised over dumb animals, his companions noted with awe, was illustrated by the way in which he could make the most different species—cats, dogs, even mice— eat quietly together off the same plate. One of the most delightful stories told of Fray Martín is how he dealt with a plague of rats. "The rats were playing havoc with the infirmary linen which he kept in his cell; but he still would not permit any of them to be killed as that seemed too heavy a punishment for so light a crime. But in view of the damage they were doing the monastery he one day allowed a trap to be set. Then, when a young rat had been caught in it, the servant of God picked it up without doing it the slightest injury and said to it: 'Run off now, brother rat, and tell your companions that they are doing a great deal of harm to this community, and that I feel sorry for them going short of food and so have not let any of them be killed. But they must not be a nuisance and do any harm to the linen. From now on, they can go out into the garden and each day I will bring some food out to them'. When he had said this he let the rat go and —wonderful to relate—the little creatures behaved just as if they had understood and they did what they had been told so obediently that they all came out of the wardrobe and the next morning, there they were all together in the garden. Fray Martín did as he had promised and brought them food. This went on day after day. As soon as the servant of God appeared, swarms of rats would come out to meet him, as if they were answering a bell, and they would get their food from his hands, to the great wonder of all the monks who beheld this singular sight."

The explanation given by Fray Martín's biographer for a love of animals which seemed so unaccountable to his contemporaries is probably not far wide of the mark. "His charity extended even to brute animals, for although charity does not lay upon us the obligation of loving creatures which lack understanding and the means of attaining the glory which is the object of charity, yet man can love animals as creatures of the Creator, directing this love towards God and taking delight in preserving those animals for the honour of God and the benefit of his neighbour." Nevertheless, this concern for the lower creation could also have its inconveniences. The monks, in time, tired of seeing their priory serve as a clinic for sick animals and told Fray Martín to find another home for them. Once again, it was the long-suffering Juana who came to his rescue, though this burden soon proved almost too much for her. "So many cases of this sort occurred that, in order to care for the dogs, cats and other animals without causing a nuisance in the monastery, he transferred them to a room in his sister's house. But as there were so many of them that they could not help making a mess of the place, his sister could not put up with it and complained to her brother and asked him to remove them from her house. When Fray Martín came to see them they all swarmed round him licking and caressing him as they always did, and he then addressed them in these words : 'You must not be a nuisance, my brothers, to those who are kind enough to look after you. Keep out of the rooms which are not set aside for your use. And when you need to relieve nature, go out into the street'. Wonderful to relate, it seemed just as if the animals understood what he said, for never again did any of them set foot in his sister's quarters, and they only left their own room to go into the plaza in order to relieve nature, so that all who knew of it marvelled greatly."

The sick, the poor, the hungry, whatever their condition, whatever their need, would turn to Fray Martín and receive at his hands what often seemed to them miraculous relief. "On leaving the refectory he would put his own portion of food into a pot, together with the scraps left over from the meal, and would then go to the infirmary where a crowd of poor folk—Spaniards, Indians, negroes, and children—would be waiting, bowl in hand, for him to relieve their hunger. Even the animals looked to Fray Martín for help. Before distributing the food, the servant of God would pronounce a blessing over it saying: 'May God, in his infinite mercy, grant it increase.' And this, it seems, is indeed what happened." Much of his time would be spent out of the priory, going from house to house collecting alms from the rich and distributing to the poor, not in any haphazard fashion, but according to the need and condition of each, whether it was the substantial sum of 4,000 pesos required for a girl's marriage dowry or a few penny-worth of bread to keep the starving prisoners in the city jail alive. (Once he had recourse to pawning his own hat for this purpose.) Fray Martín was a familiar figure in Lima. Pious ladies and charitable merchants would give generously, for they knew that the money would be wisely laid out. The Viceroy himself, the Conde de Chinchón, con-tributed 100 pesos a month and would sometimes call in person at the priory to visit the friar, 'seating himself on a chest where the patients' clothes were kept, for there was no chair in the cell'. Fray Martín helped as many as 160 needy families every week, besides collecting and dispensing alms according to a regular pattern; on Thursdays and Fridays, for needy students and clergy, on Sundays, clothes and blankets for the use of negroes and Indians, on Tuesdays and Wednes-days for other poor folk, on Sundays and Mondays, to pay for masses to be said for souls in purgatory.

The homeless urchins roaming the streets of Lima excited Fray Martín's special compassion. Some he would take to the priory, but as their numbers grew, as the numbers of his human and animal patients had grown, a home had to be found for them elsewhere. With the help of a friend, a well-to-do apothecary called Mateo Pastor, a house was purchased where waifs and strays, girls as well as boys, could be housed. This orphanage, the College of the Holy Cross (an establishment of this name, though not, it seems, the direct descendant of Fray Martín's foundation, still exists in Lima today) appears to have been the only institutional form taken by Fray Martín's charity, though his spirit of service was to remain an inspira-tion for many future generations. Some of Fray Martín's orphans, particularly a Spanish lad called Juan Vásquez whom he had found wandering destitute in the priory cemetery and who was later to leave us many interesting details about the saint's life, became his com-panions and helpers in these works of mercy.

Fray Martín was to find another helper in the person of his own sister, Juana. The relationship between a brother resolved to dedicate himself entirely to his vocation of universal service and a sister, humble half-caste like himself, warm-hearted and generous but without the heroic quality of the saint's charity, emerges movingly through the pages of his biography. When Juana married and moved from Guayaquil to Lima, she would come to the priory and reproach him for never coming to see her. "Can you not spare a few hours for your own flesh and blood, brother? Must you spend them all with your brethren the friars, and not one with your own sister?" Fray Martín's reply, as recorded by his biographer, seems uncharacteristically harsh; perhaps it was some time before he came to realize that family ties could serve not as a distraction, but as a means of promoting his works of charity. "Go back to your home," he answered, "and leave me to mine. God has not called me to work in the infirmary only to be constantly interrupted by you!" But Juana was not to be so easily deterred from her sisterly concern. "As his office was commonly to look after the sick and to bleed them, and to sweep out the dirty places of the monastery, his sister noticed his unkempt appearance and offered to make him another tunic and habit." Later, she must have offered the use of her own house to serve, as we have seen, as a place of refuge for Fray Martín's human and animal sufferers.

Fray Martín had his own way of returning his sister's affection. Juana, it seems, was not always happy with her husband. As he kept her so short of money, Juana had an extra key made to his money-box and resolved to help herself to meet the needs of her family. Though no one had breathed a word of this to Fray Martín, he seemed to know all about it, took her sternly to task, and made her throw away the key. As long as he was there, he told her, she need never worry that she or her family would go lacking. Fray Martín proved as good as his word. Juana's daughter Catalina was growing up to marriageable age, but was too poor to buy the *manta* indispensable to any respectable girl in Lima. One day a servant arrived from a milliner's with seven or eight *mantas* and a message from her uncle that she could choose the one she liked best and send the others back. Fray Martín seemed to have an uncanny insight into people's problems and weaknesses and would appear as if by magic just when his presence was most needed. Catalina relates another occasion when her parents had taken her out for a day in the country but had quarrelled violently. They were sullenly preparing to come back to the city when a smiling Fray Martín arrived, as if miraculously apprised of what was afoot, and quickly restored them all to good humour.

We read, too, of another close and enduring friendship in the life of Martín de Porres. This was with the porter of the other and smaller Dominican monastery dedicated to St. Mary Magdalene on the outskirts of the city. The porter, a Spanish lay-brother called Juan Macías, was almost as extraordinary a character as Fray Martín. Left an orphan when he was four, he had tended pigs and sheep in his native Estremadura and then wandered about doing casual jobs until, at the age of 34, deciding to leave Spain. But Juan Macías was no ordinary adventurer. "When, in the year 1619, I took ship to the Indies," he later declared, "it was not with the intent and desire of getting rich, but that God's will might be accomplished in me." From his tenderest years, whilst guarding his flocks in the hills of Estremadura, Juan had been favoured by heavenly visions. His guardian angel, moreover, was none other than St. John the Evangelist himself, who had constantly accompanied him on his wanderings and had once rescued him when the innocent youth wandered into a brothel in Seville under the curious impression that it was a church. Juan, the very embodiment of *sancta simplicitas,* continued to be favoured by the divine protection. On reaching Cartagena, he wandered overland to Bogotá, Quito, and finally to Lima, where he arrived unharmed and resumed his old calling as a shepherd. During the two and a half years that he remained in the service of his master, a wealthy butcher, he declared that "St. John the Evangelist was constantly at my side, and he would carry me off far, far away, whether in the spirit or the body I know not", in the comtemplation of his heavenly visions. Finally, St. John told him to join the Dominicans, which he did, dividing the rest of his life between his humdrum tasks as a porter and an unremitting round of prayer and penance. Juan became famous for the zeal with which he collected and distributed food to the many who came to the monastery for help, and for the miraculous way in which the food seemed to be multiplied in his hands so that none was ever turned away hungry. The pious porter seldom left his lodge, but preferred to send the monastery donkey off on its own with messages to his former master the butcher, and to other charitable folk, who would load the beast up with the food asked of them and send it back to the monastery. We do not read that Fray Juan had his friend's gifts of healing, "agility" or "subtility", or even his green fingers and love of animals, but in the severity of their self-imposed penances, their burning charity, and their dedication to prayer, the Spanish lay-brother and the mulatto *donado* found much in common.

In addition to their two monasteries, the Dominicans owned a number of farms which were worked by negro slaves and sent in their produce for the support of the communities. One of these farms was at Limatambo, half a league outside the city, which Fray Martín would often ask permission to visit. "When he was at the farm in

Limatambo, after spending all the day in devout works, he would go
at night to the negroes' quarters, bringing with him ointments and
other medicines which he had brought with him from the city, and
there he would treat their pains and aches, speaking to them words
of encouragement but also of reproof for their vices, telling some of
them what they had stolen that day. Afterwards he would go to the
quarters where the old and sick negresses lay, nursing and healing
them as best he could, for his charity extended to all, and he did it
for God, whom he loved."

These excursions gave Fray Martín the opportunity to turn his hand
to a self-imposed task which shows his personality in a peculiarly sympathetic light—the planting of fruit trees and medicinal herbs for the
benefit of his brethren in the monasteries and for the public at large.
This was a labour of love in which he sometimes found willing helpers,
though none had the mulatto's green fingers which enabled the seed-
lings to take root and yield fruit in an astonishingly short time. Limatambo was enriched by a fine and extensive olive grove in this way.
Often he could be seen planting camomile and other herbs by the
wayside for the benefit of those who were too poor to buy them from
the apothecary; at other times "he would go out into the fields and
hill-sides and there plant fig-trees; and that to such good effect that
they would take root marvellously. And when the lad who accompanied him and other devoted friends asked him why he put himself
to what appeared to be such unnecessary labour, he would answer
them : 'In two or three years' time, these fig-trees will bear fruit, and
any poor folk who pass this way and lack food will be able to sate
their hunger somewhat by eating the figs without any need to break
into the orchards and pick fruit there against the wishes of their
owners. And although the fig-trees will not belong to them, they will
be able to eat of their fruit without committing the sin of touching
what is not theirs' ". Another account speaks of Fray Martín planting
not only fig-trees, olives and herbs but even sweet-smelling flowers by
the wayside for the refreshment and delight of wayfarers and the
greater glory of the Creator.

In the light of such testimony we might be inclined to look on
Martín de Porres as some sort of pioneer of voluntary social service,
a "man of the trees", or enlightened forerunner of the nature conserva-
tionists of our own day. This would be to ignore a whole dimension
of the man, the dimension which indeed he strove to keep from prying
eyes and to practise as a secret between himself and his God—the
dimension of a personal sanctity forged from prayer and penance. But
try as he might, Fray Martín could not wholly conceal the rigours of

his mortification from those who lived closest to him. His knees, as one witness graphically puts it, were calloused like those of a camel from the long hours spent in prayer. His biographer writes that his recreation was "to toil tirelessly, digging and sowing healing herbs for the poor. Then he would withdraw to the most secluded part of the farm and turn to his prayers and penances". At night, in the privacy of his cell, he would scourge himself mercilessly, "from the thighs down to the calves of his legs and the soles of his feet, repeating at the same time all the offensive words addressed to him by irritable patients so that he not only lacerated his body with the discipline, but lashed his soul with the memory of the insults received". Sometimes he would inflict his penances in the burial vaults so as to impress upon his mind still more deeply the sense of his own nothingness and the transitoriness of human life. We are told of him too, as of St. Luis Bertrán, in the marshes of New Granada, that he would bare his body to the bites of mosquitoes. If this is the voice of legend, it comes to us with the unmistakable accents of Fray Martín, for we read that he did this "not only that the insects might mortify him, but also to sustain them with his own blood, for they too are God's creatures". The moments of respite which Fray Martín allowed himself from such penances were of the scantiest. He would snatch a little sleep stretched out on the monastery catafalque or at the foot of some patient's bed in the infirmary. According to another account, "his custom was to retire at night to some tall chests where the patients' clothes were kept and there he would remain, his arms folded on his breast in the shape of a cross and half his body hanging out of the chest in a way more conducive to mortification than to repose. He would sleep like that until a cat, prompted surely by some impulse from above rather than by any natural instinct, would start pulling and clawing at his habit when he would wake marvellously in time to ring the dawn bell, a custom which he observed throughout his life".

Nor could the friar's humility always hide his state of ecstasy from the eyes of others. Once when the monastery was shaken by one of the light tremors which are so often felt in Peru and sometimes herald the imminence of a serious earthquake, a lad came rushing into Fray Martín's cell and found him, rosary in hand, prostrate on the ground. The boy shook him, and failing to rouse him, took him for dead and hurried off to fetch help. But the monks at once recognized Fray Martín's state, and before long the friar had come to himself and was going about his usual duties. Sometimes his raptures would be accompanied by the phenomenon of levitation. A fellow *donado* called Ignacio de Santo Domingo swore on his death-bed that he had seen

4. San Toribio de Mogrovejo

5. San Francisco Solano

6. San Martín de Porres

Fray Martín caught up in prayer and suspended in the air six times, and that it had been the sight of this marvel which had first moved him to seek entry into the Order. The lad who accompanied him on his errands of mercy declared that Fray Martín would often go off by himself to pray in the solitude of the fields, and that he had seen him many times suspended in ecstasy several feet above the ground. Two monks also related how they had once come into Fray Martín's cell and, not finding him there, were about to leave when one of them felt something lightly brush against the cowl of his habit. He looked up to see the man of God suspended in prayer above the door of his cell.

Fray Martín was widely credited with two further supernatural faculties—those of "agility" and "subtility". It was believed, in short, that he could literally be in two or more places at the same time, and that he could be supernaturally conveyed through solid objects such as stone walls and locked doors. It was not only a question of the multifarious activities, far beyond the powers of ordinary mortals, which the friar seemed able to cram into every 24 hours; nor even of the uncanny speed with which he would appear by the bedside of the sick, knowing their needs and anticipating their whims to a degree that seemed due to more than intuition. Stranger things still were recounted and solemnly sworn to by many respectable witnesses in his beatification process. For many of them the scene was the novitiate, a building which stood apart from the main monastery and was kept locked and bolted every night by the novice-master, who slept with the keys under his pillow. Fray Martín was reported to have come frequently to the aid of some novice taken ill in the night, without disturbing the novice-master or even being summoned from the main building. One day when the friar was urgently needed for some emergency in the priory, five monks were sent to scour the monastery for him and told to meet together later at a given rendezvous to report whether they had found him. They gathered together, their errands completed, as instructed, and *each* reported success; *each* said he had found Fray Martín busy about his labours in five different parts of the priory, and he had at once left to go where he was now needed. Nor was this phenomenon of bi-location confined to Lima. One merchant friend had gone on a journey to Mexico and had fallen ill there. What was his surprise to receive an unexpected visit from Fray Martín there, only to discover, when he recovered and returned to Lima, that his friend had never left the priory. Others claimed to have benefited from Fray Martín's ministrations in Spain, France, Africa and other parts of the world.

Fray Martín did nothing himself to promote this aura of the supernatural with which his contemporaries were apt to surround him. His calling was simply to serve. Wherever men were in need, Fray Martín's place was at their side. When, in 1639, at the age of 60, he lay in his cell stricken with a mortal illness, word was brought that a negro had been brought into the infirmary in great pain and required urgent attention. Fray Martín reproached himself most bitterly for lying there uselessly whilst others had need of him—he, a mere mulatto dog, the least and most worthless of God's creatures. To the very end of his days, Fray Martín remained deeply aware of the urgency and universality of man's need and of the call which he had received from God to relieve it. It is the fullness of his response which marks the life and work of Fray Martín de Porres with the true stamp of the supernatural.

CHAPTER 6

The Rose of Lima
Santa Rosa de Santa María

In the time of Fray Jerónimo de Loaysa, predecessor of *el santo arzobispo,* a picturesque ceremony took place in the Cathedral at Lima. In the presence of a numerous congregation, the Archbishop knelt before the image of the Blessed Virgin Mary and reverently placed a rose at her feet. It was the first to be grown from seed introduced into Peru by some pious flower-lover in the year 1552. The seed had been blessed and then planted in a plot of ground on which there came to be built the Hospital del Espíritu Santo, and not long afterwards, a more modest house where an old soldier called Gaspar de Flores went to live with his family. The roses flourished in the fertile soil and the mild climate of Lima and continued to grow in profusion in the garden of the Flores family. The Archbishop's floral offering had a deeper symbolism than he could have foreseen. The child who grew up amongst the roses and took her name from them dedicated her life to the same Virgin and became known to history as Rosa de Santa María—St. Rose of Lima.

Rosa's parents could be classed as *hidalgos de segunda fila,* gentry of the second rank and of somewhat straitened circumstances. Her father had come in his youth from Puerto Rico and fought for the Crown in the civil wars which followed the conquest of Peru. Later in life he served as an arquebusier in the Viceroy's guard and married María de Oliva, a high-spirited, quick-tempered Creole girl much younger than himself, who gave him 13 children. The one who was to become famous was born in 1586 and christened Isabel, after her maternal grandmother, Isabel de Herrera, and figures in the baptismal register under that name, with the curious annotation *hija de estima,* instead of the more usual *hija legítima,* indicating perhaps some special mark of affection on the part of the parents. The child was certainly remarkable from earliest infancy for her fair and flower-like beauty. "A perfect rose!" the Indian maid-of-all-work, Mariana, is said to have exclaimed when she set eyes on the babe. Some biographers add that she was born enveloped in a fine membrane or caul, just like a rose-bud, whilst others declare that a rose of unearthly beauty appeared on the infant's cradle to indicate the supernatural destiny in store for her.

Rosa, then, seemed in every way an appropriate name for the child. But it was not to gain unanimous acceptance in the family without a battle—the first, it seems, of that long series of bitter trials and tribulations which was to be her lot throughout life. The grandmother after whom the child had been christened felt slighted and insisted on calling her Isabel and on punishing her if she answered to the hated nickname. Her mother no less obstinately declared that she was Rosa and must answer only to that name. For a sensitive, submissive and affectionate child this battle of wills and the divided loyalties resulting from it was a distressing experience.

Gaspar de Flores and his wife must soon have become uneasily aware that their youngest daughter was no ordinary child. There was something odd about the games which, as a mere toddler, she played or refused to play. She would never, for instance, touch dolls, and when asked why, would answer they seemed to her to be idols—an astonishing remark unless we bear in mind that, even today, the dolls still played with by Peruvian children do have an unmistakable look of fetishes or little "idols" about them, and that the Indian population of Rosa's day, though nominally Christian, often cherished their ancient gods in secret. Rosa liked to steal away to some nook in the house or garden when the other children were playing and remain hour after hour in silent initiation into the life of prayer, contemplation and penance for which she already showed a precocious vocation. She hated to be interrupted in those pursuits as other children hate to be interrupted in their games. Her mother, a woman of some education despite a rough tongue and violent temper, tried to teach her daughter to read but met with little success. The little girl showed no interest in the lessons and looked on them as a waste of time; why could she not simply be left alone with her prayers? Her mother stormed and declared that the family confessor would make her see reason. When the priest sat down beside the girl, opened a book and told her to try and spell out the letters, both he and her mother were amazed to hear Rosa begin to read aloud with no apparent difficulty. Given a pen, she wrote down a few sentences with equal fluency. It seemed uncanny; she had learned to read and write with no help from anyone. A similar story is told of Rosa when she had grown older. She loved music and had a pretty voice, but no one had ever taught her to play a musical instrument. Yet it happened one day when she was carried away in spirit and felt an overmastering impulse to give vent to her emotions that she took down a guitar which was hanging on the wall and started to accompany herself with complete sureness of touch. Later, we are told, she became proficient, without the help of any tutor, with a number of other instruments.

Rosa was a quick, precocious girl in everything—precocious, above all, in a craving to submit herself to a course of self-denial which, starting with a refusal to eat of the many delicious fruits produced in the country and leading on to the most fearsome self-imposed penances, she persisted in following with a single-minded zeal bordering at times on masochism. Yet Rosa was not a gloomy child; she loved flowers, birds and all living things, and had an artistic sense which found expression in her spontaneous music-making and little poems, in the skill and loveliness of her embroidery and in her cultivation and arrangement of flowers. A sweet and sensitive nature was accompanied by what her foremost biographer describes as her *peregrina hermosura*, a strange or rare beauty—rare in part, no doubt, because of her fair hair, an unusual and much admired feature in women of hispanic stock. These golden tresses were to give rise to a memorable incident in Rosa's childhood. Her brother Fernando, playing one day in the garden, thought he would see what they looked like with a few handfuls of dirt rubbed into them. Did not his little sister know, he taunted, with the superior wisdom of one two years her senior, that a woman's beautiful hair was a snare with which to catch men and send their souls to hell? Rosa was horror-stricken; less by the dirt in her hair than by the thought that she might be the cause of another's perdition. Rushing into the house and seizing a pair of scissors she cropped the offending locks as closely to her head as she could.

Fernando was nevertheless devoted to his sister, though her imaginative and hyper-sensitive nature sometimes left him exasperated as well as puzzled. Merely to set eyes on a cross was enough to move Rosa profoundly, not only in church or wayside shrine, but even at the chance sight of some natural object recalling that sacred symbol. When she grew older, Fernando took to accompanying her to church and we are told that "if she should happen to see on the way some twig or piece of straw or anything at all lying on the ground in the form of a cross, she would stoop down and remove it so it should not be trodden upon. This happened so often that it took a long time for them to reach church as she was always stopping to perform this act of piety in the street." Fernando not unnaturally found this intensely irritating and told his sister that such behaviour was indecorous and absurd and that she would only make herself a laughing stock. Rosa replied that people might laugh at her as much as they liked, but for her it was agony to see anything which recalled the cross of Christ being trodden under foot.

As she grew up, a resolve began to form in Rosa's mind which was bound to provoke a major crisis in the Flores family. Her biographers tell us that she was no more than five when she "vowed her virginity to Jesus Christ". Perhaps, in its early stages, this was little more than part of the game of "playing at nuns"; an element of devout make-belief may even still be seen in the famous episode when she later commissioned her brother to have a marriage ring made for her and received it in a solemn ceremony before the image of Our Lady of the Rosary in token of her spiritual betrothal to the divine Spouse. Whether entered into at the age of five or formalized later in the Priory of the Rosary, the concept of the mystical marriage was to lie at the heart of Rosa's contemplative life and to provide both the goal and the justification for the path of renunciation and dedication which she felt called upon to follow.

*   *   *   *

Extraordinary as such a destiny might appear to Rosa's contemporaries in Lima, and as it still seems to us today, it becomes less so when viewed as part of the traditional pattern of Spanish spirituality. From early times women, as well as men, had responded in Spain to this call to extreme asceticism and often frightening mystical experiences. Nor had they always had the shelter of convent walls; sometimes their vocation had been to continue in, if not of, the world. The 13th Century poet Berceo has left us a picture of an eccentric maiden who chose to live virtually walled up in her parent's home, the holy virgin Oria "in whose prayers God took such delight that He opened the heavens to grant her great visions, by which men's hearts might be turned". By the end of the 15th Century, when the epic of the Reconquista had ended with the triumph of the Cross, religious exaltation reached a new peak and resulted in a proliferation of *beatas,* some of whom were no longer content to tread the mystic path in seclusion but gave public utterance to the favours they claimed to receive. This was a disconcerting phenomenon which the conventionally pious found hard to explain. "For the last two centuries", wrote the Hieronymite friar José de Sigüenza, who had chronicled many such singular cases, "there have been saintly women in these parts whom Our Lord has been pleased to treat—be it said with all reverence—in a novel fashion, making Himself so open and accessible to them that one can only suspend judgment and leave it all to the verdict of the Church, from whom, as His beloved Bride, He will not conceal the secrets of His heart".

But these *beatas* believed that they, and not merely the Church in general, were in a particular and personal sense the Brides of Christ. A sect of men and women known as *alumbrados,* who claimed to be "illumined" by direct revelation, made their appearance in Spain. Their pretensions smacked of heresy and seemed to call in question the authority of the Church. The latter looked very warily on all who claimed to be receiving special spiritual graces; were they indeed favoured servants of God, or were they imposters or—still worse—the objects of diabolical possession? An enigma of this sort had been posed in the early years of the 16th Century by Sor María de Santo Domingo, commonly known as the Beata of Piedrahita from the small town near Avila which became the centre of her cult. The *beata,* as Rosa was later to do, took the habit of a Dominican tertiary, became famous for her austerities and ecstasies, and regarded herself in an almost literal sense as the Bride of Christ. But unlike the modest Lima maiden, she seems to have had a strong streak of exhibitionism. Sor María claimed to be on familiar terms with the Blessed Virgin and her Divine Son and would chat with them familiarly in public. The local Dominican friars vowed that she was a saint destined to reform their Order; the great Cardinal Cisneros spoke of her as an "angelic soul" and even King Ferdinand regarded her with veneration. But there were many others who looked upon the *beata* as a deluded fanatic or worse, and nothing ever came of her pretensions to ecclesiastical reform.

Dreadful cases had occurred of women, reputed for years for their sanctity and miracle-working powers, being suddenly detected as frauds. The most notorious case of this sort had been that of Magdalena de la Cruz, the revered abbess of a Franciscan convent in Córdoba, who had enjoyed the confidence of the Spanish King and his Queen before being unmasked as one who had been all those years— according to her own confession—betrothed not to Jesus Christ but to the Devil! Another impostor, known as the Nun of Lisbon, was at the height of her fame when Rosa was born. The saintly but over-credulous Luis de Granada, whose works were to be amongst Rosa's favourite reading, had just finished compiling an edifying Life of this nun when the latter's impostures were unmasked by the Inquisition.

Saint or sinner—deluded, deceitful, or divinely inspired? It was not always easy to say. There had, for example, been the puzzling case of Juana de la Cruz whose strange life and miracles served Fray Gabiel Téllez, the famous dramatist who wrote under the name of

Tirso de Molina, as the subject of one of his plays, completed some four years before Rosa's death; *Saint* Juana he called his heroine, though the Censor prudently pressed him to substitute the safer epithet "servant of God". Juana was a beautiful girl whom her parents were anxious to marry off to advantage. But Juana vowed that she would take no other spouse than Jesus Christ and declared that it had been vouchsafed to her in a vision that her prayer would be granted. To prepare for her spiritual union, Juana subjected herself to frightening penances. She kept gall and wormwood in her mouth in memory of Christ's passion, encased her young limbs in a sort of coat of mail, bound sharp stones and shards to her knees, and stood on tiptoe against the wall of her cell, into which she had driven nails, in a manner of self-crucifixion. The consolations vouchsafed to her were commensurate with her pains and it was also given to her to speak with tongues. Then suddenly all these favours ceased and obscurity descended upon Juana de la Cruz. Perhaps the singularity of these happenings brought suspicion of diabolism, if not of heresy, upon her and caused her to be silenced. But Juana de la Cruz was never shown to have been an impostor and there were many who continued to revere her as a saint after her death. When her tomb was opened in 1609, it was said that her body had been found uncorrupted and fragrant.

Then there was the great Teresa of Avila, whose seven brothers had all sought their fortunes in the New World and whose life and writings spoke eloquently of her sanctity though the Church had not yet canonized her. Rosa may have heard too of doña Sancha Carrillo, a young lady of noble birth who had been converted when about to become a lady in-waiting to the Queen and had then retired to live in prayer, solitude and penitence near her parents' home. Luis de Granada had written movingly of the mystical "favours, consolations and gifts" vouchsafed to this youthful recluse and of her early death, brought on either as the result of plunging into a tank of cold water "when she was suffering mighty temptations from the spirit of fornication and saw that this was to the peril of her faith and virginal purity", or because of "the great drought and famine which so distressed and moved her to compassion for the poor that she offered up to Our Lord her own health and life for them, if only their necessities might be relieved". There were, in short, many examples of heroic if singular sanctity which Rosa may have found exemplified in the lives of these other near-contemporary Brides of Christ and resolved to take as patterns for her own.

It was, however, to an earlier saint, a native of Italy and not Spain, that Rosa looked for her chief inspiration—Catherine of Siena. Born in that city-state of strife-torn Italy two and a half centuries earlier, the youngest member of a prosperous dyer's household (nearly twice the size of Rosa's large family, for she had more than twenty brothers and sisters) Catherine defied convention and her mother's scoldings for refusing to consider marriage and chose instead, whilst still living at home, a life of extraordinary mortification and mystical contemplation. Becoming the centre of a spiritual "family" of her own, she had then embarked on an unprecedented career as teacher, mentor and peacemaker amongst the feuding factions of the time, travelling to Avignon and pleading successfully with the Pope to return to Rome, and whilst never departing from her life of strictest poverty and penance, keeping up a correspondence of deep spiritual insight and shrewd practical wisdom with popes and princes. Rosa did not aspire to imitate the saint in her role as a great public figure, but in the severity of her mortifications and self-denial. She lacked Catherine's charismatic personality, eloquence and virile intelligence, being blessed instead—or handicapped, as she deemed it, in her passion for self-abasement—with unusual personal beauty. She must have recognized from her reading of Catherine's life those same yearnings and experiences which, albeit on a humbler scale, were her own, and become aware of new depths of self-surrender which she felt moved to emulate. From the childish impulse to cut off her hair, through such matters as abstaining from food and the taking of a Dominican tertiary's habit, to the whole range of preternatural experience, Rosa trod resolutely in the footsteps of the Sienese saint. When an insensitive confessor dismissed her revelations and visions as no more than the vain fantasies of a mind unhinged by too much fasting and penance, Rosa consoled herself with the thought that her dear mistress had likewise at first been disbelieved and misjudged.

*　　　　*　　　　*　　　　*

We do not know exactly when Rosa began to take Saint Catherine as her model; probably at a very early age, for the cult of the saint had spread to the New World and her parents may have owned some image or painting of St. Catherine, probably crudely executed but vivid enough to have caught her childish imagination. When she grew old enough to read, there came into her hands a Life of the saint, which we are told she came to know almost by heart. One trait which Rosa shared with the Italian saint was her extraordinary and precocious fortitude under suffering. Her biographers relate many stories from her early childhood to illustrate this; the thumb crushed by the lid of a heavy chest, the corrosive agony of a mercury salve misguidedly applied to her scalp by her mother. All such things the little girl bore with gentle stoicism remarkable even in descendants of the hardy *conquistadores.*

More extraordinary still were the ingenious and ferocious torments which Rosa herself devised for her mortification and which are described in often macabre detail by her biographers. By the age of six, she had learned to live on bread and water, not as a punishment, but as a self-imposed penance. The very taste of meat later became so repugnant to her that whenever she tried to take some to please her mother she only became ill and vomited. María de Oliva, tired of storming at her to eat properly, eventually let the peculiar child subsist on a diet which she concocted for herself consisting chiefly of raisins and bitter herbs, some of which she grew specially in the garden, sometimes seasoned with ashes instead of salt. This she referred to light-heartedly as her *gazpacho,* or soup. She also concocted a brew from bitter herbs and sheep's gall of which she drank, in memory of the vinegar offered to quench Christ's thirst on the cross, whilst preparing herself for Holy Communion and during Lent. Her abstinence reached astonishing extremes. It became customary for Rosa to take no food from Thursday evening until Sunday. We read of her going for 15 days without eating, and on one occasion of her consuming nothing but a single loaf of bread and no water at all during a mammoth fast of 50 days. There were times when Rosa seemed to subsist, like her beloved Catherine of Siena, solely on the Holy Sacrament administered to her. Before communicating, she would often be so weak through fasting and other mortifications that she could barely struggle to church on her mother's arm, but after receiving Communion, she felt so invigorated physically as well as spiritually that her mother could not keep up with her as she strode joyfully homewards.

The body's need of sleep had also to be vanquished. As Rosa grew older, her mother expected her to take over more and more of the household work—the washing and mending, the cooking, the care of the younger children—as well as to earn all she could through her sewing and embroideries and the sale of their garden produce. María abused her daughter for spending on her devotions so much of the time that might have gone to these tasks. Rosa meekly accepted her reproaches and prepared to submit herself to a regime which seems beyond human power to endure. Out of every 24 hours she would set aside 12 for the prayer and contemplation which her nature craved; ten hours would be devoted to work and the remaining two to sleep.

Much of the night Rosa would spend leaning against her bedroom wall, knocking her head against it and pinching her arms to keep herself awake, or even twisting a lock of her hair to a nail high up on the wall to keep her from drooping forward in weariness. But the greatest deterrent to sleep was the bed that Rosa constructed for herself. The mere thought of getting into it, we are told, was enough to set her trembling. And no wonder; the bed was made up of bare boards, unevenly laid together and decked out with an assortment of stones, scraps of wood and broken crockery which Rosa was careful to hide away from her mother's eye in the morning. María nevertheless found a pillow filled with these unpleasant odds and ends and ordered Rosa to throw them away and fill it with wool instead. Rosa obeyed, but found a way, as she so often did, of pursuing her ends even in obedience. She stuffed the pillow so full of wool that it became as hard as a rock. We are told that Rosa spent her ration of sleep on this appalling couch for fifteen years until sickness made such external torments superfluous and her confessors ordered her to have done. María, with a sigh of relief, then threw the whole contraption into the river.

The hair-shirt and the scourge or "discipline" had long been part of the mediaeval ascetic's stock-in-trade and were still to be found in the convents and monasteries of Lima. Rosa did not easily come by a hairshirt which met with her exacting requirements. The first one given her proved too short and soft. A larger one, presented by an obliging nun, had the advantage of sleeves, to which Rosa attached linen cuffs so that the wearing of it would not be apparent. It was long and stiff, and its weight and discomfort served as a suitable mortification. Rosa nevertheless made sure that it would feel really rough to the skin by sticking a number of pins into it. The disciplines currently in use were made of knotted cords and these too seemed to her inadequate. Rosa preferred chains, and applied one to her back to such lacerating effect that her confessors forbade its use. But they did not tell her to give it up altogether, and so Rosa pulled the chain around her as tightly as she could, locked it with a padlock and threw the key into the garden well. The torment of the chain lasted until a severe attack of sciatica proved too much even for Rosa's superhuman powers of endurance. Her groans brought the Indian servant Mariana hurrying to her chamber and together they tried to loosen its grip. Mariana then went off to fetch a stone and a piece of iron with a view to forcing open the lock whilst Rosa lay gazing up in agony at the crucified Christ. Suddenly, in merciful answer to her prayer, the links of the chain fell apart and Rosa was free. The chain was surrendered at the behest of her confessor, but the iron had eaten deep into her flesh and left angry weals.

To her confessor, too, was confided the secret, long kept from her family, of Rosa's most ingenious and refined instrument of self-torture —her crown of thorns. The craving to share in this way in her Saviour's sufferings had come to her when, still a small girl, she would gaze upon the drawn features of an Ecce Homo in her parents' home. Rosa experimented on herself first by inserting a sharp pin into the garland of roses which her mother liked to see her wearing, then by improvising a chaplet of string and nails which she wore concealed under her veil. These were preliminaries for the metal crown which she was to wear, similarly hidden, for the last ten years of her life. It consisted of a silver band into which three rows of nails, each numbering 33 in honour of the years of the Saviour's life, had been firmly embedded. How Rosa managed to have this fearsome object made, or where she found the silver for it, we are not told. Silver was almost a common metal in Peru, which was then the greatest silver producer in the world. Probably her brother Fernando was the intermediary in this, as in many other of his sister's pious whims. However this may be, Rosa let her hair grow in front the better to conceal her crown, but the rest of her head she kept cropped beneath the veil so as to expose the scalp to the full effect of the nails.

For a time Rosa kept her secret. Then one day her father lost his temper with one of his sons. Rosa interposed herself to shield the offender and received the blow on her own head. She fled from the room with blood streaming down her face. María, horrified, followed her to her room and discovered the crown and the lacerated head. The confessor was sent for and delivered a homily on the dangers of excessive penance. But no one, we are told could resist Rosa's pleading, and she was allowed to keep her crown provided the nails were filed down. Soon she was wearing it again, beneath her veil and her garland of roses, and would do what she could to make up for its bluntness by every now and then giving it a sharp blow with her fists.

The mere enumeration of Rosa's self-inflicted tortures can hardly be read without a shudder, perhaps even a frisson of almost prurient fascination when we remember that the sufferer was a young and beautiful girl. But before we dismiss this side of her personality as an abnormality, if not a perversion, it is well to bear certain things in mind. In the first place, the times in which she lived were not far removed in spirit from the middle ages, with their acceptance of savage penance as a norm of the pious life. Spanish society, both at home and in the New World, seemed to have passed straight from the tortured asceticism of the mediaeval to the convolutions of the baroque, without experiencing the humanizing influence of the Renaissance. The hair-shirt and the discipline were still the familiar possessions of the devout, as we have noted from our glimpses into the life of Rosa's contemporaries, Archbishop Mogrovejo, Fray Francisco Solano and Martín de Porres. It is not the practice of penance by Rosa which need surprise us, but the ingenuity and fanatical intensity which she brought to it.

Only by attempting to understand the motive behind such seeming excesses can we hope to find the matter intelligible. The basic justification for asceticism is that it is a means of bringing the body into subjection to the spirit. The recalcitrant flesh has to be whipped into obedience, temptation driven out by the lash. Now in the case of the innocent Lima maiden all this might seem well nigh superfluous. Her life, from the cradle to the grave, appears to have been as blameless as any human life could possibly be. She had gone through no period of "unconverted" youth nor been worsted in tempestuous struggles against the flesh. We do not read that she had recourse to her excruciating penances, as Luis de Granada writes of doña Sancha Carillo, "when she was suffering mighty temptations from the spirit of fornication". It is true that Rosa, like all saints, was oppressed by an overwhelming sense of personal sin. But she intended her penances not only to expiate the guilt of her own sins but to offer her suffering to God in atonement for those of others. We read that she had worked out a regular schedule of mortifications in this sense. One night would be set aside to make amends for her own sins; the next, to invoke God's mercy and spare his people from "public calamities", a third in intercession for Lima and "the lands of Peru", a fourth for souls in purgatory, a fifth for the dying, a sixth for those living in mortal sin. It was a whole programme of vicarious suffering mapped out and humbly offered to God in atonement for the crimes of the Conquista and the callousness and frivolity of the colonial society in which she lived. Sometimes she would offer up her own sufferings to the credit side, as it were, of someone else's spiritual balance-sheet. There survives a letter written by her to a certain Fray Bartolomé de Ayala undertaking, as some return for the charity he had shown her, "to take Your Reverence's faults upon myself, and I pray God to require of me the punishment due for them, for I repeat that I wish to suffer this for the love of Jesus Christ", and she calls on saints Augustine, Dominic and Francis to bear witness that she wishes to make him a co-beneficiary of all her fasts and penances. On another occasion, a confessor fell ill and sent Rosa a message that he would be unable to preach at an important church festival. Rosa, who knew that this would be a keen disappointment to him, sent him a reply bidding him take heart as she knew he would unexpectedly recover in time and be able to preach his sermon "although this would be on a condition grievous for another person". This other person was Rosa herself, who suddenly fell ill with excruciating pains and a high fever. But the friar was able to preach his sermon as she had predicted.

But this eager acceptance of suffering was fed from still deeper springs. On the walls of Rosa's home there hung an Ecce Homo— Christ looking down in suffering and compassion beneath His crown of thorns. The picture stirred the imagination of the small child with an answering compassion and an irresistible impulse to share in His passion. Here was her chosen Bridegroom—the Man of Sorrows with whom union could come only through a willing participation in His agony. It was folly, of course, for a normal child in a normal home to have such notions—the precocious folly of the lover or the mystic. For what is a mystic but one who is mad with the love of God? Rosa belonged to the company of those beneath whose divine madness can always be glimpsed the stern logic of the Cross. This she was later to express in her beautiful vision of the Scales, when Christ was revealed to her measuring out to each mortal his share of divine grace exactly proportionate to the weight of the trials and adversities falling to his lot, and heard her Master say : "Let it be known that Grace follows upon Tribulation. This is the one ladder leading to paradise, and there is no other way by which to ascend into heaven save by the Cross". Christ heaped upon her an abundant measure of grace; abundant too was to be her portion of trials and suffering.

Not the least of Rosa's trials was the treatment she received at the hands of her own mother. María Oliva de Flores was, by all accounts, a woman of ungovernable temper and narrow, conventional views, who "treated her daughter as roughly and callously as if she had been a slave". María was a great believer in the rod, and would lay about her without bothering where the blows fell so that little Rosa "learned to suffer even before she learned to speak". Grandmother would take a hand too, particularly in the quarrel about her name, striking the little girl for answering to "Rosa" whilst María would whip her for responding to "Isabel". María was infuriated above all at the singular forms her daughter's piety was beginning to take. Her rage was mingled with alarm lest the neighbours and even the authorities should take an interest in these unseemly goings-on. "She feared that people would gossip about these ecstasies and revelations and that Rosa would be taken off to the Inquisition on the charge of being an *alumbrada* and made to appear in some *auto da fe,* to the shame of her parents and kinsfolk". So poor Rosa grew used to hearing herself dubbed hypocrite, fraud and *alumbrada* and reviled for bringing dishonour on her family instead of behaving like any other normal and well-bred girl. María's severest punishments and admonitions were kept for occasions when there were visitors present, for the greater humiliation of her daughter and evidence at least of her own good sense and impeccable orthodoxy.

* * * *

The course taken by Rosa's childhood was outwardly not very eventful. The chief turn in the family fortunes was the appointment of Gaspar de Flores to be superintendent of an *obraje* at Quive, then a thriving township, and now a small hamlet, in the lower ranges of the Andes some twenty-five miles from Lima. The change proved, however, to be anything but a blessing. Despite the clear air of the uplands, there was an oppressive atmosphere about the place, for its prosperity was built on the forced labour of the sullen and resentful Indians. The children's health was affected; Rosa was constantly ailing, and her elder sister fell even more seriously ill and never recovered. Her death was a great grief to Rosa, upon whom the chief responsibility of helping her mother with the care of the younger children now devolved. Only one joyous event marked their stay in Quive; the arrival of don Toribio on the second of his great diocesan Visitations. At the hands of the saintly Archbishop Rosa received confirmation and entered upon a fresh stage along the stony path which was to lead her, too, to sanctity. She was then 11 years old.

Within a few years the Flores family was back in its old home in the street of Santo Domingo. Rosa was happy to be once more in the half-wild garden, with its profusion of roses, carnations and lilies, and its clumps of fritillary and wild basil. Even the mosquitoes which swarmed in the shade seemed to her lovable fellow-creatures. "What are you doing, sister?" she once exclaimed in distress to a visitor who did not share these tolerant feelings towards the insects, "You are killing my friends!" Then she promised that her visitor would be spared from their attentions—and so it proved—as she herself was. "We have made a pact together", she smilingly explained. "I don't disturb them or drive them away, and they don't sting me or bother me with their noise. In fact they join me in singing God's praises". Early every morning, her biographer goes on to declare, Rosa would open the doors and windows of the house and say: "Now, my friends, it is time to praise God!" The mosquitoes would hum busily around for a while and then fly out into the garden. Evening would come and she would summon then again: "Come, my friends, let us praise God before we go to rest!" The air would then be full again with their cheerful hum until Rosa called out that it was enough, and silence would fall.

The garden was also a valuable economic asset where Rosa worked hard and long, though with great delight. She was blessed, like Martín de Porres, with green fingers. The flowers which she raised there for the market looked better and smelled more sweetly—so we are assured—than the common run. She also showed great ingenuity in experimenting with topiary work or "horticultural sculpture", as her biographers call it. Her rosemary bushes, trimmed so as to represent Mount Calvary surmounted by a cross, particularly impressed her confessor, who begged a specimen for himself and another for the vicereine. The latter soon had to send hers back as it had begun to wilt—"It is not used to the grandeur of palace life", was Rosa's smiling comment— but it revived at the touch of her green fingers and was sent back to the vicereine decked out with a figurine of Mary Magdalene and other adornments. Rosa lavished love on her plants, as she did on all around her. But one morning she rose to tend the sweet basil which she grew with special pride for the adornment of the chapel of the Rosary, and found to her horror that the plants lay uprooted and dead. Her love, she learned through tears, must henceforth be all for her Beloved, not for His creatures, however fair.

Rosa's garden too could be a place of terror, where devils lurked in the evening shadows. Once Satan took the form of a handsome young man who approached to pay court to her. Rosa fled into the house and reached for her scourge. At other times, the Devil would assume the shape of a monstrous hound which sought to distract her from her prayers with his snarls and foetid breath. Such diabolic apparitions Rosa faced manfully, even joyfully. Why should she fear, so long as her guardian angel was by her side and Christ dwelt in her heart? But what if the Beloved Himself were to withdraw and leave her defenceless and disconsolate? Rosa had experienced such periods of abandonment ever since she began the practice of contemplative prayer. A mood of utter desolation would then sweep over her, when it seemed that her Beloved had not only turned His face away but had wrathfully driven her from Him. It was then that she felt upon herself the wrath of the Lamb, and heard the dread words ringing in her ears : "Depart from me, worker of iniquity, into outer darkness!" Only the glimmer of the light she had once known now kept her from despair, and she prayed fervently to God that He would lead her by the common path, rather than by the terrible heights and abysses of the mystic way. Not a day passed without this hour of darkness descending upon her, she told her confessors; they could give no help, but attributed her distress to a fit of the "vapours" or the unsettling effects of excessive penances. To her mother she said nothing at all, for María was incapable of understanding such things, though she noticed the physical signs of her daughter's anguish and would sometimes call in the doctors. But they, too, were powerless; "not knowing the cause of her ills they could not prescribe the remedy". Such things as they did propose—that she should take more nourishing food or swallow some physic—only made her martyrdom the more intense. Then all at once, with no human help, the clouds would blow away and Rosa knew with overwhelming gratitude and certainty that the divine presence had been restored to her.

But above all, the garden was the place which offered Rosa the peace and seclusion she needed for prayer. In one corner of it, where the trees made a leafy shade, Fernando had helped his sister build a small bower which served as a tiny chapel with a pasteboard cross and coloured prints of the saints on its rough walls. As she grew older and her vocation for the contemplative life deepened, Rosa began to long for something more closely resembling a nun's cell or hermitage, where she could immure herself, after the fashion of the holy virgin Saint Oria and the other *emparedadas,* or "walled-up ones" of mediaeval Spain. Not that it would ever be possible for Rosa to withdraw completely into the life of a recluse; her pressing family duties would always claim a large share of her time. But every minute she could snatch from those duties Rosa wanted to spend alone and in prayer, living a double life, in the most innocent and selfless meaning of the term, and dividing her days between the charity owed to her fellows and the call to be with her Beloved. This she longed for more than anything in the world, as she dutifully confided to her parents. But María was not the sort of woman to understand, still less to grant, such a strange request. Why could not her daughter behave "normally"? "What you are asking for, daughter", she testily replied, "is not a cell or a hermitage, but a tomb, and I have no wish to see you bury yourself alive in it. Am I to let you kill yourself? This narrow box you want to have made for yourself is not a place to live but a place to die in—and die you shall when it is God's good will and pleasure, and not at *your* sweet will and whim. Do what He wants for you, and that will be what I want too. A child who obeys her parents is obeying God, for we have been put in God's place. It is all very well for you to go on inventing fresh torments for yourself day by day, which will be the death of you and of all of us too. No—I won't let you have your cell or hermitage in the garden!" It is hard not to feel

G

a certain sympathy for María and her rough common sense, albeit the latter was often altogether too rough and ultimately made no sense at all when matched against the uncommon logic of sanctity. Rosa, backed by the persuasions of some pious friends, at last overcame her mother's resistance and the "hermitage" was built. It still stands today in the garden of what is now the Sanctuario de Santa Rosa— a tiny, box-like structure of stone, measuring only four feet by five and six feet in height, with a single window and a door so low that it could only be entered on all fours.

Another place where Rosa loved to pray was the shrine of Our Lady of the Rosary in the Church of Santo Domingo. The image of the Virgin and Child which the *conquistadores* had brought with them was amongst the most venerated in the New World and many miracles were attributed to it. On her knees before Our Lady and her Holy Child, Rosa would lose herself in divine colloquy with them and receive her deepest revelations. As she gazed reverently at the Child Jesus it seemed to her "that she read in His countenance, as it were from a book, whatever He said to her, and this more clearly and forcibly than from any words or letters, and that there was born in her spirit a light so beauteous in its brightness that she perceived whatever He said to her without need of words or the exercise of the imagination, but clearly and distinctly. In the countenance of Our Lady and her most holy Son, from their eyes, lips and cheeks, she saw all these things as one might read the time from the face of a clock, more clearly revealed than any human eloquence could possibly express". As she once tried to explain to her confessors, "the mode of speaking was strange and singular, for there issued from the mouth of Christ himself a most clear and pure concept of wisdom which penetrated to the inmost depths of her soul to disclose and tell her inwardly everything which He wished her to understand".

Others might express their devotion by contributing to the rich vestments and jewels which adorned the sacred images. Rosa was too poor for gifts of this sort, but such offerings as lay within her power she fervently bestowed—the tender tribute of her prayers and penances. Several of these moving pledges are on record. One is entitled "Inventory of the vestment which I, Rosa of Santa María, unworthy slave of the Queen of the Angels, begin to weave with the help of the Lord for the Virgin Mother of God. Item, the tunic shall be made of 600 *Ave Marias,* as many *Salves,* and 15 days of fasting . . . ". Even more touching in its devotion and unflinching acceptance of self-mortification is the "Spiritual trousseau" promised for the Holy Child.

"In the year 1616, with the help of Jesus Christ and of His blessed Mother, I prepare a garment for my very dear Jesus, who is soon to be born cold, naked and needy in the stable of Bethlehem. To weave His little shirt I shall make use of 50 litanies, 9,000 rosaries and five days of fasting in memory of His most holy Incarnation. I shall make His napkins of nine stations before the Most Holy Sacrament, nine divisions of the Rosary, and nine days of fasting to honour the nine months He spent in His mother's womb. I will make the coverlet in which He is to be wrapped with five days of abstinence, five rosaries and five stations in honour of His glorious birth. I will make His swaddling bands with the Five Stations of the cross, five fasts and as many whole rosaries in memory of His circumcision. As for the trimmings of His coverlet and swaddling clothes I shall make them of 33 holy communions, 33 attendances at Mass, 33 hours of mental prayer, 33 Paternosters, Aves and Credos, with as many Glorias and Salve Reginas, 33 divisions of the rosary, 33 days of fasting and 3,000 lashes of the scourge in veneration for the 33 years He spent on earth. Finally, I shall offer to His tender infancy my tears, my sighs, my affections and my heart and soul withal, so as to bestow all I have upon Him without keeping anything back, for it is meet that I should possess nothing of my own."

*   *   *   *

The battle over Rosa's cell was only one round in the campaign which María had begun to wage to make her daughter drop her peculiar ways and go out into society. Rosa's parents had high hopes that she would make an advantageous match which would repair the family fortunes. Old Gaspar had not managed to scrape together enough to make a dowry for his daughter, but there was no lack of young men who would be glad to take her without, for word of Rosa's beauty and virtues had begun to spread throughout Lima. Father Hansen describes her as "of rare beauty—her figure graceful and well formed, her character gentle and discreet, her face oval in shape and her expression calm and serene. Her hair was fair and abundant, her brow open and her eyebrows delicately arched. She had rosy cheeks, a very small mouth, a well-formed chin and small, white, delicately fashioned hands, and she was of medium height". Another biographer refers to her as "a person of excellent parts, very capable, quick and clever. She had a keen understanding, a good memory, a gentle disposition and ready speech, and such winning ways that whenever she asked for something it was altogether impossible to refuse it".

Besides being an expert needlewoman and well versed in all the

domestic skills of the day, Rosa had a lovely voice and a natural gift
for music. She would take up the harp or the guitar and accompany
herself, either to her own verses or some poem which had caught her
fancy and to which, in her innocence, she would often impart a
religious meaning of her own. Thus, when she sang :

Las doce son dadas,	He tarries long
Mi amante no viene.	'Tis midnight past.
Quién será la dichosa	What fond arms
Que lo entretiene?	Still hold him fast?

the words, heard on the lips of her brother or of some friend of the
family perhaps, were from the famous and far from edifying tragedy
called after the old bawd *La Celestina,* but for Rosa they conveyed the
impatience which always possessed her to be alone with her Beloved.
Sometimes she would improvise songs of her own or compose little
poems which spoke always of the same theme; a prayer to her
guardian angel, bidding him go call her Beloved, or verses to the
Child Jesus, playfully alluding to the names of her own family :

Ay Jesús de mi alma	My dear Lord and Saviour
Qué bien pareces	How fair He reposes
Entre Flores y Rosas	Amongst the green Olives
Y Olivas Verdes!	The Flowers and Roses . . .

Another little poem, written later in life, is inscribed to the "nightin-
gale" probably the melodious mocking-bird, for there are no
nightingales in South America. Tradition has it that the two would
sing together as Rosa sat at her open window in the cool of the garden,
the bird adding its song in a duet of praise to their common Maker :

Pajarillo ruiseñor	Little nightingale, pray sing;
Alabemos al Señor;	We'll together praise our King.
Tu alaba a tu Creador	Thou thy Maker shalt proclaim
Yo canto a mi Salvador.	I my Saviour's holy name.

When the bird had fallen silent and left Rosa to her meditations, she
would console herself with the thought that her Beloved was always
with her :

Déjame la avecilla	Though the bird away has flown
Huye el veloz cantador.	Left me to myself alone,
Mas siempre está conmigo	Christ shall ever with me stay,
Mi dulce Redentor.	My Redeemer blest alway.

María simply could not understand why her daughter was so averse from displaying her natural charms and accomplishments in society. Rosa would beg on bended knee that she might be excused from accompanying her mother on those social visits whose purpose in the matrimonial strategy was only too clear. Even at their most harmless, Rosa found such visits embarrassing and an intolerable distraction from her vocation. To put on fine clothes, to exchange gossip, and above all, to receive compliments was torture to her. Her mother insisted; Rosa obeyed, but found a dozen artful ways, without actually disobeying, of escaping. Once she contrived to drop a heavy stone from the stove onto her foot and had to stay at home until the painful bruise healed. A lady paid her fulsome compliments on the whiteness and delicacy of her hands; the following morning Rosa plunged them into quicklime which left them scarred and blistered for 20 days. Then she developed an infection of the eyes which María was puzzled to find had a way of becoming more acute when they were about to set out visiting, until she discovered her daughter rubbing them with the ferocious chilli pepper known as *ají*. This alarmed as well as infuriated María; the perverse child might really lose her sight if she persisted in such tricks. Eventually, as always, María had to give in, or rather to agree to a compromise. Rosa need not go out visiting, but she was to stay with her mother to receive any callers at home. And callers came in increasing numbers, for curiosity was growing about the Señora de Flores' strange yet attractive daughter. Some would embark on pious conversation for her benefit, but Rosa was not to be drawn, for she kept the most discreet silence as to the secrets of her own spiritual life; "It is better to speak *with* God than *of* Him", she murmured when her mother asked with a touch of sarcasm whether she was not satisfied with all this edifying talk. Rosa had a disconcerting way of reading hidden motives, as a young gallant who presented himself at the Flores' home to be measured for a pair of lace cuffs—for customers as well as social callers were received there—soon discovered.

Rosa's physical beauty was a frequent source of embarrassment to her and gave rise to tortured self-questioning and scruples. As a child, she had sought a simple solution by snipping off her golden locks after her brother's taunt that they might be the cause of a man's perdition. Then, to placate her mother and also to help conceal the crown of thorns which she took to wearing, she had let her hair grow again, at least in the front. The fasts and other severities she practised had curiously little effect on Rosa's good looks and apparent good health. One day in Holy Week, whilst she and her mother were returning

from church, they passed a group of young bloods who quizzed her
curiously and remarked that the youthful *beata*, to judge from the
comely features behind the veil, seemed to have done better for herself that Lent than they had themselves. María, of course, grew
indignant and had to be restrained from retorting that her daughter
had, as a matter of fact, been living on nothing but bread and water.
Rosa could not find any easy solution to this problem. Her beauty
might arouse temptation not only of desire in others but of vanity in
herself; hence the savagery with which she had punished herself for
listening to those compliments about the whiteness of her hands. For
a time she prayed earnestly that God might take from her the
dangerous gift of beauty; others noticed indeed that their rose was
beginning to lose its bloom and attributed it, with reason no doubt, to
the self-imposed severities of her life. This made matters even worse;
Rosa's virtues, and not merely her beauty, were now becoming the
object of praise, and this constituted a still more invidious invitation
to pride. After much heart-searching Rosa amended her petition in a
way which does honour to her modesty and good sense. She now
prayed, her biographers assure us, that her beauty might be
"moderated"; that "her aspect should be a mean between fair and
faded, neither dazzling by its beauty nor yet revealing her penances
and mortifications". And so, it seems, in time it became. The portrait
painted of Rosa on her death-bed by the Italian Angelino Medoro
catches the expression of pain and suffering behind the still youthful
and comely features of the saint. (Plate 7).

When Rosa reached her late teens the pressure on her to accept one
or other of the offers made for her hand increased and events moved to
a crisis. Modestly yet firmly she tried to explain that she felt her vocation to be quite different and that she had made up her mind never
to marry. This was more than the irascible María could bear to listen
to; "she began to shout and rouse the whole household and told all
the family what had happened, so that each took up arms against the
poor girl, attacking her with insults and affronts and adding fuel to
the mother's passion, cursing and denouncing her disobedience until at
last her own mother laid hands on her, more roughly than she had
ever done before, and dragged her along the ground". Rosa's cup of
anguish was now full. To be an object of ignominy, misunderstanding
and even physical maltreatment was but a part of the portion she
had accepted for her own life, but she now saw that she was also
causing disappointment and resentment in those whom she most loved.
She sought consolation, as ever, in prayer and submission to the divine
will. Gradually the Flores household came to accept Rosa's choice and

to reconcile themselves to the strange prospect of seeing the beauty of the family live out her life as a spinster.

But how, exactly, was she to live? Marriage or the convent—such had long been the accepted alternatives for girls of her station. Rosa would in all probability have found her deepest satisfaction in some community of strict observance. The pious matron doña Grimanesa, sister to the late archbishop, was at that very time sponsoring the foundation of a community of Poor Clares whose rule of Franciscan poverty would have been well suited to Rosa's desires. But María, still piqued by her daughter's rejection of all marriage offers, would not consent; how would the family make both ends meet without the income from Rosa's flowers and needlework? A second opportunity nevertheless arose, and María's resistance began to weaken. Doña Mencía, widow of the ambitious Francisco Hernández Girón who had raised a rebellion and met an ignominious end in public execution, was resolved to found an Augustinian convent where the prayers of the nuns could help to expiate the traitor's guilt. Doña Mencía was so eager for Rosa to join her convent that she promised to waive the payment of the customary "dowry" which the impecunious Flores family could not afford. The girl's confessors made no objection, María was at length ready to agree, but Rosa herself remained undecided. She was drawn to the enclosed life yet uncertain whether that was intended to be her vocation. Before visiting doña Mencía to give her answer Rosa knelt in prayer before her beloved Lady of the Rosary in the Dominican's church. Fernando accompanied his sister and waited in silence for her to finish her devotions. The minutes passed and he at length approached to remind her that the ladies were waiting. There then occurred a strange thing. Try as she would, Rosa found herself quite unable to get up. She remained kneeling in the chapel as if riveted by some invisible force. Fernando, much bewildered, tried to help her to her feet, gently at first, then with all his strength. What could be the meaning of the strange power which kept her kneeling there? Suddenly Rosa became aware that her prayer for enlightenment had been answered; it was God's way of showing her that she was not to proceed with the course which the good ladies proposed for her, and that her life was to be lived out otherwise. As soon as Rosa had understood this revelation and accepted it, her limbs were mysteriously released. She rose lightly to her feet and returned home with Fernando. This phenomenon of the locked limbs, which Rosa seems to have experienced on this single occasion, has its parallels in the lives of other mystics. We read of María Vela, a nun of Avila who died in the same year as Rosa, experiencing spectacular attacks of lock-jaw from which she found release only when permitted by her confessors to follow the abnormally strict devotional path which was evidently her particular vocation.

Rosa was then to go on living the life of a *beata* at home; that much at least was clear. It was also possible to formalize such a course by seeking affiliation to the Third Order—as distinct from the First and Second Orders of fully professed men and women—of one or other of the great mendicant bodies. It is difficult to believe that Rosa had much hesitation in making this decision, which would bring her halfway towards her heart's desire and where she had the shining example of St. Catherine of Siena to follow. If doubts she had, they may well have been as to whether she should take the brown habit of a Franciscan Tertiary or the black-and-white of the Dominicans. Her Dominican biographers keep a prudent silence on this point but furnish us instead with a poetic account of the revelation which settled the matter. "When she was in sad perplexity as to whether or not to take the habit of a Tertiary, Rosa noticed that there had flown through the window of her room a butterfly, black and white in colour, which fluttered gently around her and then settled on her skirt. She fell into a wondrous long ecstasy, whilst all the while the butterfly fluttered gaily round her until it at length came to rest on her heart, where it busied itself, like a bee sucking honey from a flower, all the time she was in ecstasy. Its task accomplished, it then vanished, leaving a heart imprinted above her own, so beautifully and skilfully traced that it seemed to have been done by the hand of a master. Then Rosa awoke from her ecstasy and understood that God was well pleased that she should take the habit of a Tertiary in the Order of St. Dominic".

If, for this once, a black-and-white butterfly had served to make clear God's message, it was habitually from Our Lady of the Rosary that Rosa continued to seek guidance in her perplexities. One matter that still disturbed her conscience, now that she was entering formally upon the religious state, was the question of her own name. The days of her childhood, when she had suffered from the squabbles between her mother and grandmother on this very point, were long past, and the saintly Archbishop had himself pronounced judgment. But was not Rosa really too worldly a name for one now set aside for God's service? Did it not allude too frankly to the lower creation rather than to the Creator Himself or to one of His saints? And did it not feed vanity by implicitly ascribing to its possessor the beauty and fragrance of a flower? She was reassured somewhat when told that the Church already had a saint of her name— St. Rose of Viterbo. But scruples nevertheless remained. She laid them at length before the miraculous image and was rewarded by the assurance revealed to her that the Holy Child was pleased that she should be called Rosa, but that He wished the name to be coupled with that of His mother. Her doubts were now set at rest; from then on, she was to be known as Rosa de Santa María.

At the age of 20, Rosa received the habit of a Dominican Tertiary from the hands of her confessor. She was now dedicated to the service of her Beloved by the solemn vows of the Third Order. But was she also to be vouchsafed a still more intimate union, as her revered St. Catherine had been vouchsafed the mystical experience described as the Spiritual Betrothal? Humility forbade her to aspire to such heights, and it was only through the willing acceptance of humiliation that the call came clearly to her. Rosa had gone to the church of St. Dominic for the ceremony of the blessing of the Palms. By some oversight the sacristan passed her by when the devout received their palms. Deeply mortified by the conviction that she was not accounted worthy to receive this mark of grace, Rosa humbly took her place in the procession without a palm and then went to pour out her troubles before her dear image of the Virgin and Child. At once her grief was turned to unspeakable joy. The Virgin and the divine Child smiled upon her, and she heard Him say : "Rose of my heart, be my bride!"

Rosa's grateful obedience to this vision took a characteristically practical form. She turned for help to her brother Fernando, who promised to get a silversmith to make a silver ring which would be broad enough to have an inscription engraved upon it. Together they sketched out a design. Fernando paused for a moment as if waiting inspiration for a suitable device, and then wrote down on the paper without any prompting from his sister the words which she alone had heard : "Rose of my heart, be my bride!" The ring was made with this inscription and left on the altar for the divine blessing. Then, on Easter Day, it was placed on her finger. Rosa, now fully and finally the bride of Christ, wore it to the day of her death.

*   *   *   *

The visions and revelations described above, and likewise the extreme and ingenious severity of her self-imposed mortifications, were concealed by Rosa with the utmost secrecy from all but her confessors, and only disclosed to the latter with extreme diffidence. But even in that city of pious folk, the exceptional nature of the young Tertiary's vocation could not long pass unnoticed. The curious began to gossip and rumours to spread. Prudence required the Church to enquire into whatever smacked of the extraordinary and might be a possible occasion for error, deception or delusion. Rosa had ever shown herself to be the most submissive daughter of the Church. She had surrendered her spiritual life into the keeping of her confessors and had been brought up in the shadow of the great monastery whose inmates were also the representatives of the Holy Office. Nor did that powerful institution show itself in the Indies with quite the same scowling countenance as in Spain. Prosecutions for heresy were few, and much of its energies went into such minor matters as censorship, church discipline and disputes of precedence. But cases of sorcery and witchcraft came within its purview, and where there was talk of revelations and supernatural happenings, it was for the Holy Office to enquire whether these things stemmed from God or the Devil. The Inquisition, in short, could hardly fail to look into the case of the Dominican Tertiary, Rosa de Santa María.

Seldom can the dread tribunal have shown itself more benign or have met in more idyllic surroundings. Rosa was not summoned to appear before it; instead, one day in 1614, a commission came to talk to her in the friendly cool of the garden, outside her own "hermitage", and in the presence of her mother and of Doña María de Uzátegui, who was married to a high official of the viceregal administration and was Rosa's chief protectress and most intimate friend. The commission comprised two Jesuits as well as four or five Dominican theologians. The most prominent of them was Fray Juan de Lorenzana, who was for a time Rosa's own confessor, a Censor of the Holy Office, and a former Prior and Provincial of his Order, and Dr. Juan del Castillo, an eminent university professor of medicine. Dr. Castillo was also something of a mystic himself and the author of a spiritual treatise which is said to have been read with interest by the great reforming Pope Urban VIII but has not come down to us. It was fortunate for Rosa that a man of this calibre should have taken the leading part in her examination, for he not only recognized at once the authenticity and unique quality of her mystical experiences but was able to help her evaluate them in correct theological terms. It is fortunate too for us, for we can be sure that the answers given by Rosa to the doctor's questions were correctly understood and recorded. They offer the fullest and most trustworthy account available to us of the nature of Rosa's mystical life—an account unvarnished by legend and coloured only slightly, if at all, by the literary embellishments of the biographers who have reproduced them. They were indeed almost the only reliable account extant until the discovery, in 1923, of some notes and diagrams drawn up by the saint herself which confirm the experiences for which she had sought to find words in that memorable ordeal of the garden.

For ordeal it undoubtedly was, though Rosa received the most sympathetic of hearings and never seems to have experienced the doubts which have sometimes assailed some other mystics as to whether their visions were true or false, divinely or diabolically inspired. It was nevertheless an ordeal to reveal to her grave interlocutors the mortifications she had so scrupulously kept from the eyes of the world. Still more of an ordeal was it to speak of those things which had passed in the intimacy of her soul between the Beloved and his Bride and to frame words to convey that which by its very nature cannot be expressed. For God had been pleased to call her, almost from earliest childhood, to the summit of the contemplative life, without the long and wearisome ascent through the lower purgative and illuminative stages which are the common lot of those called to tread the mystic path. And if she had known the heights, she had also known the depths—that "dark night of the soul" whose agony neither her own mother or closest friend so much as suspected nor that tribunal of learned and virtuous men could perhaps understand.

Dr. Castillo opened the proceedings by asking Rosa how long it was that she had been following the practice of contemplative prayer and receiving divine favours. She answered simply that "she could not remember for how long, for she had had a natural inclination and propensity for prayer from her earliest years, and that to such an extent that even then her great joy, delight and consolation had been to speak of God, to think of God, and not to be parted from God." Had she then entered easily upon that path, asked the doctor? Rosa replied that "up to the age of 12 she had experienced some difficulties, but not great ones; she had never met with any obstacles preventing her from entering upon it most calmly and serenely, though she had had often to struggle against weakness and bodily exhaustion, against sleep and other distractions, and that all this happened up to the age she had mentioned; but after those difficulties had been overcome, God gently drew the soul with all its powers to Himself, with special delight of the understanding, the will, and the memory, attaching them with such close intimacy to the beauty of the Spouse that neither household cares, external disturbances, nor the most pressing concerns could divert or distract her, nor could they prevent her continuing to enjoy the most loving presence of the Lord with perfect peace and calm".

Dr. Castillo next enquired how she habitually passed into those abnormal states. Did she feel herself to be violently carried away and wrenched into them? Rosa made answer that "she suffered no violence or force, but had a sense of being firmly uplifted and sustained. The transport or ecstasy acted upon her powers like a magnet, drawing them to itself very softly and gently, and then letting them return, no less softly and gently, to their natural course, without any violence or strain whatsoever; and there then stole over her the flames of love, kindling so sweetly and peacefully that there were no terms in which to express it, irradiating the inmost recesses of her heart with the serene and loving presence of God, and favouring her with the bestowal of celestial delights; and of this presence she felt absolutely certain, for the singular joy and delight she experienced could stem only from that most loving and lovely presence, by which she knew with manifest clarity that the Lord had made His dwelling within her".

Dr. Castillo was a man of letters, and the next question he put to Rosa suggests that he may have suspected that her experiences might have been coloured by those of St. Teresa or of others who had written of the mystic way. What books of this nature, he asked, had she read? To this Rosa replied that "in no book had she read any part of what she knew; that the book in which she commonly read was that of continuing and persevering in prayer; that experience and practice served as her notebooks; that the interior joys which she experienced could not be described since she found no words with which to explain them; that never, in her ignorance and simplicity, could she find any name by which to express this union; that she could only enjoy and not describe it, though she did know that it was through prayer that it was reached and attained".

And when the soul tired of contemplating heavenly things, the Doctor continued, did she seek relief in turning her thoughts upon the lower creation? "No created thing in this mortal life could serve as relief or consolation", Rosa declared without hesitation, "for this she found only in the presence of her divine Spouse in the soul, and such was the certainty and truth with which she felt this presence to be there that if it were to be taken from her for one moment, for but a single instant, this would be the greatest misfortune which could befall her, the annihilation, as it were, of her very soul, more terrible and cruel than the pains of hell itself".

The Doctor next questioned Rosa as to the "contrary impulses" which must have assailed her mind to deflect it from the path of mystic prayer. How long had she to struggle against them, and how had she managed to subdue them? Rosa, in her innocence, could only say that "she did not remember ever having had such struggles, since from her earliest years she had followed the path of virtue by natural inclination and unhindered by the pull of passion, and that once she had gained her first knowledge of God she had conceived such a horror of sin that if perchance some involuntary impulse sought to deflect her from the right path she would at once place herself in the divine presence and drive and cast it out from her, so that it left not a shadow or trace of having beset her".

Yet the path had not been easy; far from it. If she had been spared the onslaughts of the lower passions she had been constantly racked by the more terrible and relentless agony of the spirit. In answer to further questioning from Dr. Castillo about the nature and frequency of these torments Rosa replied that "she could not reduce them to number, as she had suffered them since she was a very small child and not a single day passed without them coming upon her, not just one at a time, but many together, for what the spirit suffered at those times of desolation she had never found words to describe, convey or express; neither the torments of the martyrs nor the agony of men condemned to death nor any pain or affliction suffered by any created things whatsoever could equal in number or weight the martyrdom of those times of desolation".

Dr. Castillo gravely explained that this sense of spiritual dereliction which Rosa had suffered was the "chaos of darkness, the very likeness of hell" which commonly assailed those who sought to tread the mystic path. But what passed in her soul, he asked, once the clouds began to lift, when the "blindness of that horror" was taken from her? At this point in the interrogation, Rosa began to falter and remained silent. Her listeners seemed to have understood her when she spoke of the "dark night of the soul", but how could she find words to express to them that mystery of mysteries, the most intimate union of Lover and Beloved which passed in the depth of her being? So at Dr. Castillo's question "the humble Rose grew troubled, the colour left her cheeks, and she fell silent. The servant of God marked this, and after leaving her a little time to recover, he asked her a second time to reply to what he had asked, but she answered never a word. At last, making a show of righteous anger and prudent indignation, he said :

"Mark, Rosa, that this is no time or place for silence, for we have come to look into this business of yours. If you conceal or keep back anything I ask you about, you will be denying the favours for which you owe God gratitude. And if you do not reply to everything I ask you, it will be neither possible for me to understand you, nor for you to understand me, specially in what appertains to the confusion of

horrors which you have suffered and which I have begun to tell you
about, and which must be fully explained".

"Then Rosa, with humble modesty, broke silence and with downcast eyes (as was her wont) she said : 'When I feel carried away quite
beyond myself in that confused whirlwind of darkness and shadows,
and all in tears, I suddenly find myself restored to the arms of my
beloved Spouse, as if I had never left them, and in the clear light of
the first union. I feel the ardent impulses of love sweeping me along
as it were a river or stream, whose course is not hemmed in by banks,
but flows on swift and strong to lose itself in the calm of the sea. The
divine grace blows fresh and serene, and there arises a glorious tem-
pest in which the soul sinks in that immense ocean of goodness and
sweetness, ineffably transformed into the Beloved, casting off her own
nature and becoming one with Him. Amongst the favours vouchsafed
in this closest of unions, the greatest seems to me to find myself as it
were motionless and rooted in God Himself, sure of His friendship
and Grace, and then to feel a gift so strange and rare that I can find
no words to describe it; but the effect is that it seems to render me
altogether free of sin, as when St. Paul says—"Who can separate me
from the love of God? Neither Life, nor Death, . . ." And all this that
has happened to me, and continues to happen to me today, I have
not dared to say or reveal to anyone, nor would I dare to say it now
unless compelled to do so under this examination'."

Pressed to say in what form the celestial figures appeared to her,
Rosa answered "that the Lord granted her such favour that He manifested Himself to her in His sacred Humanity, now as a Man, now
as a tender Child, with a serene, smiling and loving countenance, as
did often the elected Queen of the Angels, Most Holy Mary, with the
same loving-kindness". Did these figures appear before her visually,
the Doctor asked, or as if apprehended by the understanding? Were
they, in short, what the theologians call "imaginary" or "intellectual",
and for how long and how clearly were they granted her? Rosa
answered that "the differences between these different visions were
unknown to her until now, and she did not know what name to give
them; but the Humanity of our Lord Jesus Christ appeared before
her, glorious, clear and distinct, like a beam of light which gleams
brightly, is seen and is gone, yet not sudden and fleeting, but slowly
lingering; and that she did not see His full stature but the head and
breast, whereas the Most Holy Mother of God she saw in full, for the
favour of her presence was granted her much longer".

Dr. Castillo pronounced such visions to be "imaginary"—not in
the sense that they were mere figments of fantasy, but that spiritual

reality had been manifested in visual form to a mind ravished in ecstasy. But when Rosa went on to speak of her apprehension of the Godhead itself, the revelation vouchsafed to her seemed to him to be nothing less than the authentic "intellectual vision" of mystical theology. Rosa apprehended the presence of God "as a light which had neither shape, nor measure, nor end, incomprehensible yet comprehending all things, subtle, steady and firm, most clear and pure, supremely one yet supremely many, supremely far off yet near and intimate, noble, sublime and not to be compared with anything created. The soul perceived it more by nature of the marvellous effects of the life-giving properties which flowed from it rather than in its very substance. These effects were a tender feeling of love, a strong and sweet joy above all imaginable joys, a sense of the divine kinship, an inner renewal in the very heart of our old nature; a fullness reaching into the recesses of the will, imparting everywhere and to every feeling a strong, holy and ineffable life".

At this point the learned Doctor broke off the examination in amazement that a simple girl could give such answers on these profound and difficult matters. He turned to question Rosa about her mortifications and penances and after listening to what she had to say "he remained still more astonished and persuaded that the path which Rosa was treading was most assuredly that of true virtue and vocation, and that she suffered none of those delusions with which the Devil, under the guise of an angel of light, is wont to beguile the most spiritual persons". The inquiry was declared at an end, leaving the servant of God as astonished as he was edified.

But though Rosa had come through Dr. Castillo's cross-questioning with flying colours, the inquisitors had not done with her yet. The Doctor had hitherto monopolized the proceedings, and there were others who also wanted their say. The following day the commission resumed its sessions in the garden. It was now the turn of Fray Juan de Lorenzana, "not so much to examine", Rosa's biographer explains, "as to check what had already been examined". This done, the commission finally dispersed, though Dr. Castillo seems to have continued seeing Rosa from time to time, for it was to him that she later confided one of her most beautiful and symbolically significant visions—that of the rainbows and the scales.

Rosa saw in this vision a rainbow of unearthly splendour, in the midst of it the figure of Christ in glory. Above it rose another rainbow, equal to the first in size and beauty and surmounted by a gleaming cross. As Rosa gazed at the sacred Humanity in rapt contemplation, she felt "indescribable flames of glory reaching and penetrating to the core of the soul, so that I seemed to be totally free of the prison of this corruptible flesh and transported to the enjoyment of eternal bliss". She beheld too a host of angels measuring out on a pair of scales the trials and tribulations which were to be the lot of every human soul. As she gazed, Christ himself took the scales into his own hands, weighing out for every man his appointed share of affliction and then a corresponding share of divine grace. Rosa herself received a great portion of each, as she heard Christ say: "Be it known that Grace follows upon tribulation, and that without the weight of affliction there can be no rising to the heights of grace. Let no one be deceived; there is but one ladder leading to Paradise, and no other way to ascend into Heaven save by the Cross". So keen an awareness of this truth then swept over Rosa that she felt a mighty urge to rush out into the streets calling upon all and sundry to share in the revelation that grace is only granted through suffering, and that such is the power and joy of that grace that men would gladly go through the world seeking trials and torments if only they might gain more of it. None would complain of the pain and suffering which fell to their lot in this life if only they knew on what heavenly scales, and for what rewards, these had been meted out to them.

    *   *   *   *

The truth enshrined in this great vision helps us to understand the paradox of how the solitude of contemplation may nurture a powerful urge to action. This was at first restricted by pressure of domestic duties and social conventions to Rosa's family circle. But as her younger brothers and sisters grew up, she was able to extend the range of her charity to sick and needy neighbours. Being poor herself, it was not easy to find money with which to help them, but she sometimes managed to save some out of the family budget by cutting her own diet to bread and water and thus "relieve their hunger by suffering hunger herself". Once, when her father procured a bale of cloth so that the family could make new clothes for themselves, Rosa quickly gave away all her own share after making sure from her mother that "she might do whatever she liked with it". Rosa had a disconcerting way of taking others at their word in order to further her own charitable purposes. But when she began visiting the hospitals to help nurse the women suffering from venereal diseases, and came back home with her white habit soiled with the stains and stench of the sick-room María altogether lost patience. Her daughter would sooner or later catch some horrible illness herself and die, and then what would become of them all? Rosa should know that charity begins at home, María sententiously remarked, and that she had a duty to look after herself. Rosa replied with the unanswerable logic of the saint; by devoting herself to the poor she was indeed looking after herself, for in the poor she saw Christ, the same Christ who dwelt in her own heart and was her very life. And how could she mind about her dress being soiled, when He let men defile and spit upon His sacred body?

María's patience was further taxed when the sick and needy came knocking at the door in quest of attention and when Rosa brought back her patients to the house. This seems to have begun after Rosa learned that a lady called doña Juana de Bobadilla y Azevedo was living in the outskirts of Lima with no one to look after her in her illness. Rosa went to visit her and persuaded her to come back to the Flores' house where there was an empty room which María was proposing to rent out. Rosa promised her mother that she would herself find the money for the rent and managed to do so for the four months that doña Juana stayed with them until she was well enough to return home. Other patients followed, and the room became a regular infirmary. Rosa nursed them all, dressing their wounds and treating them with the medicinal herbs she grew in the garden. María, as always, ended by accepting the situation. A little statue of the Child Jesus which Rosa placed in her infirmary became known as "el Doctorcito" —the little doctor—on account of the many miracles of healing attributed to it, and it is still venerated in Lima today.

One episode which occurred in the course of Rosa's ministrations cannot be read without an incredulous shudder, though similar feats of fearsome mortification are related of St. Catherine of Siena, St. Elizabeth of Thuringia and other saints. Rosa had gone to the house of her friend Isabel Mejía to help nurse a sick servant. The patient had been bled and the doctor had sent word that the blood should be kept for him to examine. He had then been delayed for a couple of days, and by the time he reached the sick woman's bedside the blood had begun to coagulate. A slave was told to empty the basin, a mere glimpse of which was enough to turn Rosa's stomach. But even stronger than the nausea was the wave of self-recrimination which at once swept over her. Was not this the blood of her own sister, for whom Christ had died and who was infinitely precious in His sight? Was this the charity and compassion she felt—she, a creature infinitely more vile and loathsome than the thing she looked upon with such horror? Taking the basin from the slave and leaving the room as if to empty it, Rosa raised it to her lips and drained its contents. The deed may fill us with horror; yet it was no less heroic, in its way, than that of St. Luis Bertrán in quaffing his poisoned draught.

But heroic deeds were commonly held to be the prerogative of the *conquistador* and missionary. Only occasionally might an exceptional woman venture onto this male preserve—Alvarado's widow governing the province of Guatemala in his stead, or Pedro de Valdivia's mistress stoutly organising the defence of the Spanish settlers in Chile. Rosa too burned with a desire for conquest—the conquest of heathen souls through the weapons of self-sacrifice. If only she were a man, she would exclaim to her friends, and could find martyrdom preaching to the ferocious Indians! One biographer declares that, since she was unable to go to the mission-field herself, she adopted a boy and raised money to pay for his upbringing and training so that he could go in her stead. How this project prospered we are not told.

We do know, however, that when Rosa was in her twenty-ninth year, the opportunity suddenly arose for the old *conquistador's* daughter to show her mettle. From the end of the previous century the Dutch had begun to penetrate into the Pacific and would sometimes descend on the coasts of Chile and Peru. In 1615 Joris van Speilbergen sailed round Cape Horn, defeated a Spanish fleet and threatened Callao. Rumours reached Lima that the heretics had landed and were marching on the capital. As the Viceroy called out the levies, the Archbishop ordered the Host to be displayed on the altars of the churches where the population was already flocking in alarm to pray and seek shelter. The Dominican tertiaries gathered in the chapel of St. Jerome. Rosa, far from sharing in the general panic, was filled with exaltation and fervently exhorted her sisters to prepare for martyrdom. As she spoke, she drew a pair of scissors, "slipped them inside her habit and cut off the train which trailed decently behind her on the ground, and shortened the hem all round, rolled up her sleeves, hitched up her over-skirt and scapular to above the ankle, and kicked off her sandals. All this she did most nimbly and gracefully. Those who were with her asked what she was doing, and she answered that she was preparing for martyrdom and did not want her clothes to get in the way, for if the heretics came, she would be able to climb up freely onto the altar and offer up her life there at the foot of the Spouse, who offered His for us all; and she declared she would not desist from this nor come down from the altar until her body fell mortally wounded to the ground, and that she would call on them not to kill her with one blow but to go on striking her until her body was cut into small pieces, in which business, she said, they might tarry and stay the affront which— oh woe is me!—they would surely do the Holy Sacrament, my Spouse.

"All this was said not with voice alone, but with her eyes and every gesture and movement, so that others took courage from her resolve, for she who was commonly as meek as a lamb now seemed a very lioness. Such resolution did she show by these actions that they gazed at her with awe and amazement, for so modest was her usual deportment that no commotion ever caused her to raise her eyes or her voice. Yet here she was cutting off her habit, rolling up her sleeves, kicking off her sandals, throwing back her cape and taking her stand with superb defiance as she waited the moment to join the battle of martyrdom, so that all who saw her were thunder-struck". But the report of the pirates' approach proved a false alarm. Word eventually reached Lima that the sails of their fleet had disappeared over the horizon. The dénouement, as related by her biographer, if something of an anti-climax, is not without a touch of humour which lends verisimilitude to the strange episode. "Rosa was grievously disappointed to find herself defrauded of her hope of suffering martyrdom. And since she had cut off her habit and was no longer decently clad, she was abashed to see that she could not go out into the street and so had to wait for nightfall before she could return home". It was not the courage to face martyrdom that she lacked, but the occasion for it.

*　　　*　　　*　　　*

Perhaps the most important event in the last six years of Rosa's life was the chance meeting with Doña María de Uzátegui, wife of Gonzalo de la Maza, a high official who had been sent by the Crown to inspect the Tribunal de Cuentas, or Commission of Audits, in Lima and to establish another important fiscal institution, the Tribunal de la Cruzada. The Contador was a man of standing and unquestioned probity. He and his wife, who had seen Rosa at her devotions in church and been moved to speak to her, were also a devout and perceptive couple. They at once recognised the exceptional quality of the young tertiary and a deep friendship quickly ripened between the three of them. One curious incident is related which may be taken as illustrating both the almost telepathic solicitude which doña María showed for her young friend and the latter's clairvoyant sensitivity. One evening, we are told, when Rosa was in poorer health than usual, her mother grew alarmed and declared that the one thing which might put her right would be a good dish of hot chocolate; for chocolate was then highly praised for its supposed medicinal qualities. But there was no chocolate in the Flores' home and the shops were shut. María was nevertheless on the point of sending out a servant to rouse the apothecary when Rosa stopped her. The chocolate, she assured her incredulous mother, would soon be brought to them and was indeed already on the way. A few minutes later a messenger knocked at the door from her friend María de Uzátegui, the Contador's wife, with a great bowl of chocolate. We might dismiss this little incident as part of the accretion of picturesque legend which veils the figure of our saint were it not for a curious piece of independent evidence. One of Rosa's few surviving letters is a note to María de Uzátegui thanking her "for the gift which you sent me last night and which reached me just when I was most in need of it".

So close an interest did the Contador and his wife take in their prottégée that the proposal was made and accepted that Rosa should go and live with them. María de Oliva had less need of her daughter now that the younger children in the Flores household had grown up. Fernando, the brother who had been closest to Rosa, had gone off to the wars in Chile. Her parents may well have felt gratified at don Gonzalo's invitation. Next to an advantageous marriage, against which Rosa had long since set her face, adoption into a family of such impeccable reputation and social standing had much to commend it; could the Flores family itself ever suffer serious want if linked to such a charitable and upright protector as the Contador? Rosa's health, always delicate, may also have begun to give grave cause for alarm, though she was to lead the same sternly ascetic life in don Gonzalo's more commodious house that she had always lived. Perhaps she needed more time and seclusion not only for the prayers which absorbed so many hours but also so that she could make some record in writing of her spiritual experiences. That such a record was made we now know, though only its fascinating outline has been preserved in the form of sketches and notes. In these she also refers to the accounts "I have written at various times to the glory of God and hell's confounding, for the consolation of many souls".

Despite the extreme modesty and seclusion in which she lived, Rosa became the centre of a group of devotees who looked to her in various ways for spiritual help and guidance. Girls who believed they had a vocation for the cloister would consult her, and might sometimes be told to their surprise that they should become wives and mothers, whereas others, whose thoughts seemed directed to those very things, learned incredulously that they would take the veil. Rosa seemed to possess an unerring insight into the minds of those around her and would speak out, when grave issues were at stake, with great boldness. Once, when she learned that the novice-master had come to doubt the suitability of a certain novice with whom she was acquainted and had recommended that he should not be given the Dominican habit, Rosa went straight to the priory, asked to see the novice-master and the prior, and persuaded them to reconsider their decision. The novice, as she predicted, made in time an exemplary monk. Others, whose lives reflected less credit on their Order, discovered for themselves the efficacy of Rosa's prayers and counsels. We read of one who, for over 30 years, had been addicted to the "odious, stupid, loathsome, abominable and harmful vice of smoking" which had ruined his health and defeated all his efforts to give it up in obedience to his superiors. Yet Rosa prayed and reasoned with him to such good effect that he soon conceived a loathing for the very smell of tobacco-smoke and broke the habit of a life-time. The most violent of tempers, too, could be tamed by Rosa's gentleness. María de Mesta, wife of Angelino Medoro, an Italian painter who had settled in Lima, would fly into such tantrums that "she became intolerable to her whole household and to herself". Yet after she had been persuaded to lay her problem before Rosa, her very nature seemed to change and she was henceforth as mild as a lamb. Such transformations earned a reputation for Rosa which the modest tertiary found highly embarrassing. We read of one of her devotees, doña Luisa Melgarejo, who "would never address her or receive her in her house without falling on her knees and kissing the earth she trod on. If doña Luisa had to write her a note and consult her on some spiritual matter, she would always kneel down to write it". It is no surprise to learn from her biographer that "such signs of veneration were for Rosa thorns which pierced her very heart".

Rosa responded by redoubling her own practices of humility and obedience. She had always lived in her parents' house under as strict a vow of obedience as the most observant of Orders would require. "She lived in such submission to her parents that she did nothing without their leave; whether it was taking up her needlework, starting or finishing sewing, sitting down, drinking or eating—absolutely nothing without first asking permission of them, for she rightly believed that God had made her subject to her parents in the smallest matters, although her mother often scolded and chided her, for she had a rough and quick-tempered nature and kept her daughter busy without bothering much about such maidenly scruples". It is clear that her parents were simply not equal to responding to such a degree of deferential submission. Old Gaspar must by this time have become senile, whilst his ill-tempered and insensitive wife, though she may perhaps at last have come to recognize her daughter's exceptional vocation, was hardly the person to guide it. Perhaps it was the urge to offer her obedience to those who had the insight to respect the mode of life she had chosen which led Rosa to accept the invitation to live under the Contador's roof. She addressed him always as "Father" and treated him with the most affectionate and submissive deference. "If she needed to drink, eat, work, sleep or to speak with someone outside the house, she would first fall on her knees before the Contador and beg his permission". Nor was submission to the master of the house enough to satisfy Rosa's craving for self-abasement. "She obeyed and humbled herself before everybody—before the master and mistress of the house, before the children, the servants and the whole household, even submitting herself to the slaves, as if they were her masters, serving them and doing whatever they asked of her".

In don Gonzalo Rosa found a generous and influential supporter for the project to which she now increasingly gave her thought and prayers—the founding of a Dominican convent in Lima dedicated to St. Catherine of Siena. Rosa had always sought practical ways of expressing her devotion to the saint on whose life she had sought to model her own. There was, of course, the thrice-yearly ceremony of taking the statue of the saint out in solemn procession round Lima. First, the statue had to be lovingly decked out with all manner of jewels lent for the occasion by pious devotees. Rosa, with her fellow tertiaries, took this duty very seriously and she once made new robes for her mistress with money provided for this purpose by an anonymous well-wisher in answer to her prayers. Towards the end of her life, when her right hand was racked with arthritis, Rosa found it miraculously restored to health so that she could handle scissors and needle once more for this good purpose. But longing to show her veneration for St. Catherine went far beyond this ceremonial doll-dressing. Though without resources or social influence herself for the founding of a convent in the saint's honour, Rosa was so firmly convinced that this great undertaking should and could be accomplished that others were inspired by her faith. The Contador and his wife took up the idea with ardour, and after their death, the large house which had been their home became an enclosed convent dedicated to St. Catherine of Siena. Rosa seems to have begun working on this project when still quite young. One of her few extant letters, dated 4 May, 1613, when she was 27 years old, is written to a Fray Gerónimo Batista in Spain, asking him to expedite matters for the foundation and referring to the two previous letters she had sent him giving proposals for the site and endowment of the convent, and to the 100 ducats enclosed for expenses—the gift of the Contador—out of which he was to pay an image-maker in Seville who had been commissioned to produce a new statue of St. Catherine for which Rosa and her friends had already made a suitable habit.

But opposition or scepticism towards Rosa's project persisted; even the pious Dr. Castillo, though he was a close friend of the Contador and a firm believer in Rosa's gifts of spiritual perception, believed that nothing would come of it. The Procurador who had been sent to Spain to obtain the necessary licence returned empty-handed. Rosa remained serenely confident. She had already made the acquaintance of doña Lucía Guerra de la Daga, a married lady with five children, whom she surprisingly saw as the prioress of the future convent. She confidently assured one of the Dominican fathers, Fray Luis Vilbao, who was luke-warm at the time, that he would say the first mass in the convent. Both prophecies were fulfilled; doña Lucía was left a widow and devoted her considerable fortune to the new foundation of which she became prioress. Rosa even predicted that her own mother would become a nun. María dismissed the idea with her usual irritable incredulity. Amongst the artless little poems left by the saint we find some verses addressed to St. Dominic calling on him to take María under his protection after Rosa had gone. And so indeed it came to pass. 12 years after Rosa's death, when her large family had dispersed, the irascible woman took the Dominican habit herself, just as her daughter had prophesied, and found peace—or so at least we must hope—in the convent whose foundation Rosa had foreseen and worked so hard to bring about.

*   *   *   *

The greater comfort of don Gonzalo's house in no way mitigated the austerity of Rosa's life. The bed of planks and shards had gone, but sleep was still rationed to two hours a night, the remainder of which would be given up to her devotions. A friend who once shared the bedroom with her relates how she awoke to find the room bathed in a soft light which emanated from the rapt face of her companion; the priests administering the sacraments to Rosa saw her features transfigured by the same radiance. As soon as there was enough day-light Rosa would take up her needlework, for she still had to help support her parents. She had learned to let her nimble fingers run whilst her thoughts remained absorbed in contemplation. To work was truly to pray. Her confessors had, at her request, drawn up a list of 150 attributes of God culled from the scriptures, and with each stitch of the needle her mind would ponder one of these divine attributes. The list, arranged by Rosa in the form of a Litany to the Trinity, has come down to us and was thought, until recently, to constitute the only expression, from her own hand, of the saint's spiritual life.

We now know that Rosa not only experienced mystical graces of a high order but wrote about them too. Evidence of this was discovered less than 50 years ago by a Dominican friar who had occasion to visit the convent which was once the Contador's house. The discovery adds a fresh dimension to the figure of our saint. We can no longer think of her as the passive recipient of mystical favours, ingenuous and inarticulate, of popular belief. We see her as striving, in the tradition of the great Spanish mystics, to analyse and record her experiences, tracing the progress of her spiritual development and constructing from them the outline of her own system of mystical theology. We know that she made this attempt, though the *cuadernos* or notebooks to which she refers have not come to light. What does survive is set out on two sheets of paper in a highly original and moving way. It takes the form of a series of notes and diagrams designed to summarize and illustrate the longer accounts we may presume the missing *cuadernos* to have contained. Other mystics had sought a similar way of conveying their own experiences and the universal truths which they reflected; Ramon Lull, the 13th Century Majorcan mystic, by geometrical figures symbolising the multiple attributes of God, St. John of the Cross, by sketches of mountain peaks and valleys to indicate the soul's ascent. Rosa was more at home with scissors and needle than with pencil or brush. Her diagrams are a set of collages, formed from scraps of coloured paper and material deftly cut out and superimposed upon each other. The range of symbols is modest—spears, nails, crosses, wings, hearts. Hearts, above all; for is not the heart the very symbol of Rosa herself, recurring constantly in her thoughts and visions, the heart overflowing with love, the heart suffering the wounds of Christ, the heart chosen by Him for His abode—"Rose of my Heart, be my Bride"? The combination of these hearts, crosses, spears and nails forms a sort of mystical scrap-book, devised with a child's freshness and ingenuity to record the tremendous odyssey of a rare and child-like soul.

The first of the precious pages records three successive phases or "favours" experienced by the soul, which is represented in each case by the symbol of a heart with a cross superimposed upon it. The first bears a gash through which a spear has been inserted and bears the legend: *The first favour of wounds received from God. With a lance he wounded me and hid Himself.* We are reminded of the beautiful verse of St. John of the Cross, the great mystic who wrote so movingly of "the dark night of the soul" and the agony of separation from the Beloved. Rosa cannot have known his poem but it alludes to the same spiritual experience:

A dónde ti escondiste	Where can your hiding be
Amado, y me dejaste con	Beloved, that you left me thus
gemido?	to moan,
Como ciervo huíste	While like the stag you flee,
Habiéndome herido;	Leaving the wound with me.
Salí tras tí corriendo, y	I followed calling loud, but
eres ido.	you had fled.*

The second heart bears a likeness of the child Jesus in its centre and the legend : *Here Jesus makes His resting-place and sets my heart aflame.* The third shows a winged heart : *Taking wings towards God. God fills the whole heart with His love and makes His dwelling there.* The following gloss, in Rosa's clear and well-formed handwriting, accompanies the diagrams : *These three favours I received from the Divine mercy before the great tribulation which I suffered in the general confession made at the behest of that confessor who gave me such occasion to gain merit, and after the general confession and some two years of suffering great pain, tribulation, desolation, loneliness, temptations, battles with demons, calumnies of confessors and fellows, sicknesses, and the cruellest torments of hell imaginable—in the course of those two years, which is now about five years ago, I received from the Lord those favours set down on this sheet of paper through the inspiration of God and the experience of my own heart, unworthy though I be. I confess in all truth, and in the presence of God, that all the favours which I have both recorded in the note-books and pictured and illustrated on these two sheets of paper have not been seen or read by me in any book. God wrought them in this sinner, by the mighty hand of the Lord, in whose book I read, who is eternal wisdom, who confounds the proud and raises up the humble, and so reveals to the meek what he hides from the learned and wise. All these favours were granted on many different occasions which I cannot enumerate, for I received them repeatedly, great sufferings alternating with most exquisite purifying joys, as I have written at various times to the glory of God and hell's confounding, for the consolation of many souls, at the Lord's command. On the eve of the festival of my father, the apostle St. Bartholomew, I did the two works which I here remit on two sheets of paper.*

The second sheet of paper bears a series of 13 diagrams with the following heading : *All these favours were granted to a heart tenderly enamoured of God, a slave of Christ unworthy to be numbered*

---

* Translation by Roy Campbell

amongst the children of God, and depicted here with special light from heaven; may any error be corrected.

It is again the story of a heart, a drama in 13 acts—for St. Teresa it was seven—in which the soul is drawn by love of God towards the consummation of divine union. The inscription which accompanies each diagram elucidates its meaning or takes the form of a simple ejaculation. In the first collage, the writer's hand dips a pen into the heart itself; *Here the soul suffers a holy restlessness. The heart writes, beside itself with divine love.* A wisp of paper inserted through a slit in the heart shows a *heart pierced by the lightning ray of God's love.* Another heart traversed by a shaft shot from a bow is a *heart pierced by the arrow of divine love.* Next, accompanying the collage of a hand clasping a crucifix, comes a quotation from the Song of Songs: *I found Him whom my heart loved; I hold Him fast and will not let Him go.* More pierced hearts follow, each with its gradation of spiritual ecstasy; *Oh happy heart to receive the Passion nail as its marriage pledge!—Heart wounded in the fire of God's love and forged in His furnace! Healed only by Him who forged it in His love!* Again some verses from the Song of Solomon, that inexhaustible well of mystical inspiration, *I am sick with love and die of its fever,* followed, rather unexpectedly, by a quotation in Latin from the same source: *Adorn me with flowers, comfort me with apples, for I am sick with love.* Then we are back amongst the pierced hearts: *Oh sweet martyrdom; I am wounded with a lance of fire—Heart pierced by the dart of divine love cries out to Him who wounds it—Purify thyself, heart. Receive the spark of divine love that thou mayest love thy Creator.* The soul is now nearing its supreme goal and words falter before the ineffable. The heart is borne up by two small wings, one inscribed *Holy Fear* and the other *Pure Love.* It is still traversed by a cross under which stands the legend *Life is a Cross.* From this cross hangs a thread and the supplication *Untie, Oh Lord, the knot that binds me!* The soul is now borne up by wings which have grown full and strong; *Ecstasy. Drunk amongst the wine-skins. Secrets of divine love. Oh Blessed union, God's close embrace.* The last tableau symbolizes the Trinity. Gone are the crosses, the darts, the spears. Words find no place. Only the heart is left, merging into the symbols which veil the mystery of the Godhead.

*　　　　*　　　　*　　　　*

We know the day and the month—24 August—but not the year when Rosa composed her mystic collage. The day, the feast of St. Bartholomew, held a special significance, for she had long had the

presentiment that it was to be then that she would be called away to
meet her Bridegroom. A few months before her death there occurred
an event which the Contador's household, and many others in Lima,
regarded as a portent, or at any rate as a marvel, but which left
Rosa's serenity unclouded. Don Gonzalo's chapel was hung with
sacred pictures, amongst them a poignant painting of the suffering
Christ by Angelino Medoro. Rosa would draw aside the curtain which
veiled this painting and gaze upon it with deep emotion. Sometimes
she was unable to suppress the exclamations of love and compassion
which involuntarily rose to her lips. One evening she was praying in
the chapel together with Doña María and her daughters. The others
stole away and left her to her devotions. After a while, one of the
daughters returned to the chapel to trim the lamps, and her mother
heard her give a cry of amazement. What appeared to be beads of
perspiration had appeared on the hair and beard of Medoro's Christ
and were running down his flushed cheeks. Soon the whole household,
including don Gonzalo and a friend who had dropped in to see him,
were in the chapel staring in astonishment at the phenomenon. The
Contador, a prudent and level-headed man, sent at once for Medoro.
The artist examined his work incredulously, testing the canvas and
wiping off the moisture and sniffing it to see if it had been exuded
by the oils, before pronouncing that he could find no natural explanation. Two Jesuit fathers were hastily summoned. By the time they
arrived the picture had been "sweating" for some three hours. Twice
they wiped the surface of the painting dry with a fresh cloth, and
each time the drops of moisture began to re-form. Don Gonzalo was
most distressed. He feared that the portent betokened divine displeasure at some unsuspected wickedness in his household or a public
calamity which was about to befall Peru. Only Rosa seemed unper-
turbed. For her the explanation was quite clear. Christ had been
moved by compassion for the sufferings of mankind and by a craving
that they should love him more. The sweat of his agony was already
bearing its sweet fruit, for "there was not one of those who beheld it
who did not feel an inner kindling of wonder and love".

Soon Rosa was herself to experience a still more startling demonstra-
tion of the picture's miraculous power. Shortly after this event, Rosa
fell and injured her arm so badly that the surgeons feared that she
would never recover its use. Then the cloth which had been used to
wipe the sacred sweat from the surface of the picture was applied to
the injured limb and Rosa went to the chapel to pray. At once the
swelling began to subside and three hours later the dressing was
removed and the injured limb found to be as sound as the other. A

public clamour had now arisen for the miracle-working picture to be removed to a church where all might venerate it. Don Gonzalo was distressed at the prospect of losing such a treasure but could not refuse. Rosa consoled him by assuring him that he need not worry, for the special grace which God had imparted to Medoro's painting would now be extended to all the other pictures in the chapel. And such, we are assured, proved to be the case. Not the least curious feature of the whole affair is the impressive body of testimony which surrounds it. The portent of the sweating Christ is recorded as having first occurred at 6 o'clock in the evening of 15 April, 1617.

The fall and injury to Rosa's arm were probably an outcome of her increasing physical frailty. Ever since the sickness which had fallen on the Flores family at Quive and carried off her elder sister, Rosa had been subject to frequent and not easily identifiable bouts of illness. Those listed by her biographers include angina, asthma and other respiratory complaints, sciatica, arthritis, painful stiffness of the finger-knuckles and other joints, even gout, not to mention acute pains in the stomach and side and the abnormally high temperature charac- teristic of many mystics. All these things were borne with smiling fortitude by Rosa who, when she mentioned them at all, would refer to them as gifts from the hand of her Beloved. Some may well have been of psycho-somatic origin brought on, or at least aggravated, by the austerities she mercilessly imposed upon herself, so that the doctors were probably justified in pronouncing that "these sicknesses are not subject to the common laws of medicine".

During the last months of her life, Rosa continued to return from time to time to her old home in the street of Santo Domingo to see her parents, and perhaps to go on nursing, as best she could, the sick to whom she had given shelter there; but the journey through the rough streets, though not long, was increasingly difficult for her and she would often be obliged to accept the offer of a carriage which a wealthy friend, doña María Eufemia de Pareja, put at her disposal for this purpose. She found the rose-filled garden as lovely, and her tiny hermitage cell as inviting, as ever, and there was still music to brighten her last days with its solace. María de Oliva heard her daughter singing softly to herself to the guitar in the shade of the garden, but the words of her song now gave her pause. It was a prayer to St. Dominic to take her mother under his protection when Rosa was no longer with her.

At the beginning of August, 1617, Rosa was forced to take to her bed in atrocious pain. Soon her left side became paralysed and her fever increased. She had predicted that in her last illness she would suffer the torments of thirst and had begged María de Uzátegui not to deny her then a sip of water. But the doctors believed that water would only redouble her fever and forbade it to be offered her. To the very end, Rosa was to share in the sufferings of the crucified Christ. Besides her confessors and the Contador's family and friends María de Oliva and other members of the Flores household were at the bedside. Old Gaspar, now in his nineties and so infirm that he had to be carried to the Contador's house in a chair, was brought to take leave of his dying daughter. After she had received the last rites, Rosa asked to be laid on the ground. This too was denied her, but one of her brothers took the pillow from beneath her head so that at least she could have the feel of wood, as of the cross, at her passing. She died, as she had prophesied, on the feast of St. Bartholomew, with the prayer which had so often been on her lips: *Jesús, sea conmigo!*— "Jesus, be with me!"

CHAPTER 7

The Lily of Quito —
Santa Mariana de Jesús

To turn from St. Rosa of Lima to St. Mariana of Quito is to catch an echo of celestial strains to which our ear is already attuned. In personality and the circumstances of their lives the two saints have much in common. Each divided her time between penance, mystical contemplation and works of charity. Each chose to follow her austere vocation in the bosom of the family rather than in a convent, and each died young. Each was blessed with a singularly sweet and gentle disposition, gaiety even, and charm of manner, though Mariana's beauty does not seem to have been of Rosa's superlative order. Each of them had a love of music, a quick intelligence, and for all their submissiveness to authority, remarkable independence of mind and firmness of purpose. They were both consumed by a craving for martyrdom and the achieving of great deeds for God for which the conventions of the day and the disabilities of their sex allowed little scope. Mariana's life was shorter and even more withdrawn than Rosa's. The provincial capital in which all of it was passed offered a more modest scenario than the city of the viceroys. Nor did she leave more than a few written lines to posterity or figure largely in the records of her contemporaries. We know, in consequence, very little about her. The resonance of her life is muted—dissolved, we might think, in the rarefied mountain air which she breathed.

Mariana Paredes y Flores was born in Quito at the end of October, 1618, just over a year after Rosa's death. Her father, Jerónimo Zenel Paredes y Flores, had come as a young man from Spain, where some say his family was connected with that of Rosa's father, Gaspar de Flores. This seems unlikely, as don Jerónimo was of gentle birth, and Flores is by no means an uncommon surname in Spain. In Quito he married a Creole lady, doña Mariana Jaramilla de Granobles, and set up house in the city where he and his wife took their place in society as *personas principales,* persons of rank and substance. Eight children were born to them, of which Mariana was the youngest. Left an orphan at a tender age, she was taken into the household of her elder sister, Jerónima, whose husband, Captain Cosme de Caso, acted as guardian to his little sister-in-law, and in their spacious house—later, as Mariana prophesied, a Carmelite convent—Mariana lived until her death some 20 years later. Doña Jerónima had three daughters of her own—María, Juana and Sebastiana. With these nieces, her sister Isabel, and other little girls of her own age, Mariana spent an active and not unhappy childhood.

The lot had fallen to Mariana and her playmates in a fair ground. Quito lies in the centre of a delightful and fertile valley only a few miles from the Equator, but nearly 10,000 feet above sea level, so that the clear sunshine is never scorching and the nights are always cool. Conquered first by the Incas, then by the Spaniards, Quito had grown into one of the most beautiful of Spanish colonial cities, and though it came within the general jurisdiction of the Viceroy in Lima, enjoyed a fair measure of autonomy under its own *audiencia*. By the middle of the 17th Century its population numbered some 50,000 souls, of whom the 2,500 or so Spanish and Creole households, of which don Cosme's was one, formed the core. Privileged and pleasure-loving, but punctilious in its religious observances, this elite set the tone to Quiteño society. Its pride was in the many magnificent churches and other ecclesiastical buildings, adorned by the rich baroque carving and polychrome sculpture of its own native school of artists and craftsmen. The Cathedral, the Sanctuario, the Franciscan monastery—probably the major building of its type and time in all Spanish America—and the Jesuits' magnificent church, with its baroque facade and gold and crimson interior, known as the Compañía, were amongst the many splendid and solidly built masterpieces which, earthquakes and other disasters notwithstanding, still impress and delight us today. The celebration of the cult within them was correspondingly sumptuous and well calculated to impress the imagination of a child as sensitive and piously brought up as Mariana.

A good deal of worldliness, and even occasional turbulence, were mingled with the prevailing religiosity. Its spirit was epitomized in the figure of Dr. Antonio de Morga, whose long career as President of the *audiencia* ended with his death in 1636, when Mariana was nearly 18 years old. An intelligent and efficient administrator, Morga was at the same time much given to gambling, speculating in contraband and don-Juanesque adventures. Assiduous in his attendance at mass and all church functions and a frequent visitor to Quito's many monasteries—the Franciscans enjoyed his particular protection—the President threw himself into the current ecclesiastical disputes with equal zest. He met his match at last when the formidable Licenciado

Juan de Mañozca, lately Inquisitor in Cartagena and a future Archbishop of Mexico, was appointed by the Crown to look into the
alleged irregularities—no less than 73 charges were preferred against
him—of his administration and personal life. Mariana was probably
too young and innocent at the time to hear much about these scandals.
But a few incidents were so sensational—the fracas of December,
1625, for instance, when an armed posse of Dominican friars raided
St. Catherine's convent in an attempt to recapture one of their
brethren who had sought refuge there—that they could hardly have
been kept from her. Mañozca intervened in the affair by invoking
inquisitorial powers and ordering the arrest of the friars. The leaders
of the Orders retaliated by declaring him excommunicated. The
Bishop, a man of peace, prudently left Quito on a long diocesan Visitation until the storm had blown over.

The regular clergy in the *audiencia* of Quito numbered at this time
some 300, and the secular clergy about 200. A sad decline in standards
had already set in. The Bishop estimated that about one-third of the
Augustinians left their communities as apostates every year. In addition to the prevailing vices of merchandising, gaming, licentiousness
and inter-Order rivalry, the first stirrings of nationalism—ill-feeling
between the American-born Creoles and Spaniards from Europe—
were already making themselves felt. It was this which had exacer-
bated the clash between the Visitor General, a staunch upholder of
the Spanish faction, and the Creole-orientated heads of the Orders.
The Jesuits, thanks to their greater care in recruiting and their
superior training and discipline, were less prone to these defects. They
maintained a deep level of spirituality amongst their devotees in the
city and an active, if ultimately unsuccessful, missionary campaign
amongst the Indians of the Amazonian jungles. Mariana, whilst still
a very young girl, felt herself drawn towards them on both counts.
She was to entrust her spiritual development to the sons of St. Ignatius
and to remain throughout her life, as she liked to put it, "all Jesuit".

It need not surprise us to read that Mariana's childish games were
to imitate the ceremonies and devout practices she saw around her. She
developed a taste for decking out little altars, marshalling her playmates in processions, and even forming them into two choirs which
would alternate in reciting responses and chanting litanies. She had
a pleasant voice and learned to play the guitar and other instruments.
In all this, she no doubt differed little from other small girls of her
age and station. Where she did show signs of singularity was in her
early addiction to self-inflicted penance, from the childish trick of
putting hard peas into her shoes to the more serious business of

staggering around under a heavy wooden cross and beating herself with home-made scourges. To the catalogue of such tortures were in time to be added the hair-shirts, crown of thorns, and unspeakable bed which recall the *via crucis* of St. Rosa. We read, too, though few details are given us, of her initiation through the *Spiritual Exercises* of St. Ignatius into the practice of mental prayer, to which, one biographer says, she would devote five hours daily from the age of ten. A strange and precocious child, certainly, whose peculiar quality her elder sister was quick to recognize, with the result that she was confirmed, placed under the guidance of a spiritual director, and received her first communion at the tender age of seven. Soon she was begging her confessor for the privilege of communicating three times a week, then every day. This was an unheard of thing, specially in a child not yet in her teens, and when it became known, aroused a great to-do in ecclesiastical circles. The Bishop even took cognizance of it, and after consulting his advisers and satisfying himself as to Mariana's maturity and exceptional progress in spiritual matters, eventually endorsed the permission for daily communion given by her confessor. We are accustomed to hearing of the precosity of genius in the arts and sciences; religious genius, too, may display itself precociously. It can coexist in a child together with other characteristics which seem quite normal.

There survives a portrait of Mariana at the age of eight. It shows us a small girl with a broad smooth forehead, pleasantly rounded features, a small sweet mouth, a firm chin, and exceptionally large and intelligent dark eyes. The expression is not that of a shy and dreamy child but of a very alert little person, confident and eager. The active, rather than the contemplative, side of her nature was then no doubt most apparent. Mariana experienced and survived the usual hazards of childhood; she fell from the roof of the house but picked herself up unharmed, and slipped from the back of a mule whilst crossing a stream but came safely to land—without even getting her clothes wet, if we are to believe the hagiographers. Once, when busy with her playmates in a courtyard putting together crosses for a pious game, she was seized with a premonition of danger and dragged them out into the street just before a wall came tumbling down on the very spot where they had been sitting. There were to be many later instances of the clairvoyant gifts which Mariana, like many another mystic, seems to have possessed.

It is worth lingering over such stories as have come down to us from Mariana's childhood, since her life was so short that childhood took up about one-half of it and set the tone for the other. One thing stands

J

out from her early infancy : she was the leading spirit amongst her playmates, the dominating, but not domineering, personality amongst the children brought up under Captain Cosme's hospitable roof. Two examples are on record of the direction her powers of leadership were taking. In 1629, when Mariana was 11, the churches of Quito celebrated the canonization of three Japanese martyrs who had suffered crucifixion for their faith not many years before. As they were sons of St. Ignatius, we may suppose that the occasion was celebrated with particular pomp and devotion in the church of the Compañía which Mariana attended. Their sacrifice had too a special relevance in Quito, for it was from that city that the Jesuit fathers sustained the great missionary effort, at constant risk to their own lives, to christianize the savages of the province of Maynas in the Upper Amazon valley. Father Juan Camacho, Mariana's own confessor, himself later left for this daunting mission field, from which he was to return with his health broken by perils and privations. Mariana was seized with a craving to give her own life in so glorious a cause. Firing her playmates with her own ardour, she planned to set out by stealth, secured the keys of the house, and retired to bed without saying a word to the grown-ups, but promising to arouse her nieces soon after midnight when the household was asleep. But the great missionary enterprise came to naught for the simplest of reasons—Mariana overslept. In the morning, the servants reported that the keys were missing and the girls had to confess. Her biographers see in this childish fiasco the hand of divine providence. Mariana, they declare, was already at this time so accustomed to spend the greater part of the night in prayer and penance that it was inconceivable she could have been overcome with drowsiness at so critical a moment without some miraculous intervention.

Mariana does not seem to have been discouraged by the failure of this venture. She felt within her the same urge to heroic action which had prompted the youthful St. Teresa to set out with her brother for the "land of the Moors". Her motives must have been much the same as those described by the saint of Avila : "When I saw the martyrdom which the saints had suffered for God, it seemed to me that they had bought the enjoyment of God very cheaply, and I longed greatly to die like them, not for the love I felt for Him but to enjoy as soon as possible the great treasures which I read were stored up in heaven. Together with my brother I discussed how it could be possible to accomplish this. We agreed to go to the land of the Moors, begging our way for the love of God, there to be beheaded".

Mariana was soon busy planning her new escapade. Thoroughly

alarmed by an eruption of the volcano in 1580, the citizens of Quito had raised a statue of the Virgin on the crater rim of Mount Pichincha. With the passage of time the memory of the disaster had grown dim, the volcano seemed reassuringly dormant, and the faithful ceased to make pilgrimage to the mountain-top shrine. Mariana conceived the notion of reviving the cult. Once again, she had no difficulty in gaining the enthusiastic co-operation of her nieces. This time they laid their plans with greater care and waited until Captain Cosme and his wife had left Quito for a few days and then one morning, disguising themselves in old clothes and taking with them some food for the journey, they slipped away quietly and made for the mountain. To heighten the excitement of the venture, the children had slashed their faces with a piece of glass and rubbed coal-dust into the scratches in imitation of the tribal markings which they had seen adorning the faces of the Indians who sometimes came into the city from savage parts. Their idea was to live as anchorites, "poor slaves of St. Mary", and guardians of the shrine, high up on the slopes of the volcano, from which one of their number might return to Quito once a week to buy provisions. All went well until the children—according to the biographers—suddenly came upon a wild bull barring the path. They hid in a ditch and waited for the beast to make off. But there he stayed, making as if to go for them whenever they showed signs of moving. Mariana was in no doubt as to what this could mean. God had sent the bull to show them that they were not, after all, to become "poor slaves of St. Mary" on Mount Pichincha. Her companions again followed her lead and they decided to abandon their adventure and return home. As soon as they had taken this decision, the bull ambled off placidly into the bushes, his mission accomplished.

The second of these pious pranks must have alarmed Captain Cosme and his wife considerably. It was the more disconcerting in that Mariana was now 12 years old and under the care of a confessor, to whom however she had not breathed a word of her madcap scheme. To her worried brother-in-law, prudence suggested an obvious solution; she ought to go into a convent. Whether he reached this conclusion out of conviction that she had a vocation for the contemplative life or whether it was more by way of precaution to keep an unconventional and high-spirited girl out of mischief we are not told. At all events, he confided to Mariana what he had in mind and the girl seemed to acquiesce. She replied at least that she would do what seemed to her to be God's will. The prioress of St. Catherine's convent showed herself quite ready to accept Mariana until she was old enough to take the veil. But nothing came of this proposal. The explanation given by Mariana's biographers—that the prioress sent for Captain Cosme to arrange the final formalities for her acceptance but he was unaccountably nowhere to be found in all Quito, although in fact he was going about his usual business there quite normally—is clearly fanciful. Whatever the reason for this set-back, Captain Cosme tried again and turned to the Poor Clares who declared themselves equally prepared to accept his sister-in-law. But this time it was Mariana who put an end to the negotiations. She announced firmly that she would never enter a convent; she had reached the conclusion, she declared, that this was not God's will for her. The family was taken aback and Captain Cosme inclined to feel aggrieved. He had already let it be known what Mariana's future was to be and was tempted to insist that, as her guardian, he knew best what was good for her and that she was to do as she was told. But the girl now seemed so calmly resolved, so wise beyond her years in spite of her recent escapades, that he agreed to let her have her own way—or rather, the way she now believed that God wished her to follow.

The convents of Quito, as Mariana had probably perceived, were not really conducive to leading the extremely rigorous life which she had decided to embrace. The ladies whose dowries assured them a place in a convent could generally count on leading a secure, comfortable existence, attended by their servants, and given to genteel pursuits such as making jam and sweetmeats, when unoccupied by the not very exacting religious observances required of them. Mariana's ideas were quite different. She was resolved to live in the world, yet not of the world, in the tradition of St. Catherine of Siena and St. Rosa of Lima. Don Cosme and doña Juana agreed to set aside an apartment for her in their roomy house, and in return Mariana made over to them her whole dowry, depending for the rest of her life on their charity for her food and other simple needs. The vow of virginity which she is said to have first made at the age of seven was now renewed in solemn earnest, and to it she joined the further vows of poverty and obedience. She let it be known that she no longer wished to be called doña Mariana, as befitted her station in life, but simply as Mariana de Jesús. Some biographers say that she lived under the rule of the Third Order of St. Francis, as Rosa had lived under that of St. Dominic. This seems unlikely, from what we know of her single-minded devotion to the Jesuits. However this may be, at the age of 12, or little more, Mariana took the great decision of her life and embraced the calling of a recluse.

*   *   *   *

Mariana set about ordering her new life in grim earnest. The first thing she did was to have the hangings and furniture removed from the apartment assigned to her so as to make it as bare as possible. The inventory of what remained is given by her first biographer, Fray Jacinto Morán de Butrón, as follows: "an image of Our Lady of Loreto, some pictures of St. Ignatius, St. Francis of Assisi and other saints of her devotion, a small sewing-box, some books of devotion and lives of saints, a great number of hairshirts and disciplines, three crosses, a coffin, and a guitar to which she would sometimes sing before a crucifix which she had". The coffin contained a dummy skeleton which she had somehow procured and dressed up in a Franciscan habit that she intended to serve as her own shroud. A crucifix was placed round its neck and a skull at its head. At night Mariana would set lighted candles on either side of the coffin and muse on that state to which all must come, exclaiming—so we are told—"God have mercy on you, Mariana! What is your lot to be—eternal death or life everlasting?" No wonder that a lady of her acquaintance who once came to visit the young recluse fell down in a dead faint at this gruesome sight! Another macabre object which Mariana had had made as an aid to her devotion was "a small painting of a half-decomposed head, full of loathsome worms and maggots", which suggests one of the nightmare canvases of Hieronymus Bosch and something more than the common Hispanic predisposition to necrophilia.

Such was the setting in which the young Bride of Christ chose to pass most of the remaining fourteen years of her life. Her time was not however given to morbid reveries, but plotted out according to a meticulously regulated time-table, interrupted only by the frequent bouts of sickness to which she was subject and to which her austerities no doubt contributed. As she grew older, these austerities became more intense, and the regimen of her devotions and penances more severe. Amongst the documents preserved for her Process of canonization is a copy of the schedule which she drew up for the approval of her spiritual director towards the end of her life. It reads as follows:

"At four in the morning I will get up and take the discipline kneeling down, and I will return thanks to the Lord and recall the points of my meditation on the passion of Jesus Christ. From four o'clock to half past five, mental prayer. From half past five to six, recollection; I will put on my hair-shirts and recite the canonical hours as far as nones; I will make my general and particular examination of conscience and then go to church. From half past six to seven, I will go to confession. From seven to eight, during the time of one mass, I will prepare a dwelling place in my heart for the reception of my Spouse. After receiving him, I will return thanks to the Eternal Father, for the space of a mass, for having given me His Son, and offer him up to Him, asking many graces in return. From eight to nine I will pray to gain indulgences for the souls in purgatory. From nine to ten, I will recite the 15 mysteries of the Rosary of the Blessed Virgin Mary for the space of a mass. At ten, for the space of a mass, I will commend myself to my patron saints; but on Sundays and Festivals, I will continue this exercise till 11. After this, if I stand in need of it, I will take some refreshment. At two in the afternoon, I will recite vespers and make the general and particular examination of conscience. From two to five, some manual labour, raising my heart to God, making frequent acts of love. From five to six, spiritual reading; and I will say compline. From six to nine, mental prayer, renewing the presence of God with more attention. From nine to ten, I will leave my room to go and get a glass of water and take some moderate and seemly recreation. From ten to 12, mental prayer. At midnight, the life of some saint as my spiritual reading for an hour; after that, I will say matins. From an hour after midnight to four o'clock in the morning I will take my repose; Fridays on my cross, the other nights on my ladder. Before going to my rest on Mondays, Wednesdays and Fridays, I will first take the discipline. During Advent and Lent, I will place peas in my shoes, wear a crown of thistles and six rough hairshirts; I will fast the whole week, without tasting a morsel of anything. On Sundays I will eat one ounce of bread. And I will begin every day with God's grace".

The regimen which Mariana prescribed for herself, with the approval of her spiritual director, allows us a glimpse of those fearsome mortifications which her biographers catalogue at some length. "That which commonly served this rare maiden as a bed", we read, "was a triangular-shaped ladder of seven rungs". The cross, which she preferred to it on special occasions, was of timber and massive enough to support her as she contrived to hang suspended from its arms for an hour or two. In Holy Week she would stagger round under its weight to make the Stations of the Cross. She possessed "two crowns, one commonly in use, of thistles, the other of iron", a whole armoury of scourges—over thirty were found in her rooms at the time of her death—and a wardrobe of hair-shirts, two of which she would normally wear under her black gown, though when they prepared her body for burial they found it to be clad in no less than five. Her sleep was rationed to three hours a night, and even this, Father

Camacho assures us, she managed to reduce towards the end of her life to a single hour. Her fasts, too, seem to us of quite incredible severity. Even the once-weekly ounce of bread, soaked in water and eaten with a few herbs or the juice of some fruit, seems in time to have been dispensed with, so that virtually her sole sustenance, like that of St. Catherine of Siena, was the Host she received daily at the hands of the priest. Little or no trace of the tortures Mariana inflicted upon herself was however visible even to her intimates. Like Rosa, whose austerities she emulated, she prayed that her face should bear no tell-tale lines.

These penances were not devised, as is clear from what we know of the lives of St. Rosa and other heroic souls, as a mere exercise in masochism, a morbid end in itself. They were simply considered essential to the training of all spiritual athletes. And what trials and tribulations the latter had to overcome! Those listed by Morán de Butrón make curious reading. They range from quaint tricks played by the Devil to distract Mariana from prayer—a little dog which kept up a continual yapping, or a handful of egg-shells mysteriously ejected from under the altar with a great clatter—to the alarming apparition of "a very sharp curved sword" or "a gleaming knife which flew round the room and made as if to strike her and cut off her head". There were also unrecorded combats with the powers of darkness which "left her in the morning black and blue with bruises so that she could not lift a finger". One particularly macabre experience occurred "when she was praying one night, and the light was suddenly extinguished, she knew not by whom. Without any fear, she groped her way to the coffin, turned out its contents and lay down inside— not to sleep, but to continue praying. When it grew light, she got up and opened the window. Then she noticed that the skeleton, which she had thrown out onto the floor, had picked itself up and was sitting with folded arms, in a most horrible and frightening way. The sight struck fear into her, but she soon recovered and dispelled the apparition by sprinkling holy water over the skeleton which she then put back into the coffin, saying as she did so: 'God have mercy on you, Mariana!' "

As for temptations of the flesh, her confessor Father Alonso de Rojas declares with his usual sweeping rhetoric that "so admirable was this servant of God that in all her life her body never once felt a lustful urge, nor did a single sensual thought spring to her mind, so that she seemed an angel rather than a woman". Morán de Butrón, on the other hand, suggests that Mariana was exceptional less for any immunity to carnal temptation than for the fulness of her victory over it.

"The Devil assailed her", he states, "in the form of naked men and women, who strove to trouble her most chaste body with abominable gestures, but they were driven back in confusion for their pains". She was at least spared Rosa's fate of being pestered by importunate gallants and suitors. So complete was her seclusion that, as one of her biographers observes, there were few in Quito, outside her own family circle, who had so much as set eyes on her face. When a young man once accosted her in church, she silenced him with these solemn words: "Pray leave me, señor; I am preparing to meet my death. If you would save your soul, I beseech you to do likewise". One episode which distressed her greatly occurred when she was on the way to church. An *oidor,* or judge of the *audiencia,* met her and signalled his appreciation of her sanctity by giving her a hearty embrace. Mariana wept bitterly to think that the body which she had vowed to keep inviolate for her heavenly Spouse had felt the touch of a man's arms. Nor should we be too ready to dismiss her scruples as needless prudery. The *oidores,* as we know from the annals of the period, often belied their grave mien. One of their number, don Manuel Tello de Velasco, had to be censured by the Council of the Indies for deflowering three Quiteño virgins.

The most harrowing trials of all which Mariana had to undergo in following her chosen path were not carnal but spiritual, and are only fleetingly alluded to by her biographers. Like all mystics, she passed through "the dark night of the soul". Morán de Butrón simply says that "for some time her soul suffered periods of notable desolation and aridity, and only her hope in God served as an anchor which kept her from foundering in the storm". Probably her confessors were of little help in such crises, the exact nature of which is not known to us. Father Camacho, who understood her best, had been succeeded by others—Father Antonio Manosalvas, Father Antonio de Rojas, Father Lucas de la Cueva, and at some stage, Father Luis Vásquez. The latter seems to have misunderstood his penitent completely. Perhaps it was he who ordered her to abstain for a time from taking Communion and to eat more solid food—to behave, in short, like any "normal" young lady of conventional piety. All we can say, from the fragment of a letter written by Mariana after she had at last found a spiritual director after her own heart, is that she "made her peace" with Father Vásquez. His name figures amongst those of the priests who later kept vigil round her death-bed.

From none of these confessors, who should have been best placed to gain some insight, do we find anything but the most generalised allusions to the nature of Mariana's mystical experiences. We are told that she first began to practice mental prayer at the age of seven or eight. Father Manosalvas observes that "after some years Our Saviour raised her to such contemplation, and to so close a union with her Spouse, that she did not cease for an instant to live in His presence, and she had no need of books to know what should be the object of her contemplation, for whatever she read or heard furnished her with matter enough to inspire her with love and praise for her Spouse for days and nights on end". Father Rojas, with that taste for rhetorical metaphor which gained him a great reputation for spiritual oratory, declared that "she gazed within herself, in the presence of God, and mused so deeply on the Most Holy Trinity that her spirit was raised to heaven and she joined the Virgins singing their hymns to God; so profound was her recollection that she often seemed as if beside herself, like a bee sucking nourishment from God's side". Father Camacho states more simply that "Our Saviour raised her to the height of contemplation, which is to know God and His perfections beyond the reach of reason and to love them without ceasing". "This", concludes her first biographer a little lamely, "is what her Confessors say about Mariana's prayer-life, and it seems there is no more to be said".

It would be nearer the truth to say that Mariana preserved throughout her life the mystic's impenetrable reticence about those secret things which pass between the soul and God. When the mystic—as distinct from the expositor of "mystical theology" who may be more learned but lack direct personal knowledge of such matters—attempts to record and analyse his experiences, it is nearly always at the behest of his confessor or spiritual director. The latter, concerned lest the apparent graces vouchsafed to his penitent may in reality be self-deception or even a manifestation of diabolical possession, calls for a written account which he can scrutinize himself or refer to his superiors. To this concern we owe the *Life* of St. Teresa and other spiritual autobiographies of unique interest. But in Mariana's case, the penitent had been from her tenderest years under the constant guidance of the Jesuit fathers who had themselves trained her in the practice of mental prayer through the *Spiritual Exercises* composed by their founder. She had submitted her life, in every detail, to their care and formed her mind in their doctrine. Her orthodoxy was impeccable, her decorum irreproachable. There could be no reason to exact from her an account in writing of what she had always been frank in confiding under the seal of confession. The nearest they came to requiring such a thing of her is recorded by Morán de Butrón for reasons which strike us as somewhat inadequate, and with an outcome which seems agreeably appropriate, even if we discount the miraculous element he ascribes to it. "The venerable Father Camacho," writes her biographer, "in order to put her obedience to the test, told her to give a full account of her conscience, penances and supernatural favours to one of her nieces. She was most distressed at this, but complied with the exacting demand without keeping anything back. Mariana called her niece and related everything that had passed in her soul—her virtues, the penances she set herself, and the favours her Spouse bestowed on her. Her niece was greatly edified, and desiring that nothing of what she had heard should escape her memory she took leave of Mariana in order to write down what she had been listening to. But when she reached the threshold of her room—marvellous to relate—she found herself quite unable to recall anything at all of what had gone before, and she returned to Mariana in sadness and confusion and begged her to repeat everything she had related as she could remember nothing. Mariana smiled and replied: 'I described to you under obedience what passed in my soul; tell my Confessor that I obeyed him, and that my Spouse did not wish that these matters of mine should become known so long as I am alive' ". Nor indeed, it seems—to our disappointment—after His bride had passed from this life.

But however carefully she attempted to conceal it, the unusually austere nature of Mariana's life could not pass unnoticed in Quito. The reputation which this earned her she felt not only as an insidious invitation to pride but as a cause of genuine distress. One day, as she was returning from church, she overheard a group of children whispering together; "La Santa! La Santa! the saint is coming!" Mariana regained the solitude of her room in deep confusion and took good care in future to vary her way to and from church so as to avoid the stares of the curious. She would make her daily communion in La Compañía when the congregation was at its smallest and kneel in the corners of the church where her dark-veiled figure was likely to be least conspicuous. She denied herself the pleasure of joining in pilgrimages or even watching the colourful processions when the famous Madonna of Guápulo was borne through the streets of the city. It was not for the Bride of Christ either to indulge or to arouse curiosity.

* * * *

There was another side to the personality of the young recluse which we have not yet considered—the burning desire to give practical expression to the second of Christ's commandments, that we should love our neighbour as ourselves. To one who had herself vigorously embraced poverty, the poor were in a special sense her neighbours. We have seen that in the daily schedule set down for the approval of her spiritual director Mariana had allotted the hours between two and five for "manual labour". It was this time of her day that she devoted, we may assume, to caring for the needs of those who found in Captain Cosme's house a sort of combined clinic, school and kitchen. We are not told much about her labours as a teacher. No doubt she taught the children to read and write, and perhaps instructed them in St. Toribio's Catechism. The other duties which Mariana took upon herself were certainly not for the squeamish. The most deplorable of her ragged visitors had to be deloused and generally cleaned up. "To the poor who came to the house", Morán de Butrón writes, "she distributed food with her own hands, and those whose condition was most loathsome and apt to inspire the greatest revulsion she cleansed of the *animalitos* which are commonly to be found in the Indies and are enough to fill the most mortified nature with horror. After this work of heroic mortification, she would line them up, kiss their feet, and often bring from her room a basket filled with bread of very fine quality which she distributed amongst the needy". This bread became famous in Quito—a celestial manna dispensed by an angel. But there was nothing other-worldly in Mariana's way of dealing with those in need. "There was a small window in her room looking out onto the street", Morán de Butrón continues, "and beneath it those in need would come and throw up pebbles to attract her attention. If she had anything in her room with which to relieve their necessity, she would pass it down to them; if not, she would have recourse to the charity of her sister, who had given her the keys of the larder, for the relief of the poor. The only thing which made her sorry that she had taken a vow of poverty was, it seems, the lack of anything of her own to give away to those in need".

In this charitable work Mariana had the help of the girls who were growing to womanhood with her. Her influence over them seems, if anything, to have grown even stronger since she began to live her retired life. Her niece Juana wished to emulate her vows of poverty and celibacy, but Mariana declared that her lot was to marry and have children. In due course, Juana did so, devoting herself as well to many works of charity, particularly the care of the Indians stricken down by epidemics. But the attraction of the contemplative life never left her, and when her two daughters were in their teens, Juana begged her husband to give the three of them leave to withdraw together to a convent. The father refused and Juana died disconsolate, leaving one daughter, Caterina, to become a Carmelite nun in the house where her mother, Mariana, and all the Caso family had once lived.

Juana's younger sister Sebastiana was even more devoted to

Mariana and determined to follow in her aunt's footsteps. Captain
Cosme betrothed her to a young man of suitable family in Quito, but
Sebastiana steadfastly refused to consider matrimony, claiming that
"she already had a far better Spouse, and that she would rather give
her life than break the troth plighted to Him". Her father, holding this
to be no more than girlish waywardness, insisted and went ahead with
the marriage arrangements. In desperation, Sebastiana turned to
Mariana who was convinced that she was right to persist in her refusal.
Together they went to consult Father Camacho who confirmed what
they both felt and is reported to have told her: "Pray your Spouse to
look to His honour and—if there is no other way—to take away your
life and let you celebrate your nuptials with Him in glory!" If the
good father did offer such counsel, it would seem he has much to
answer for. Sebastiana earnestly took his words to heart and, there and
then, before the image of the Lady of Loreto, offered up in sacrifice
the life which she had vowed she would never share with any human
partner. Almost at once she was seized with a high fever, returned
home and took to her bed. Five days later she was dead. Mariana,
who saw in Sebastiana's death a sacrifice required of God and willingly
offered to Him, assured her before she died that within a short time
she, too, would be called to take the same path.

Before this and other misfortunes befell the Caso family, we have
pleasant glimpses of life in don Cosme's patriarchal household. In the
evenings Mariana would emerge from her solitude to join the family
seated at table. She would never touch a morsel herself, but would
have her share of the food sent out to a neighbouring family which she
knew to be in need. After serving the others she would then go to the
kitchen to help do the washing up. Mariana's own diet was already
diminishing to vanishing point. Solid food, which she would sometimes
take in compliance with her confessor's orders, only made her vomit.
She was approaching the stage when, we are assured by her
biographers, the Host which she received daily would be her sole sustenance. The schedule which she had submitted for the approval of
her spiritual director included provision for "some moderate and
seemly recreation". Her chief delight she found in music. Some verses,
touching in their artless and heartfelt piety, have come down to us
which she used to sing and may have composed herself, though she
seems to have lacked Rosa of Lima's graceful facility in this respect.
Mariana would accompany herself on the guitar, and there is a charming story of her being carried off into ecstasy, her fingers still resting
on the strings, in the company of a startled friend. Such tales of rapture and other mystical phenomena are rare in the accounts of

Mariana's life. That she was subject to them, specially when deep in her devotions at church, there is no doubt, but Father Antonio de Rojas assures us that "she was no friend of revelations, raptures or ecstacies, but held them in abhorrence rather". Another confessor, Father Manosalvas, makes the same point even more strongly in his sworn evidence: "What she most earnestly begged of her heavenly Spouse was to be excused visions and such favours in this life, praying that they might rather be laid up for her in glory".

At the age of about 19, Mariana reached a turning-point in her spiritual life. It was a time of doubt and desolation when, as Father Gijón y León, the Procurator later sent to press the Process of her canonization in Rome, puts it, "those holy exercises in which she used to delight now became a heavy burden to her, and where she had once felt only a natural inclination to good, dark phantoms now drove her to fear and despair". She had no confessor at hand capable of guiding her through this dark night of the soul. Father Camacho, who knew her best, was away, and though she continued to correspond with him, could be of little use. Between Father Vásquez, her confessor at the time, and the unusual young woman who stood in such need of help, little sympathy existed. Despite her unquestioning submission and obedience to those set in authority over her, Mariana still retained— as was the right of every penitent—an irreducible core of spiritual autonomy. She remained free to choose her confessor. In her desperation she would gladly have done so. But to whom should she turn? The answer, vouchsafed after hours of anguished prayer, was as disconcerting as it was unexpected. "God took pity on her," writes Father Gijón y León, "and spoke of her quite clearly one night saying—'Go to the Church of the Compañía, which you are wont to attend, and speak to the first man to enter the church from the monastery through the door of my Javier's chapel. Tell him that he is to be your spiritual Father and he will examine you' ".

Mariana lost no time in carrying out this startling command. Early next morning she was at the Compañía waiting for someone to enter from the monastery. The first person to do so was a Jesuit lay brother called Hernando de la Cruz. Mariana asked the sacristan to tell him that she wished to speak with him. Brother Hernando was taken aback by the request. It was forbidden to speak to a woman without permission, and the lay brother had first to ask leave of his superiors before he could comply with it. Permission was granted and Brother Hernando went over to speak with the slim, black-veiled *beata* who told him in calm but firm tones that God wished her to take him as her spiritual director and would make known to her through him how to emerge from the dark night in which her soul was enveloped. For some time the two remained in earnest converse. As they talked, the clouds began to lift from Mariana's troubled spirit. A few days later, she was able to write to Father Camacho :

"God mercifully consoles the afflicted. Father, ever since I began to treat with Brother Hernando de la Cruz on matters touching my soul, my life has turned to joy. His words are a great solace to me; truly, Father, he is a saint".

As for Brother Hernando, the first encounter left such an impression on him that he could not help exclaiming to the sacristan : "Do you know, Sebastian, with whom it is that I have been speaking? Know then—for God is marvellous in his saints—that it is with another St. Catherine of Siena—a veritable angel in the flesh !"

So began the long and fruitful spiritual intimacy between Brother Hernando and Mariana which was to last until her death some seven years later. We are told that during all this time they saw each other for about two hours daily, as well as exchanging frequent messages in writing. Father Alonso de Rojas, as a priest, was responsible for hearing her confessions and giving absolution, but it was Brother Hernando who was to become Mariana's true spiritual mentor. That the superiors of a college noted for its piety and learning should have entrusted the direction of a young woman of such manifestly exceptional sanctity to a lay brother is surprising but not unprecedented. St. Alonso Rodríguez, the famous doorkeeper of the Jesuit college of Montesión in Palma, was for years given the spiritual direction of the novices and of others who sought his guidance. Brother Hernando de la Cruz was likewise no ordinary layman. Born nearly fifty years before in Panama of Spanish parents of gentle birth, he had led a gilded youth, abandoning himself to his three passions for fencing, poetry and painting, in the last of which he showed special talent. His only sister, to whom he was deeply attached, conceived a vocation for the religious life and wished to join the Poor Clares. As there was no convent of that Order in Panama, her brother accompanied her to Quito where, partly under her influence and partly as a result of a duel in which he had all but killed his opponent, he underwent a spiritual crisis and entered the Society of Jesus under the name of Hernando de la Cruz. Lack of education kept him from the priesthood, but, as a lay brother, he soon gained a reputation for fervour and holiness. For 20 years, we are told, he never left the Jesuit College except to pay a visit to his sister with the Poor Clares. The one feature of his old life which he retained was his passion for painting. The Church, cloisters and walls of the College soon bore evidence of Brother Hernando's skill and devotion to his art.

To the pure, all things are pure. No breath of scandal clouds the memory of this unusual intimacy between the artist lay-brother and his spiritual protégée. Mariana's biographers compare it to that between St. Francis and St. Clare. Yet it was a relationship so close and privileged as to be fraught with danger. The Church had known many cases where men of irreproachable virtue and holy zeal had succumbed to charms more sentimental than spiritual. In the previous century there had been the affair of Fray Francisco Ortiz, the rising star of the Franciscan Order in Spain, who became infatuated with a young *beata* of reputedly celestial purity but shady antecedents, ruining his career in his championship of her dubious sanctity and even denouncing the Inquisition for daring to have her arrested on suspicion of *alumbrismo* and immorality.

Mariana, irreproachable in her orthodoxy and in the decorum of her personal life, was spared the prying eye of the Inquisition. But she had other trials to contend with in the closing years of her short life. First, there was the misfortune which overtook the affairs of Captain Cosme de Caso. What the exact nature of this trouble was we do not know, but Morán de Butrón states that it involved the loss of his entire fortune, including the portion of it which had come from Mariana's dowry, and left the whole family in penury. Another biographer adds that the Captain was sent to prison. Secondly, there was the death of Sebastiana in the distressing and dramatic circumstances which we have already noted. Thirdly, there occurred a grave deterioration in the health of Mariana herself. Her biographers speak of "a pain in her side which, she said, if it had lasted a quarter of an hour longer, would have been the death of her"; but, it was characteristically added, "this she bore cheerfully, in memory of the wound suffered by Christ her Redeemer, the object of all her love". She had been afflicted by other painful ailments too; fevers, accompanied by a burning thirst, headaches, digestive disorders, and oral haemorrhages which perhaps indicated consumption. She may also have been subject to occasional epileptic fits, for Morán de Butrón recounts how they found her one morning almost lifeless, "her tongue so bitten through that it was only hanging by a thread", but it was marvellously made whole again once she had communicated. Some of Mariana's troubles were undoubtedly of a psychosomatic nature, brought on by her suggestibility to the thought of the sufferings endured by Christ and his martyrs. Once she lay ill for three months, half paralysed on one side, as the result of an attack which the doctors could not diagnose but which she had no hesitation in describing as "sent from heaven on account of the great desire she felt for suffering martyrdom for love of her Spouse". The accounts she had heard of the martyrdom of the Jesuits in Japan had left the most vivid impression on her, and when she went to bed the following night she dreamed that she, like them, was being torn limb from limb, and she awoke with the excruciating pains which were the beginning of the seizure.

This passion for vicarious suffering and the urge to offer herself as a propitiatory victim help to explain the circumstances of Mariana's death, at the age of 26, in the spring of 1645. The year had been one of unparalleled disaster. Quito and its surrounding district had been swept by epidemics of measles and diphtheria which are said to have claimed the lives of 2,000 Spaniards and five times as many Indians. A series of earthquakes had caused the death of another 2,000. Mount Pichincha itself had begun to belch forth smoke and send streams of lava pouring down its slopes towards the city. The terrified population crowded the churches where the priests exhorted them to repent if the wrath of the Almighty was to be appeased and Quito saved. At the foot of the pulpit in the gold and crimson splendour of the Church of La Compañía Mariana listened to Father Antonio de Rojas assuring the frightened congregation that Quito would soon share the fate of Riobamba, which had already been razed to the ground, unless God took pity on them. He concluded his sermon with what Morán de Butrón describes as "a most tender appeal, in which he offered up to God his own life for the salvation of his people, praying that what would otherwise befall the whole community might descend upon his own head".

Mariana, who had been listening to the words of her confessor with growing emotion, then rose to her feet and declared, in calm but confident tones, that the Father's life was too precious to be taken in this way, but that hers was worthless and of no account, and that *she* would gladly offer it up to God if thereby His wrath might be turned from them and the city saved. Then she quietly left the church and for the last time took the familiar path back to her home. Quito was never to see her alive again.

"It seems," observes Father Morán de Butrón, "that God accepted the offered sacrifice, for there was an end to the earthquakes, and an end to the epidemic, and the very day that this occurred she fell ill and never left her bed again." The church of the Compañía, the great monastery of St. Francis, and the other splendid monuments raised by the piety of the Quiteños are still with us today. And it is a fact that the Indians of that part of the sierra of which Quito is the natural centre were never decimated by disease to the same extent as elsewhere on the once densely populated Andean plateau. It is certain too that Mariana's publicly offered pledge of her own life marked the beginning of the illness which was rapidly to prove fatal. After a few days of intense pain, the sufferer lost the power of speech. Making signs for pen and ink, she was able to write a few lines confiding to Brother Hernando that St. Catherine had appeared to her and shown her a most beautiful garland with which she was shortly to be crowned, and had declared that she would come again, accompanied by her divine Spouse and his Virgin Mother, to fetch her away to glory on the evening of the 26th of May. On the following day, she was just able to scribble a few lines reminding the devoted band of relatives and priests who stood round her death-bed that it was her wish to be buried before the altar of Our Lady of Loreto in the Compañía. She died, as she had predicted, on the evening of the 26th. Shortly before she expired, those keeping vigil noted a movement of her eyes and a sudden expression of joy steal across her face. The heavenly visitors had come for her.

Brother Hernando knelt by the death-bed absorbed for a while in ecstatic prayer. Then he rose to his feet and announced in the confident tones of one who brings good news; "You have no reason to grieve, señoras, for the death of this most blessed woman. For she is not in purgatory, but God has taken her straightway to Himself. Let her rest in the church of the Compañía where she wished to lie, and make no show of grief or mourning, for she who has been taken from us has given us only cause for rejoicing".

Brother Hernando then hurriedly left the chamber and returned with canvas and brush to paint a rapid portrait of the young *beata* whose modesty had never permitted her likeness to be recorded during her life-time. His moving yet unsentimental impressionistic portrait (Plate 8) accords with the description which Morán de Butrón has left us of his heroine; "Her face was pale and rather full but pleasantly proportioned, with a calm and tender expression, her eyes were large, dark and expressive, her eyebrows thick, dark and arched, her nose a little less than moderate size, and her mouth small".

During the course of Mariana's last illness, the surgeons had ordered her to be bled. An Indian servant had emptied the bowl in a corner of the courtyard of Captain Cosme's house. A few days after the death of her mistress, the same servant then noticed that a clump of beautiful lilies had sprung up on the very spot where she had poured out the sick woman's blood. The sudden growth seemed miraculous; no lilies had ever blossomed there before. The servant hastened with the news to Captain Cosme and soon all Quito was marvelling at the portent. From that time on, the memory of Mariana de Jesús has been associated in the popular mind with the flower whose delicate fragrance and immaculate purity seems a fitting emblem for the maiden who had wished to live and die as the Bride of Christ.

CHAPTER 8

The Martyrs of Paraguay—

Fathers Roque González, Alonso Rodríguez and Juan del Castillo

WE have seen the Jesuits in their rôle of confessors, spiritual directors and scholars and caught a faint echo of their work as missionaries amongst the Indians. It is now to this latter field that we must turn. Maynas, the jungle province in the Amazonian lowlands to which Mariana and her companions once set out in their childish zeal to suffer and die for the faith, was one of the five main zones to which the Society of Jesus directed its missionary endeavours in South America. Taken together, these zones formed a great arc spanning the whole interior of the sub-continent from north to south, and skirting the Andean Cordillera to link with the other great field of early missionary activity by the Jesuits, Brazil; to the north, along the upper Orinoco; then Maynas itself; south of Maynas, along the valley of the Madeira River, an affluent of the Amazon; the region of Chiquitos, north of the Upper Paraguay River; and what was then known as the Province of Paraguay. The latter region, where for a century and a half their work was to bear its most remarkable fruit, comprised an area perhaps ten times larger than what we now call Paraguay and covered most of the future Viceroyalty of La Plata or the modern republics of Uruguay, Paraguay, and part of Argentina. Its core was the irregularly shaped quadrilateral lying between the rivers Paraná and Uruguay. The name of the Argentine province of Misiones and a few crumbling but still impressive ruins in the woods are all that remain today of what was the most flourishing and extraordinary of missionary ventures.

It was not until 1540—nearly half a century after the discovery of the New World—that the Society founded by St. Ignatius Loyola received papal sanction and began its astonishing expansion. Two years later, Francisco Javier started his labours in India, and seven years after that, Manoel de Nóbrega and the first party of Jesuits sailed to Brazil to launch their great missionary and educational work in that country and their long campaign to save the Indians from enslavement. Eight years later the Jesuits were in Peru. But another 50 years were to pass before they were ready to form their Province of Paraguay and start their campaign to convert and civilize the Guaraní Indians. During the intervening years they were learning from the experience of the other Orders and from their own, not always successful, attempts to discover how best to approach primitive natives and consolidate what gains they made. The Franciscans, with their *pueblos de indios* in Mexico and their later settlements in the Amazon valley and elsewhere; the *pueblos-hospitales* founded by Vasco de Quiroga, Bishop of Michoacán, on lines inspired by Thomas More's *Utopia;* the valiant if ultimately futile attempts by Fray Bartolomé de las Casas to replace armed conquest by the peaceful persuasions of missionaries in Cumaná and Tuzutlán—these no doubt were amongst the experiments studied with profit by the Jesuits. The latter later started a pilot project of their own in the Indian settlement of Juli on the shores of Lake Titicaca. The idea underlying all these differing initiatives was the belief that the gospel should and could be propagated by peaceful means, that even the wildest Indians were capable of receiving it and of being gradually led into civilized ways, and that the best means of achieving these ends was to group the Indians into communities under the care, material and spiritual, of trained and dedicated priests.

The Province of Paraguay had remained remote from the mainstream of Spanish conquest and colonization. The wide estuary of the Rio de la Plata, into which are poured the great Paraná, Paraguay, Uruguay and Pilcomayo rivers, might be thought to invite access from Europe. But the fierce tribes which inhabited its shores had effectively discouraged colonization. Juan Diaz de Solís, the first European to set foot on the Uruguayan side in 1516, had been seized and eaten. Pedro de Mendoza founded Santa María de Buenos Aires in 1532, but the settlement was soon destroyed by the Indians. The fort of Asunción, built a 1,000 miles up-stream, managed to hold out and became the chief bastion of Spanish power in the region, and it was colonists from Asunción who descended the river to refound Buenos Aires in 1580. In the meantime, other Spaniards pushing down from Peru founded new cities east of the Andes such as Santiago del Estero and Córdoba. But the vast plains and forests, through which the rivers offered the chief means of communication, continued to be roamed by war-like Indians, most of them of Guaraní stock, who stubbornly resisted the attempts made by the Spaniards to subdue them. Precarious alliances were indeed from time to time concluded, some fusion of races occurred as a result of miscegenation, and the weaker tribes were subjected and their men sent to labour on the *encomiendas*. But the Spaniards had neither the force nor the skill to establish their authority far beyond the radius of each scattered settlement.

Could the missionaries succeed where the soldier-settlers had failed? Such, at least, was the hope of Hernandarias de Saavedra, several times Governor of Rio de la Plata and the first Creole to be appointed to such high office by the Crown. After suffering more than one reverse at the hands of Guaraní warriors, Hernandarias had become convinced that those savages could never be overcome by arms alone and he warmly welcomed the Jesuits. Fathers Ortegoa and Fields had come for a time from Brazil, as had three Fathers from Peru, and their pioneering work had yielded promising results. The Franciscans too were active. Fray Luis de Bolanos had laboured long and fruitfully amongst the Indians and his translation into Guaraní of St. Toribio's Catechism was to stand his successors in good stead. Even more spectacular success, as we have seen, had attended the apostolic fervour of St. Francisco Solano amongst the Indians of Tucumán. But the saintly friar had been recalled, and though the Indians still spoke with awe of his miracles, they had lapsed, with none to guide them, into paganism. Something more was required than the heroism or holiness of any single missionary. It was to meet this need that the Jesuits, under their first Provincial, Father Diego de Torres, with many years in Peru and the experience of the Juli "pilot project" behind him, evolved the system of the mission-villages or *Reducciones*.

The *Reducciones* or Reductions were all built on broadly the same plan (Plate 9). On one side of a large square rose the church, flanked by the Casa Parroquial, the priest's quarters and the administrative offices. On the other side of the church lay the burial-ground and beyond that the alms-house for widows and orphans. Round the other three sides of the square were ranged the homes of the Indians, all more or less alike and grouping together several families under one roof. Each building was flanked by a loggia or covered gallery providing shelter against sun and rain. In the centre of the square stood some sacred monument, and at each corner of the square a cross, often with two small chapels flanking the main entrance to the square opposite the church, all of them designed to play a role in the ceremonial processions which were an important aspect of community life. Beyond the church were grouped other communal buildings—store-rooms, work-shops, infirmary, stables and kitchen gardens. The population of each Reduction varied from little more than 1,200 to some 8,000. The buildings consisted at first of no more than mud-and-wattle huts but came to comprise well-built houses of adobe or wood and churches of stout timber or hewn stone, built on a lavish scale with three or even five naves and adorned with statues imported from Europe or skilfully carved and painted by native craftsmen.

The life of the Reductions was organized on a communal basis and geared to agricultural production. Not only in food but also in clothing—thanks to the cultivation of cotton and in some cases to their flocks of sheep—each settlement was almost self-supporting. Such commodities as they lacked—salt, for example—they obtained by barter from each other or by purchase in Asunción. Their main cash crop was the tea-like beverage *maté,* which the Indians not only drank themselves but were permitted to sell in prescribed quantities so that they could pay the tribute due to the King and purchase necessities out of the proceeds. The settlements were based on what we would call a mixed economy, each head of family being allotted a plot of land for his own needs, whilst other land, the Tupambaé or God's Portion, was held and worked in common, its produce being either consumed or disposed of by the community. Horses, cattle and oxen, as well as reserves of food, seed and cloth, were also held in common.

Each Reduction was directed by a Jesuit Father, with the help of an assistant priest and perhaps a lay brother skilled in agriculture, building, or some other craft. Improvident and indolent by nature, the Indians were prone, if left to themselves, to consume the seed-corn alloted to them and to slaughter the oxen loaned for ploughing. The strictest order and decorum were maintained by means of over-seers, recruited from amongst themselves, and there was the whipping-post for serious offenders. The Indians still had their own *caciques,* now dignified by the office of *alcalde* or *corregidor.* But real power lay always with the Jesuit Fathers, who ruled their flock without the sanction of any secular force—no armed Spaniards set foot in the Reductions save on the Governor's rare visits—but only through the moral authority of their priestly office and their unrivalled understanding of the native mind. The Fathers persuaded the Indians by their eloquence and convinced them by the devotion and integrity of their lives. They preferred to coax and charm, rather than coerce, their converts. The Guaraní were musically and artistically gifted and readily impressed by the splendid liturgy of the Mass and the solemn pageants which the Jesuits devised for them. Each day began with attendance at Mass and a procession, to the sound of flutes, to the fields where they worked, bearing an image of St. Isidro, the farmer-saint of Madrid. It ended with a return procession, the office of the

Rosary, and "the singing of a short motet in honour of the Blessed Sacrament or the Holy Mother of God". The Indians formed excellent choirs and orchestras of their own and learned how to make their own instruments, including organs for the churches. Many of them showed great talent too as wood-carvers, painters, masons and craftsmen of every description.

To persuade a people of nomadic, or semi-nomadic, mode of life to form permanent settlements, submit to the routine of agricultural labour and the tutelage of strangers was something achieved only after many set-backs. Crops might fail, famine threaten, and the Indians would melt away again to seek what sustenance they could in the woods. Epidemics would sweep through the settlements and decimate the population. Sometimes the call of the old wild life would simply prove too strong, and the docility of the Indians towards their mentors would turn to sudden fury. Often the Jesuits had to face the hostility of their own compatriots. If enlightened governors like Hernandarias backed their work, there were others, in high positions in church and state, who looked with envy on the extraordinary influence the Order came to wield and on the wealth and cosmopolitan connections of their establishments. Ill feeling was most widespread amongst the *encomenderos,* who would have liked to see the Indians labouring for themselves instead of for the Fathers and who resented the support which the Jesuits had always given to the Crown's attempt to abolish, or at least to limit, the forced labour exacted from the Indians. One of the first actions by Father Diego de Torres on assuming charge of the Province was to declare all Indians on the Society's estates free of "personal service" and to institute payment for their labour. This provoked a storm of indignation amongst the *encomenderos* who forced the Jesuits for a time to leave Córdoba, Santiago del Estero and Asunción. But the settlers needed the Jesuits, however much they resented their liberal treatment of the Indians. They needed them for the schools which the Fathers opened for the education of their sons. They needed them above all for their ability to pacify the warlike tribes which still endangered their settlements. Whilst some detested them and others respected them, most came to accept the Jesuits and the existence of the autonomous Indian Reductions. A few even admired them so fervently that they sought admission themselves into the Society. Amongst this select band was one who was to become an outstanding pioneer in the establishment of the Reductions and in so doing to win the crown of martyrdom.

*   *   *   *

Of the early life of Roque González we know very little. He was born in Asunción in 1576. His parents, don Bartolomé González de Villaverde and doña María de Santa Cruz, were people of wealth and importance. Of their numerous children, one daughter married a son of Hernandarias de Saavedra, one son—Francisco—became himself for a time Lieutenant Governor and Captain General, whilst two other sons held lesser posts under the Crown, and three others, including Roque, entered the priesthood. He was given such education as the still primitive township was able to provide. But if his studies of Latin and Theology could do little more than pass muster, he became skilled in riding, handling boats, and the other pursuits common to the boys of his own station, and showed a bent for carpentry, building, farming and other practical matters which was to stand him in good stead when pursuing his work amongst the Indians. Like other young Creoles, too, he was equally at home in the Guaraní and Spanish tongues. We are also told that, from his earliest years, his life was adorned with all the Christian virtues, including that of chastity, a rare quality in a frontier community commonly dubbed "Mahomet's Paradise" where, a scandalized chaplain had earlier complained to the King, "some men have as many as 70 women, and the very poorest does not have less than five or six". At the time of Roque's birth, 39 years after its foundation, Asunción had a population of less than 300 Spaniards, but the mestizo inhabitants engendered by them numbered more than 5,000.

One of the few stories which has come down to us from Roque's childhood and was recounted in the Process for his beatification, relates an attempt, made when he was aged 14 or 15, to go off with some other lads "to the forest and wilderness, to do penance and read the lives of the saints". This pious escapade came to an end when his angry relatives caught up with the boys, some 12 leagues outside the city, and brought them back home "with persuasion and threats". At the age of 22 or 23 Roque was ordained by the Bishop of Tucumán and was able to begin his pastoral work in good earnest. He chose to start it amongst the Indians of the Maracayú region whom the Spaniards had compelled to toil on their *maté* plantations with scant regard for their physical or spiritual welfare. There he began to gain his unrivalled insight into the native mind and to learn how to present the gospel message in terms which it could grasp. After some time he was recalled to Asunción for work amongst the Spaniards and mestizos. Aspects of a strong and energetic personality began to reveal themselves, and after ten years in the priesthood he had won such repute as an organizer and administrator that the young priest was selected to be Vicar-General, an important post since the Bishop resided far away in Buenos Aires and his Vicar would normally be left in virtual charge of Asunción. But Roque González declined this honour and the promise of a brilliant ecclesiastical career. He had made up his mind that his vocation was to work amongst the Indians, and that the best way of doing this would be to seek admission into the Society of Jesus, whose members were debarred from accepting senior posts in the church hierarchy, and which was preparing to launch one of the most remarkable missionary enterprises in its history.

In May, 1609, at the age of 33, Roque González began his work with the Society. The application of this promising Creole postulant came at an opportune moment and was readily accepted. Fray Diego de Torres, with a nucleus of some 45 Jesuits, had recently arrived to begin the evangelization of the new Province. Roque González started his novitiate in the small Jesuit College at Asunción, but after only one year's grounding in the Founder's *Spiritual Exercises* and the *Constitutions* of the Society, he was considered ripe for the mission field. With one other companion, the Italian Father Griffi, he was detailed for pioneering work amongst the Guaycurúes.

The Guaycurúes were not of Guaraní stock. They were a race of hardy hunters, fishermen, and warriors inhabiting the swamps and forests of the Chaco on the western bank of the Paraguay opposite Asunción, who preyed equally on the Spaniards and on other Indian tribes. Time and again the Guaycurúes had launched surprise attacks on the colony, killing without mercy and carrying off the women, including even a sister of Governor Hernandarias. The Provincial, writing to Rome in June, 1610, gave a graphic description of the savages amongst whom he was sending his missionaries. They were, he assured his General, "so warlike and fearsome that they have never been able to be conquered. They wage war against the Spaniards, and have killed many of them and laid waste their properties. They keep the city armed and in great dread and they ravage the other Indian tribes who are their neighbours. When the Spaniards first came, there could not have been more than 500 of them, but now they are far more than double that number, which is something unheard of in all the Indies, where the inhabitants have suffered greatly from the ills and injustices inflicted on them by the Spaniards. Amongst the ruses which have helped them to survive is that in the wars they wage against other Indians they seize young children and bring them up with their own just as if they were their sons. They take great pride in always going around with horribly painted faces and they themselves declare to the others that they are Demons. . . . The land they inhabit is full of great swamps in winter and so parched in summer that the Spaniards cannot pursue them, and if they occasionally do manage to do so, the Indians scatter so that there are never two of them together, and in this way they can never be caught". Nevertheless, concluded the Provincial, these savages were not without virtues of their own. They seldom got drunk, they gave great obedience to their chiefs, lived in chastity until the age of 25 or 30 and then would take to wife only those women who freely chose to live with them, and once the fury of their blood-lust had passed, they treated their captives well.

There were sound strategic reasons for attempting the conversion and pacification of the Guaycurúes. Their territory lay athwart the direct route to Peru, and if safe passage could be assured through it, communications with Lima would be conveniently shortened. But Father González and his companion found themselves faced from the outset with difficulties which might have deterred less resolute men. They were delayed from setting out by ill-health, Father González first falling sick, then Father Griffi developing a high fever. By the time they had both recovered the rains had started and the river was in spate. They crossed it nevertheless, taking with them only a couple of Spanish lads to help with the celebration of the mass, and a Guaraní Indian who had lived amongst the Guaycurúes and knew their tongue. For three days the party struggled on through the marshes and forests on the far side of the river, seeing no sign of any Indians, though their own movements were being watched and reported by invisible sentinels. At last they came to a clearing where they found the *cacique,* whom the Spaniards called don Martín, and explained as best they could that they came as friends to tell his people about God and to help them in their harsh struggle against nature. They then distributed the gifts they had brought with them—fish-hooks, axe-heads and a few ornaments—and were allowed the use of a reed hut, whilst the *cacique* secretly sent his spies to Asunción to ascertain whether what the Jesuits said was true. The reports they brought back confirmed the missionaries' statements, but the Indians still remained suspicious. When they saw Father González and his companion writing down the words which they were trying to learn in the Guaycurúes' difficult tongue, they wondered whether they were not drawing up reports which would help the Spaniards conquer their land.

After a time, however, it became clear that the missionaries were beginning to win the Indians' confidence. The Provincial was able to report to Rome that the Fathers "come and go in perfect safety", and some months later, that "though it has not been possible to baptize many of them, they are at least being tamed. Whereas they used to cross the river in order to pillage and do harm, they now come in their scores, go through the streets, enter the houses and sleep safely in the town. Not only have they lost the name of Demons, but they are held as friends. They show the Fathers extraordinary affection and obedience. Fathers González and Griffi have been teaching them with great devotion to plough, sow, tend the land, and harvest the crops". To see those nomads learning the skill of the husbandman, the Provincial concluded, was a miracle; still more miraculous was the way in which such dread warriors were turning from their ancestral pursuit of war. He described how he had himself been invited to visit don Martín in order to help select a site for a church and settlement. He had ventured across the river, much against the advice of his compatriots who vowed that he was going to his death, and been escorted "with great rejoicing" by the Indians, who carried him shoulder-high through the swamps until they reached a place which seemed not unsuitable for a settlement.

But the rains came again, the land was flooded, and the Guaycurúes dispersed in search of higher ground. Father González and Father Griffi followed their Provincial back to Asunción and waited for the waters to subside. Don Martín then invited them back to his land, and for the next year the two Jesuits lived amongst the Guaycurúes in conditions which Father Nicolás del Techo, writing his *History* of the missions half a century later, describes as follows: "Their food differed in no wise from that of the Indians except that they did not eat poisonous creatures. Their hut was made of reed mats and extremely small. They suffered day and night from the bites of mosquitoes, from the noxious airs rising from the marshes, from lack of fresh water and in danger from tigers and vipers. To this was added the stench exuded from the bodies of the Indians smeared over with rancid fish-oil; worst of all was the obstinacy with which the Indians persisted in their ancient customs, breaking the silence of the night with their horrible howls and orgies. Little by little, the Fathers managed to disinfest this pestilential atmosphere. They preached often, travelling through the country and penetrating to its remotest parts, teaching the children, and conveying by signs what they could not express in words".

Though the Guaycurúes had now accepted the missionaries, they still showed little disposition to accept the faith they preached. Don Martín did indeed have a mortally sick daughter baptized and given Christian burial. The missionaries even managed to prevent the usual holocaust of the companions selected to accompany the dead child in the other world. When a smallpox epidemic spread amongst the Indians, others also consented to receive baptism and Father Griffi reported to his Provincial that 50 souls had been saved in this way. All this nevertheless appeared a meagre harvest to Father Torres who was seriously considering whether to withdraw his missionaries from the Chaco when don Martín sent his son to Asunción to seek baptism and to announce that the *cacique* himself wished to visit the Spaniards' city. The chief's son was duly received into the Church, the newly arrived Governor, don Diego Marín Negrón, and don Francisco Alfaro, the Visitor sent to enforce compliance with the royal ordinances for the just treatment of the Indians, standing god-parents to him. Don Martín appeared in person and was likewise solemnly received. The missionaries then recrossed the river and resumed their labours.

Father González was not to remain amongst the Guaycurúes for long; he had proved himself in a singularly difficult and unrewarding field and was destined for work where the harvest promised to be more abundant. As for the Guaycurúes, the high hopes which Father Torres had set upon their speedy conversion were to be disappointed. The Jesuits continued working amongst them for a time, and don Martín himself eventually accepted baptism. But his people never took to the settled life of agriculturists or to the new faith offered them. The Fathers were recalled and the mission abandoned. Perhaps the Provincial realized that the very proximity of the Guaycurúes to a large Spanish settlement must mean that they could never escape a contact which was bound to prove fatal. If the Indians were to be nurtured in the purity of the faith, it must be without danger of contamination from those who were Christians only in name and showed themselves only too ready to exploit and corrupt the native converts. The Jesuits must find more distant and secure fields for their endeavours.

*   *   *   *

The Provincial had indeed already sent two Italian Jesuits, Fathers Maceta and Cataldino, to found settlements far away from Asunción, in the distant region of Guayrá, near the great cataract of that name on the Upper Paraná. There, deep in the woods of what is now Brazil, they founded the first of a group of Reductions which they named Loreto. Nearer to Asunción itself, and not many miles from the Paraná, another Jesuit, Father Lorenzana, founded the Reduction of San Ignacio Guazú early in 1610. Lorenzana had brought some of his Guaraní converts to visit Father González in the Chaco and together

MILES

0   50   100   200

C H A C O

R. Pilcomayo

R. Paraguay

◉ Asunción

R. Paraná

R. Iguazú

S. Ignacio
†Güazú

Itapúa
†(Encarnación)

R. Yagapua
†

Corrientes ◉

†Sta. Ana

Concepción †

† S. Fr. Javier

Asunción de Iyui
†

Candelaria de.
† Caazapamini

S. Nicolas
†

† Todos Santos de
Caaró (Mártires)

Yapeyú
†

R. Ibicuy

† Candelaria
de Uncuy

R. Paraná

R. Uruguay

BRAZIL

PERU

CHILE

Buenos
Aires ◉

† Reductions founded
   by Father González
† Other reductions
◉ Spanish cities

Map 3. The Jesuit Reductions of Paraguay.

they had cut timber for a church. He had been impressed by the energy and dedication of the Creole novice and gladly accepted him as a colleague at San Ignacio when the Provincial decided to transfer Father González from work amongst the Guaycurúes. For some six months the two men laboured together until May, 1612, when Lorenzana was summoned to Asunción to become Rector of the Jesuit College, leaving Father González in charge at San Ignacio. A few days later González was joined by Father Pedro Romero, who had succeeded him briefly in the abortive mission to the Guaycurúes.

Though less intractable than the Guaycurúes, the Guaranís did not at first take readily to the settled life of San Ignacio. Many, after accepting baptism, would disappear again into the forests, and such half-converted savages, once they had had some taste of more civilized ways and decided that they did not like them, could become the most implacable foes of the missions. By the following October Father González was nevertheless able to report to the Provincial that the settlement numbered a thousand inhabitants, not all of them Christians yet, though 122 had been baptized in the past year, including a 90-year old cacique and two witch-doctors, who had publicly renounced their "lies, wiles and deceits of the Devil". The children were the special object of the missionaries' care. A school had been started for 150 boys, and as many girls, "who go every afternoon to church, in separate groups, for two hours' devotions, and they know their catechism and prayers very well. . . . We are beginning to teach them to read, write and count".

The economic basis of the settlement, though still rudimentary, had been laid, Father González reported, and held promise of better things to come. They all lived mainly on maize and wild roots at present, but they already had 40 head of cattle, as many sheep, and 14 goats, and this livestock, in the Jesuit's graphic phrase, "was multiplying like spray". The Indians knew nothing of agriculture as yet, and Father González had to teach them everything himself—how to plough, sow and tend the animals. The whole Reduction was in fact being reorganized and rebuilt. From his letter to the Provincial we get a good idea of the lines on which this was being done. The ground-plan was traced out "according to His Majesty's *cédula*", in the form of nine *cuadras* or large squares, the central one being left open to form the *plaza*. On one side of the latter was rising the church and the missionaries' house—badly needed, for they could scarce find a dry spot at present to sling their hammocks. On the other *cuadras* were being built blocks each containing half a dozen homes for native families. The church was being constructed of cedar wood, of which there was an abundance locally, though it was only thatched with straw. The Indians had set to work "with as little expense and labour as possible, and are quite happy and well paid". As for the missionaries, "they have to be fathers not only of their souls but of their bodies as well, looking for no reward here below, but in the heavenly glory hereafter, in hope of which we have come". Father Francisco del Valle, who took Romero's place as assistant to Father González, wrote in admiration to the Provincial the following year that "everything here has been built by the incredible labours of Father Roque González. He in person is carpenter, architect, mason; he wields the axe and hews the wood, brings it to the site himself with oxen which he has yoked with his own hands, for there is no one else capable of doing it. He does everything himself".

In their rôle of pioneers, founders, and settlers, the Jesuits showed the qualities which distinguished the best of the *conquistadores*. Pedro de Valdivia, the conqueror of Chile whose career was cut short by an Indian club as that of Father Roque González was destined to be, could describe, in a letter to the King, his responsibilities to his settlers as " a father to help them as best I could and to grieve for their toils, aiding them like sons to endure; a friend to speak with them; a land-surveyor to trace out and colonize; an overseer to make channels and to share out water; a tiller and worker at the sowings; a head-shepherd for the breeding of flocks; in short, settler, breeder, defender, conqueror and discoverer". But the Jesuits had also what very few *conquistadores* possessed—a sympathetic insight into the mind of the Indians and extraordinary resourcefulness in devising ways of arousing their interest and securing their willing co-operation. "As they are so young in the faith," Father González wrote in the same letter to the Provincial, "we are proceeding very cautiously so as not to burden them too much or make Christian discipline irksome to them." He realized the appeal a fiesta could have for them, and when that of the Society's founder came round, he described how they had celebrated it "with the greatest solemnity possible", after preparing many days beforehand and putting up archways around the plaza under which the procession would pass. "On the eve of the feast, there was a parade on horseback and illuminations at night, to the sound of flutes, bells, drums and trumpets, whilst they all with one voice acclaimed Saint Ignatius, invoking his name until they seemed to be quite beside themselves. And what most delighted them was the fireworks—a great novelty for them—and they spent the whole night performing their games and dances without going to bed at all." The following day a mass was sung in the church, and so great were the crowds that most

had to stay out in the plaza where there was more dancing, a procession, "in very good order", with four *caciques* wearing long shirts
specially lent them for the ceremony and bearing a reliquary beneath
an awning. The archways under which the procession passed were
decorated with a great variety of fruit and the skins of wild animals,
for the Indians had organized a special hunt in honour of the occasion.
Other *caciques* sent bizarrely painted children with gifts of parrots,
armadillos and other creatures.

Father del Techo tells us in his *History* that when the Provincial
paid a visit to San Ignacio "he grew so enthusiastic that he gave away
to the Indians everything he had—his cloak, his tent, his blankets, the
utensils he had brought with him for the journey—whilst to the
missionaries he gave the mare he rode on, his own shirts and other
articles of clothing". Most valued of all the gifts he bestowed on
Father González was "an oil painting of the Blessed Virgin to take
with him on his expeditions, which the people called the Conquistadora, and not without reason", for the picture seemed to possess some
miraculous power to soften the rude hearts of the Indians. It was
henceforth to accompany Father González on his restless travels, and
"thanks to it he gained notable victories in the regions washed by the
waters of the Paraná and Uruguay rivers".

But there were times too of bitter discouragement and soul-searching
in the midst of all this pioneering activity. Father González seems to
have passed through a spiritual crisis analagous to the contemplatives'
"dark night of the soul". As to its cause and exact nature we can
only speculate, for outwardly the Jesuit remained the same serene,
indefatigable extrovert, bearing on his shoulders the thousand and one
cares of his flock. Something of his inner conflict he must have confided to his Superior during the latter's visit, for not long afterwards,
on 26 November, 1614, when he had been for more than two and a
half years in his lonely post, we find him penning this moving letter to
Father Torres: "I have been suffering such continual anguish of
heart since those things I related to Your Reverence in this Reduction,
that I feel quite at death's door, and gladly so, or on the brink of
madness. *Sicut fuerit voluntas tua in coelo, sic fiat.* My only will is to
do that of Your Reverence, even if I am half dead, for as I have said
before, my one joy and consolation is to do whatever you would have
me do, for in doing your will I am doing God's. So that is why, though
it is a living death here and I am afraid of losing my reason through
all the scruples which torment me and such loneliness and bouts of
melancholia—in spite of all this, I say, I am resolved to stay here
though I were to die a thousand deaths or lose a thousand reasons, for

7. Santa Rosa de
   Lima

8. Santa Mariana de
Quito on her death-
bed

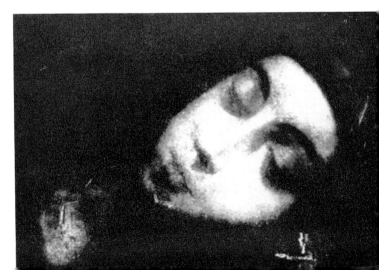

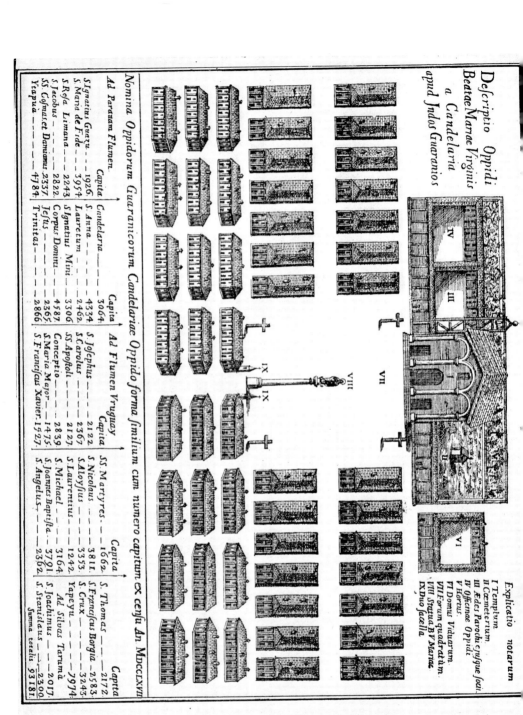

9. Plan of a Jesuit Reduction

this I would reckon rather gain than loss. And so, my Father Provincial, let Your Reverence dispose of me as most befits the service of Our Lord, for my will is only to do your will, and whether I stay here or go elsewhere is all one to me; may Your Reverence only dispose of me as you will, *ad majoram Dei gloriam."*

One thing which, we may be sure, contributed to the missionary's mental distress was the obloquy directed against the Company, and against himself personally, by the *encomenderos.* That Roque González was himself a member of the Creole land-owning class, and that the charges were voiced by his own brother, don Francisco González de Santa Cruz, Lieutenant-Governor of Asunción, made his distress the more bitter. The *encomenderos* accused the Jesuits of depriving them of "their" Indians, of attracting them away from the personal service the natives were obliged to render on the estates to the shelter of the Reductions, thereby making it impossible for the owners to gain a living and pay the royal dues. There exists a letter of 13 December, 1614, written by Father González to his brother refuting these charges with great dignity and firmness, and defending the cause of the Indians and the stand which the Jesuits had taken up on their behalf. The document, in which his brother is formally addressed as *señor general,* shows how fully the missionary had detached himself from the ties of his family and the viewpoint of his class. He takes the *encomenderos* vigorously to task for their maltreatment of the Indians in defiance of the laws of God and the King; "I say that I will not confess a single one of them for anything in the world", he concludes, "because they have done wrong and will not even admit it, still less make restitution and mend their ways".

For all the loneliness of San Ignacio Guazú, it was not far enough from Asunción to escape the harassment of the *encomenderos.* Roque González was impatient to explore virgin lands and implant the cross of Christ far from the contamination of the Spanish cities. One day at the end of 1614, as he recounts in a letter to Father Pedro Oñate, who had succeeded Father Torres as Provincial, whilst he was reciting the litany before the picture of La Conquistadora, there came to him an ardent call to labour amongst the heathen tribes of the Paraná. The new Provincial, persuaded that he would find relief from spiritual despondency in action, authorized the mission, and Father González set out to explore the land on either side of the great river and to probe the disposition of the natives for the founding of a new Reduction. Travelling mainly by canoe and bearing a wooden cross and the painting of the Conquistadora, Father González first explored the wooded plains south of the Paraná until reaching Lake Iberá. Here he found

the Indians friendly and sufficiently numerous to justify hopes of founding a settlement. The Franciscans, it seemed, had already been active in
those parts, and though there was now no sign of them, Father González thought it prudent to push on to Corrientes, where they had a
small *custodia,* to avoid any suspicion that the Jesuits were "poaching"
on their preserves. He agreed with the friars that, if they had not been
able to found a church on the shores of Lake Iberá within six months,
the Jesuits would be free to do so. A settlement there might prove the
key to opening up the whole region enclosed in the right-angled bend
of the great river as it flowed on towards the Atlantic.

Father González then returned to San Ignacio before starting to
explore the upper reaches of the Paraná. The first Indian communities whom he encountered on its banks seemed well disposed, but forty
leagues further up-stream he came upon a host of warriors in full war-
paint and armed with bows and arrows who barred his way. Their
chief boasted that "he was the only God worshipped in that land" and
declared that no European had ever set foot on it without staining it
with his blood. In recounting this incident to Rome, Father Oñate
adds that "such was the fury of the Indian that words forsook him
and he could only utter incoherent shouts". The missionary was not
in the least perturbed by this performance, but replied, in the Guaraní
tongue, that such threats left him unmoved. He was ready to shed his
blood in the service of the one true God, the lord of heaven and earth,
whom he had come to preach to them. They could see that he meant
the Indians no harm, for he came amongst them quite unarmed and
wished only to teach them about God and how to live as true men.
His boldness astonished and impressed the natives. They let him pass
on up the river, and some even accompanied him. "The marvellous
calmness of the Father", concludes the Provincial, "won the furious
chieftain over and made a friend of him".

The Jesuit continued for another fifty leagues up-stream exploring
the country on its banks and finally deciding to make a halt at a place
called Itapúa, where the town of Posadas, capital of the province,
stands today. Here, after overcoming the initial suspicions of the
Indians, he raised a large wooden cross, convinced four of the local
caciques of the advantages of coming together in a settlement under
its protection, and promised that he would go to Asunción and arrange
for a missionary to establish himself amongst them. He then headed
downstream for that city to give an account of his discoveries.

The news that a priest had been travelling up and down the
Paraná, going from one tribe to another unescorted and unharmed
and finding the Indians apparently ready to accept the Catholic faith

and come together in settlements under the care of the Jesuits produced a deep impression amongst the Spaniards. The moment seemed propitious for a great missionary enterprise. Don Francisco González was now in charge at Asunción following the death of don Diego Marín Negrón and pending the reappointment of his father-in-law Hernandarias to the office of Governor. The coolness with his brother on account of the *encomenderos'* charges seems to have passed. Perhaps family pride too played its part, for on 23 February, 1615, we find the Lieutenant Governor issuing a decree declaring that "whereas the Fathers of the Company of Jesus, by their great charity and zeal in the service of God and of his Majesty, have exhorted and prepared many heathen Indians to settle in suitable places where they may be conveniently taught and instructed in the holy Catholic faith", Father Roque González and other members of the Company were authorized, in the King's name, to found three or four Reductions at Itapúa and elsewhere. Supplies of agricultural tools and implements for the construction of the new settlement were issued to them, and thus equipped, Father Roque González journeyed back up the river. On 25 March the new settlement was formally founded and given the name of Encarnación.

Itapúa occupied a strategic position where the waters of the Paraná formed a shallow lagoon at a point about half way between Asunción and the Jesuit Reductions of the Guayrá. During the Father's absence, Indians hostile to the four *caciques* of Itapúa who were to form the nucleus of the settlement had launched an attack upon it and attempted to pull down the wooden cross. The neophytes rallied to its defence and drove the attackers off. This victory raised their morale and convinced them of the virtue of the new faith which they proposed to embrace. After four months in Itapúa Father González was joined by another Jesuit, Father Diego Boroa, and together the two priests supervized the laying out of the settlement, carrying wooden beams and loads of clay for the construction of the church and houses like any of their Indian helpers. But opposition too was gathering. The witch-doctors, who had most to lose, were spreading reports that the two Fathers were really spies scheming to subjugate the Indians to Spanish rule. The neighbouring tribes remained hostile. For two years running the crops failed. Sickness and hunger afflicted the young settlement. "Our food was sometimes a little boiled maize", wrote Father González, "at others, the manioc flour which the Indians eat. And as we used to send for some herbs to be gathered from the fields such as the parrots are fond of eating, the Indians said in jest that we were parrots too". Nevertheless, in spite of these hardships and the ravages of epidemics, many natives were baptized and the Jesuits continued their proselytizing work, either in person or through emissaries, amongst the neighbouring tribes.

Once the Reduction at Itapúa had been well established, Father González decided to return to Lake Iberá to revisit the friendly Indians there and to see whether the Franciscans had reappeared to found a church. Some eight months had elapsed since he was last there, and finding no trace of the friars, he decided that the way was clear for the Jesuits to start their mission. The Indians received him well, some accepted baptism, a makeshift church was built and a plot of land sown for the sustenance of the new settlement. Within four months the little Reduction of Santa Ana had attracted a population of some 600.

In Asunción, Hernandarias was now Governor again. This change of leadership signified no slackening in the missionary effort. Hernandarias, linked by marriage to the González family, was a warm supporter of the Jesuits. But he was also an ambitious and impetuous man whose impatience to consolidate the advances made by Father González nearly ended in disaster. He determined, despite the misgivings of the Jesuits, to make an official visit to Itapúa and take formal possession of the region for the Crown. Arriving there with a detachment of 40 soldiers, he led a solemn procession to the new church, kissed the hands of the two fathers in token of the respect which all men should pay to the servants of God, and appointed officials—the *corregidor* and *alcaldes* who were to help the Fathers administer the Reduction. These were none other than the caciques designated for this purpose by their Jesuit mentors; in this, at least, the latter had their way, for Hernandarias agreed that no Spanish layman should hold authority in the Reductions. But the ceremonies were not over before reports began to come in that hostile tribes were gathering to cut the Spaniards' line of retreat. Hernandarias decided to cut short his visit whilst there was still time. To save face, he explained that he had come to assure the King of Spain's new subjects of the royal friendship and protection, and that he had to hurry back to Asunción on urgent business. Father González, meanwhile, went to confront the hostile Indians, who had rallied, some 300 strong, down-stream. His eloquence dissuaded them from making any move against the Governor's party as it withdrew. He even tried to induce their chief Tabacambí to receive from the Governor a wand of office which would authorize him to continue ruling the region in the name of the King. To this Tabacambí haughtily replied that he had always ruled it without any wand of office, in no one's name but his own, and that he was firmly resolved to continue doing so.

Hernandarias had the grace to recognize that the Jesuits' assessment of the Indians' mood had been right. But he could not bring himself to renounce altogether the traditional rôle of the *conquistador*. Was there not room for the soldier, as well as the priest, in the spreading of the faith? Such had ever been the way of Spain. After his return to Asunción he conceived a plan for supplementing the advance of the missionaries along the Paraná by sending an armed expedition to overawe the more troublesome tribes along the Uruguay River. Father González and his brother missionaries at once saw that this venture would spell the ruin of their whole strategy of peaceful evangelization, already imperilled by the Governor's excursion to Itapúa. But if the Governor obstinately brushed aside the objections of the Jesuits, he was forced to take account of those of the Spaniards and *mestizos* whom he proposed to enrol in his expedition. They had no stomach at all for taking on the fierce man-eating Indians of the Uruguay and made it quite clear that they would not enlist. Thanks to these unexpected allies, who were the first to denounce the Jesuits when threatened with the loss of their own Indians, the missionaries were able to pursue their campaign of peaceful evangelization.

But there were set-backs and dangers from other quarters. The Guaycurúes had proved quite intractable and the mission precariously established amongst them west of the Paraguay had to be abandoned. In Guayrá, the Reductions were facing the depredations of the *mamelucos,* the ruthless half-caste slave-hunters from São Paulo, which were before long to lead to their abandonment. On the shores of Lake Iberá, the Franciscans had belatedly reappeared to claim jurisdiction, and Father González had surrendered control of the new settlement to them with a good grace; it was not destined to prosper, and the islands of the lake became a refuge for marauding Indians who had later to be flushed out by force. In San Ignacio Guazú too there was trouble. Arapizandú, the *cacique,* had deserted with some of his men and threatened to make common cause with Tabacambí, whom Father González had exhorted in vain to accept a wand of office under the Crown. Arapizandú was finally brought back into the fold after an intrepid Jesuit, Father Juan Salas, had followed him into the woods and eloquently pleaded with him to return to the true faith. It was clear that the missionaries had still only a precarious authority over their neophytes.

Father González believed that it could best be consolidated by the speedy creation of a new chain of settlements. At Yaguapúa, some 4 leagues from Itapúa and a dozen from San Ignacio, in the land of the friendly chief Tamboy, he laid the foundations of a new Reduction. He then prepared to push on up the Paraná and explore the wild region between Itapúa and Guayrá where no missionaries had yet worked. His neophytes were unwilling to go with him. They even refused to let him have a canoe or provisions for the journey. Father González sent his messengers far and wide, determined to find volunteers to accompany him. A group of Indians who had been converted by Franciscan missionaries arrived and offered to go with him, but when they listened to the fearful tales told by the men of Yaguapúa they too lost courage and hung back. Finally, Arapizandú, the *cacique* from San Ignacio who was anxious to make amends for his back-sliding, appeared in the settlement with a handful of followers and vowed he would accompany the Jesuit whatever awaited them at the hands of the ferocious tribes up-stream. His example encouraged a dozen more Indians to dare as much, and the next day the party set off up-stream, leaving Father del Valle in charge at Itapúa.

The explorers proceeded up the Paraná until they reached an island where the Indian braves had mustered under their chieftain who sent an angry message bidding them turn back. Father González replied in terms no less defiant that he was the servant of the omnipotent God and would go where his superiors sent him. The *cacique's* nephew, a famed witch-doctor, repeated his uncle's threats even more vehemently. At this point Arapizandú stepped forward, interposing his authority and vouching for the white man's peaceful intentions. The Indians let them proceed.

The next encounter proved still more hazardous. The missionary's most redoubtable foes were always those Indians who had belonged for a time to the flock and then lapsed into paganism. Three such renegades now appeared to warn the Indians against being deceived by the Jesuit and to match their eloquence against his. "I am an old fox and will not get caught again", their spokesman declared. "We know your tricks and how you come amongst us on the pretext of teaching us religion, but in reality to lure us beneath the Spanish yoke! If you want to choose slavery for yourselves and your children", he concluded, turning to the Indians, "then follow this man! If you would remain free—stay with me!"

These words only served to fan the Jesuit's fervour and indignation. Pointing to the cross, in whose sign he vowed he would overcome the treachery of the apostates and continue to win souls for Christ, Father González began preaching with such eloquence that some of his listeners were half won over. But the chief and the witch-doctors argued back, their attitude grew more and more threatening, and the missionary saw that, for the present, their hearts were closed to the gospel message. He turned back and sailed down-stream again to Itapúa, where Father del Valle welcomed him with heartfelt relief. The voyage had not been wasted. They now knew the lie of the land and the mood of the natives. Arapizandú had done them good service and proved himself strong in the faith. If the harvest was not yet ripe amongst the Indians up-stream, there was still much to be done elsewhere.

After making a fresh expedition to see Tabacambí and a further fruitless attempt to persuade that chief to sponsor the formation of a Reduction, Father González returned to Itapúa and Yaguapúa. The latter was now in the hands of Father Romero and beginning to take on the appearance of a well-established settlement. But the Indians had not yet adapted themselves to the discipline of regular agricultural labour nor had time to lay in reserves of food. Hunger set in, and sickness followed. The neophytes began to drift back into the woods. Father González went after them, cajoling, persuading and admonishing them to return. He could not absent himself from Itapúa for long, however, for Father del Valle too fell dangerously ill. The witch-doctors were busy assuring the Indians that they were dying as a result of the spells cast upon them through the rite of baptism. Some parents set about scrubbing their children to cleanse them from this contamination. One hurled a block of wood at the missionary to stop him christening a sick infant. Another flew at his throat and had to be dragged off. Many of those who had not taken to the woods forbade him access to their huts. Father González worked on undismayed. Unable to leave the settlement himself, he sent some of the few who remained faithful to seek out the members of his scattered flock and induce them to come back. Father del Valle recovered and the epidemic passed.

Later in the year 1619, Father Oñate, the Provincial, appeared in the settlements. After conferring with the missionaries, whose number had now been increased by new-comers from Europe, he decided that the time had come to organize the Reductions on a more formal basis. Itapúa was placed in the charge of Father Boroa, who was to become superior for the whole Paraná and Uruguay. The other Fathers were reassigned to different Reductions. Father González was entrusted with a new mission to the tribes of the Uruguay River. His novitiate, served in the stern apprenticeship of the Paraná mission-field, was declared at an end. After taking his vows as a fully fledged member of the Society, he set out on the new assignment.

Father González had now been in the Society for ten years and had won recognition as one of the outstanding figures in the Province. "Valiant in undertaking the most difficult enterprises for the glory of Christ, and as strong as iron in times of trial", Father del Techo writes of him, "he combined outward activity with meditation as few have ever done. He was never proud or presumptuous, though he performed notable deeds in the service of God. In temperament he was both affable and stern, his affability being blended with authority so that all men sought him out". This mixture of audacity and gentleness seems to have been the secret of the missionary's success with the savage *caciques,* but can we be sure that the worthy historian of his Order was painting the full portrait of Father Roque González as his brother Jesuits must have known him? In the register of correspondence exchanged between Father Vitelleschi, the General of the Society in Rome, and the Provincial of Paraguay, there is a marginal comment to the effect that Father González is noted for his fluency in the Indian tongue but that "since he is not of peaceable disposition and is troubled with scruples, his companions find him difficult. May Your Reverence move him to deal more gently and affably . . ." Roque González de Santa Cruz came of the race of *conquistadores.* He was a soldier pledged to the cause of spiritual conquest and for ever locked in the fiercest of battles—the conquest of self.

*   *   *   *

The great quadrilateral enclosed by the Paraná and the Uruguay comprises today the Argentine provinces of Entre Rios, Corrientes and Misiones. At its broadest, in northern Corrientes, the distance between the two rivers is some 240 miles, but to the north-east it narrows to a corridor some 250 miles long and between 40 and 50 miles wide, bounded by the Iguazú river and the great falls of the same name. Most of the corridor consists of a plateau covered by a subtropical forest of cedar, pine and broad-leaved trees, dense with a tangled growth of brilliant flowers through which tapirs, jaguars, pumas and water-hogs roam, whilst a multitude of monkeys and parrots dart amongst the branches overhead. The Indians inhabiting this Mesopotamia were as wild as its fauna. A few however had been attracted to the Jesuits' settlement at Itapúa, and these now undertook to guide Father González and a small band of neophytes into their own country towards the Uruguay.

The first Indians whom they encountered greeted the intruders with menaces before disappearing into the woods to give notice of their coming. Father González dismissed his escort and continued on his way accompanied only by two lads to help with the celebration of the mass. The chiefs proved not unfriendly. They listened curiously to the white man who expounded his strange faith with fearless eloquence. Nezú, the most powerful of them, gave him leave to stay in his village a few miles from the Uruguay. On 8 December, 1620, after a wooden cross had been set up and the Indians made to kneel in veneration before it. Father González traced the plan of a new Reduction which he called Concepción, in honour of the feast of the Immaculate Conception of the Blessed Virgin celebrated on that day. Some of the tribes remained hostile; the new settlement was raided and the cross burned down. Father González, as was his wont, went straight to the enemy chieftain and won him over. Despite this initial set-back and the continuing hazards of hunger and epidemics, Concepción slowly began to prosper. Nezú continued to give the Christians his protection and later received baptism and the Christian name of Santiago.

For the remaining years of his life, Father Roque González laboured with varying fortune amongst the Indians of the Uruguay. From time to time he would revisit the settlements on the Paraná, or make the long journey to Asunción or Buenos Aires. Once he brought to Asunción a contingent of his neophytes to take part in the festivities which marked the canonization of the founder of the Society. There Father González staged a pageant with his Indian lads, ranging them into two opposing hosts, the pagans adorned with war-feathers and armed with clubs, bows and arrows, the Christians steadfast beneath the sign of the cross. When at length the hosts of evil had been routed in mock battle, the captives were led before the Governor and the dignitaries of the Church. "They threw themselves on the ground", Father del Techo tells us, "but joyfully, as behoves willing captives, leaping up from time to time, and then suddenly running to the altar of the new saints, Ignatius and Francis Javier, to render thanks to them for having sent their sons to bring Christianity to Paraguay". Amongst the company of Indians whom Father González had brought to Asunción was Cuaracipu, a well-known chieftain from the Uruguay. He was baptized with two dozen other catechumens, amidst much public rejoicing, by the Rector of the Jesuit College, whilst the Governor, don Manuel de Frías, stood godfather to him.

In May, 1626, Father González founded a new Reduction which he named San Nicolás, in honour of the name-saint of the newly appointed Jesuit Provincial, Father Nicolás Mastrilli Durán. It stood some seven leagues from Concepción on the Piratiní river, a tributary of the Uruguay, and on the eastern side of the latter river. Don Francisco de Céspedes, the Governor of Buenos Aires, now the capital of a separate province, received news of the foundation with satisfaction. He had ambitious plans for pushing Spanish colonization along the whole course of the river Uruguay, and even dreamed of extending it to the Atlantic coast and of founding a port in the Brazilian province of Catarina. Antonio de Zayas, a Creole officer in his confidence who had a good knowledge of the Guaraní tongue, was despatched to Concepción to make contact with Father González and invite him to Buenos Aires. The Jesuit readily complied with the Governor's summons. Taking with him Nezú and a number of other Indians he set off downstream for Buenos Aires, where don Francisco gave them a solemn reception. The Society of Jesus was formally entrusted with the task of bringing the Indians of the Uruguay into the Christian faith and obedience to the Crown and was vested with full powers to this end. Nezú swore an oath of allegiance to the King of Spain, whilst the Governor gave assurances that the natives would not be reduced to forced labour on any *encomienda* but would live peacefully in the Reductions under the care of the Fathers. Father González, accompanied by another Jesuit, Father Ampuero, then returned to Concepción with Nezú and his Indians. The journey back was long and hazardous. Father González scanned the land for a suitable site for a new settlement which would make communication between Buenos Aires and Concepción less precarious. His choice fell on a place called Yapeyú, opposite the confluence of the Uruguay and its tributary the Ibicuy. But though he found the natives friendly, there were too few of them to form a stable settlement, for the open nature of the country stretching away in rolling plains towards the Atlantic seemed to invite too strongly to the nomadic life.

By the end of the year 1626, Father González had established his third Uruguayan Reduction which he called San Francisco Javier after the recently canonized martyr. It stood a few miles up-stream from Concepción and grouped together some 600 Indians whom he left in the charge of Father Ampuero. But whilst the missionaries were occupied with these foundations and with further exploration, matters took a turn which brought the whole of the Jesuits' scheme of colonization in jeopardy. Disregarding the assurances he had given only a short time before that the Reductions would be under the sole authority of the Jesuits, the Governor decided to appoint Spanish officials to them. Antonio de Zayas returned to Concepción with the rank of *corregidor*, a Spaniard called Payá appeared in San Francisco Javier, and a third, Pedro Bravo, attempted to establish himself at Yapeyú. The misgovernment and extortion commonly practised by the *corregidores* constituted, as we have noted, one of the chief slurs on the colonial administration of Spain, often nullifying the well-meaning legislation of the Crown and the exertions of dedicated missionaries. The coming of the new officials to the infant settlements of the Uruguay soon produced the results which the Jesuits foresaw but were powerless to prevent. Payá treated the Indians with such arrogance that one of the *caciques* resolved to kill him. He was dissuaded by another chief, but abandoned the settlement in dudgeon taking with him half its inhabitants. Zayas behaved little better. One night, after he had boxed the ears of a son of one of the *caciques,* he found his house besieged by angry Indians. The natives kept up a great hubbub with their wardrums and horns, declaring that the *corregidor* should leave their settlement at once and that the missionaries had deceived them by allowing Spaniards in. Father Diego Alfaro, whom the Superior had left in charge at Concepción, had great difficulty in getting them to disperse. Still more serious was the danger from the tribes who had not yet given up their nomadic life and now threatened to fall upon the settlements unless their inhabitants drove the Spaniards out.

Father Roque González was away from the Reductions when the trouble came to a head, but a message was at once sent to the Provincial who hurried to the scene with Father Romero and other experienced missionaries. He found the Indians full of indignant complaints. The *corregidores* had been behaving as petty tyrants, humiliating the *caciques* and interfering with the women. The Indians vowed that unless they were left in peace, they would all go back into the woods and resume their old life. Zayas, by this time, was only too anxious to be gone from the hornets' nest he had stirred up, but the Provincial would not let him leave until he should be ordered to do so by the Governor, and forbade the Indians to let him have transport for the journey. It was clear that the enemies of the Jesuits would be glad to seize on the apparently high-handed way the missionaries expelled the King's representatives from "their" Reductions. Father Ampuero was despatched urgently to Buenos Aires to report to the Governor and convey the Provincial's request for the formal recall of the *corregidores.* Don Francisco saw where the results of his rashness were leading and sent instructions to Zayas and his colleagues to return. "And so," the Provincial was able to report in his Annual Letter to Rome, "an end was made to this scandal and peace was restored to the land, the Indians were pacified and their minds disposed for the spreading of the Gospel which proceeds apace, to the great glory of Our Lord, despite the hell which this storm let loose". But the storm had not blown over as quickly as the good Father believed.

The Provincial's next move was to promote the establishment of a regular Reduction at Yapeyú and the conversion of the natives of the river Ibicuy, at the mouth of which the settlement stood, as a staging-post on the line of communication between Buenos Aires and the Reductions of the Uruguay. Taking with him Fathers González and Romero, he found only a few huts and around a hundred Indians living in the place. But on 4 February, 1627, after cutting timber for the church and making a clearing where manioc and maize could be sown, the Provincial proclaimed the establishment of the fourth of the Uruguayan Reductions and gave it the impressive name of Nuestra Señora de los Reyes Magos de Yapeyú. Romero was left in charge of the Reduction whilst Father González set off upstream to explore. He found the land practically uninhabited, and it was only after travelling 50 leagues up the Ibicuy that he came upon a small Indian village. The natives had never seen a European before, but they received him well, and the whole population of men, women and children helped to erect a heavy wooden cross and watched the missionary celebrate mass in front of it. Father González called the place Candelaria, in devotion to the feast of Candlemas, the Purification of the Blessed Virgin Mary. The settlement was however Christian in name only, for the missionary could not stay to catechize his flock, since he was now Superior for the whole of the Uruguay. To the east stretched a vast tract of land called Tape. This meant, in the native tongue, "thickly populated"; but here too the land seemed almost deserted. Father González determined that he would return and explore it.

A few months later he was back again. Bad news awaited him from Father Romero in Yapeyú. The Indians of the upper Ibicuy had turned hostile. They had attacked Candelaria with the intention of killing the missionary, and finding him gone, had burned down the Cross. "This news left me in perplexity as to what I should do", González wrote to the Provincial. "Before reaching any decision, I stopped for a day and commended the affair to Our Lord. When I had celebrated mass, I felt moved to go forward and find some way of righting this great wrong". The decision was typical of the man. He found the *cacique* of Candelaria and other chiefs of the district shame-faced and evasive. They had been away, they explained; in their absence, other Indians had fallen upon the settlement in such numbers that nothing could be done against them. The Jesuit upbraided them sternly and declared he would not so much as set foot on the desecrated ground; he would go on to Tape.

But the natives of Tape were hostile too, or at least intensely suspicious. They refused at first to let the missionary into their country. It was only after he had made friends with the women and children who gathered curiously round him that he was allowed to proceed. He journeyed on, he wrote to the Provincial, "most painfully, for in all the Tape there is no place suitable for a Reduction of even 200 Indians. In those parts they were once numerous, but the woods have been destroyed and they scratch their living from the hills and rocks and live in hamlets of not more than 100 Indians". When he had finished reconnoitring, a band of Indians from beyond the hills appeared and made ready to attack. Father González was, as ever, unarmed, but he had with him a saw used for cutting down trees, and with this in one hand and his breviary in the other he stood his ground, whilst the superstitious Indians, alarmed by the unfamiliar weapons, held back. They finally made off when the Indians who were with him explained that they were escorting the white man out of their country. "Never have I suffered greater trials and tribulations than in this journey to the Ibicuy and Tape", he reported to Father Mastrilli. "But all this is as nothing compared with the great debt we owe to the Lord we serve. At least we now know that there is little to be hoped from the Ibicuy, and we have seen the Tape and know in which direction we must look for the founding of our new Reductions. It has been worth while if only for this, all the more so since it has all been done in the spirit of holy obedience".

Back in Concepción, Father González learned from talking to the Indians that the Tape and the Ibicuy valley could be approached more easily from the other side, that is to say, from the direction of San Nicolás and the Piratiní river, "for there the natives were more ready to receive the seed of the holy Gospel". Soon he was able to report that he had explored this region and found it to be just as the Indians said. There he founded a new Reduction, to which he gave the name of Candelaria in memory of the settlement destroyed on the Ibicuy. The latter river, he optimistically assured the Provincial, would in time be reached by a string of Reductions from the Piratiní. The new settlement grew rapidly, and Father Romero was transferred from Yapeyú to instruct the catechumens.

*   *   *   *

We now come to the last chapter in the career of Father Roque González. For more than 17 years the indomitable missionary, explorer and founder had been toiling amongst the primitive tribes of Paraguay. The fame of his daring, his constancy, his elequence, patience and dedication to those who consented to live under his care, had spread amongst them. Did his fellow missionaries still find him at times a rather difficult companion, "not of peaceable disposition, troubled by scruples?" There is little to suggest it, for he had now won general recognition as a man of rare qualities who, with Father Ruiz de Montoya, the most remarkable of the heroic missionaries of the Guayrá, had done more than anyone else to lay the foundations on which the celebrated Jesuit Reductions were to grow and flourish. "A great pastor of souls, a deeply religious man, humble yet full of zeal", reported his Superior in confidence in 1626. "Among the Indians he is held in high repute, even amongst those who are still heathen. The Spaniards think him to be lacking in letters and scholarship. It would be the greatest pity to recall him from this work of spiritual conquest".

His extraordinary intrepidity was perhaps the quality which most impressed the Indians. Where they were hostile, Father González would go straight to the most aggressive of the *caciques* and dominate him by the force of his personality and the burning eloquence of his words. But he could be gentle, even gay too, entering into the simple life of the Indians, devising pastimes and fiestas to wean them from their wild ways and bring home the mysteries of the faith to their simple minds. Sometimes he would organize a great battue, bringing together hunters and beaters over a wide area so that rival tribes would learn to live and work together. To the children he gave his special attention, for they were the quickest to learn and to teach their elders. He held their interest by organizing games, dances and pageants in which they took part, as in the great celebrations in Asunción in honour of the canonization of St. Ignatius. He started schools for them as soon as their parents began to accustom themselves to a settled life. We have noted the pride with which he reported the progress of the classes held at San Ignacio, the first of the Paraná Reductions. But before all else, he realized the importance of providing a firm economic basis for the Reductions. The gifts which he distributed amongst his catechumens were commonly the simple iron tools they needed to make clearings in the wood on which each family would grow enough food for its subsistence. Manioc and maize were the staples, but some Reductions, such as Itapúa, had cattle as well, so that the Indians' diet could be varied by meat. He encouraged too the cultivation of *maté*, which was not only to help wean them away from their bouts of intoxication but to provide them with the cash-crop the Reductions needed for supplementing what they were unable to produce themselves. By the late 1620's, when the apostle of the Guaranís had at last ceased his labours, the features which were to characterize the Jesuit Reductions of Paraguay for the following century and a half had been firmly traced.

The pattern of colonization was now becoming clear. Expansion along the line of the Ibicuy and into Tape was, for the time being, blocked. Nor was it feasible to penetrate to the source of the Uruguay, as don Francisco de Céspedes dreamed, and thence to the coast of Brazil. The nucleus of colonization was to lie in the "waist" of Mesopotamia, where the corridor of territory between the Paraná and the Uruguay rivers was narrowest, and across the Uruguay where San Nicolás already pointed the way to the new Reductions which were to form what came to be known as the Siete Pueblos, the Seven Townships.

This expansion was made possible by the reinforcements which were now arriving from Europe. The new-comers would learn the difficult native languages with the help of their more experienced brothers and assist in the Reductions, applying themselves to the task of consolidation whilst Father González and other veterans continued their ceaseless labour to explore the land and "reduce" the Indians. Two of the new-comers, Alonso Rodríguez and Juan del Castillo, were chosen to work closely with their Superior, and were before long to share in the glory of his martyrdom. Both were young men from Spain. Rodríguez had worked for a while amongst the Guaycurúes, then in Encarnación, by this time one of the most developed of the Reductions, which he had gladly left for the greater challenge of the Uruguay. Castillo, not yet 30 and noted for his handsome bearing and gentleness of manner, had scarcely entered upon his vocation.

After laying the foundations of the second Candelaria (Nuestra Señora de Candelaria de Caazapamini), Father González, taking Alonso Rodríguez with him, turned his attention to the thickly wooded region known as Caaró. Here a number of *caciques* were living with their people in small settlements not far from the new Reductions, whose growth they watched with mixed feelings. Some had themselves resided for a time amongst the Christians and had then gone back to their ancestral ways. One of these was the *cacique* who had left San Francisco Javier with his Indians in angry protest against the misrule of the *corregidor*. In the forests of the Caaró he found a protector in Nezú who, after accompanying Father González to visit the Governor in Buenos Aires, had begun to have second thoughts about the wisdom of co-operating with the Spaniards and had withdrawn to live amongst his own people. The excesses of the *corregidores* had deepened his misgivings, and the renegade *cacique* was able to work on his mind. Santiago Nezú, who was to play a decisive if indirect role in the coming tragedy, looms through the contemporary Spanish records as a shadowy and ominous figure. His name meant in the Indian tongue, we are told, "the eloquent one". He was witch-doctor as well as chieftain, with power to command not only men—so his people believed—but birds, beasts, and the very elements. "No one in all Uruguay was more given to the diabolic arts nor so puffed up with pride", declared Father del Techo, "nor kept a greater number of concubines".

Father González realized that Nezú's attitude was still as crucial for the progress of his missionary work as it had been for its inception. The reports of the *cacique's* ambiguous stance w e r e disturbing, and the Jesuit resolved with his customary boldness to nip the trouble in the bud. He went straight to Nezú and taxed him with infidelity. The *cacique,* moved once again by the priest's compelling personality, agreed to accompany him to the neighbouring Reduction of San Nicolás where he was accorded a ceremonial reception in the church. He then returned to his own village and gave orders that a church was to be built there too. By the middle of August, 1628, Father González had laid its foundations and traced the outlines for a Reduction which he dedicated to the Assumption of the Blessed Virgin. Leaving Juan del Castillo to guide Nezú's flock, he went first to meet a party of new missionaries who had sailed up the Paraná to Itapúa, and then, accompanied by Alonso Rodríguez, made his way back to the forests of the Caaró with the intention of founding a Reduction there too. The storm clouds seemed to have blown away and the prospect to be fair once more for the continuation of his work of evangelization and colonization. On the morning of 15 November he wrote optimistically to Father Romero to say that all was going well in the Caaró, and that if only he had tools enough he could gather together more than 500 native families into the new Reduction of All Saints.

Of the events which followed we have several contemporary accounts, of which the most moving and direct is perhaps that of Father Romero. It was written from Candelaria de Caazapamini some time at the beginning of 1629 for the now ageing Hernandarias, kinsman of Roque González and the whole-hearted promoter of his early apostolate. "The instigator of this treachery and rebellion", wrote Father Romero, who himself all but fell a victim, "was that great wizard, the *cacique* Nezú whose enchantments and deceits, and the great fear in which they held him, persuaded the Indians that, if they did not obey him, do what he wished and give him what he wanted and desired, he would send the tigers to eat them up. He furthermore declared that he was the true God who had created all things, and

10. The Martyrdom of the Jesuit Fathers in Paraguay

11. San Pedro Claver

that he would darken the sun and moon and send famine and plague upon them. By such means he rallied together 400 Indians at a suitable place on the far side of the river three leagues from the Reduction on the Piratiní* and another three leagues from this Reduction of Candelaria...

"The Devil, seeing himself driven out of his old haunts, resolved to root out the holy gospel from all these provinces and cause the death, if he could, of all the preachers therein. He took them as his instrument the *cacique* Nezú, a great wizard as I have said, who was so filled with hatred of God's law and of the priests who set themselves against his evil office and his pretensions to be worshipped as a god and keep the multitude of women which he had, that he persuaded the *cacique* Caruperá, one of the chiefs of the Caaró to kill Father Roque and his companion. And that he might not hold back from that deed, he told him that after killing the saintly fathers he should send him word so that he might also kill the saintly father Juan del Castillo who was in his land, and that they should then set upon this Reduction of Candelaria, whose inhabitants would help him kill me too without more ado, whilst he and his people would fall upon the Reduction on the Piratiní and kill Father Alfonso de Aragón and his companion, and that the Indians of Concepción would then kill their Fathers as well, and so on with all the Fathers of the Uruguay, and that even those of the Paraná would kill theirs, so that not one priest would be left alive and they would be free to live just as they liked according to the way and customs of their forefathers.

"The wretched Caruperá and his people, rude and simple folk as they were, were misled by these threats and promises into believing him, and so, on 15 November, they gathered there, with no one suspecting the treachery that was brewing, for on that very morning the saintly Father Roque had written me a note to say that everything was going forward as well as could possibly be desired, and that only the lack of tools prevented more than 500 Indians settling in the Reduction. The day he wrote that and was killed was a Wednesday. After sending off this note he said Mass, and when he had given thanks, he went to erect a pole which his companion had that morning, with the help of more than 200 Indians, brought down from the forest with much rejoicing to serve as a belfry. And whilst a lad from the Paraná who was with the Fathers was piercing holes through the pole through which to pass a rope, Father Roque bent down to tie one end to the clapper so that the bell could be rung and merrily summon the people. When the murderer saw the saintly man intent on this

* *San Nicolás*

M

task and in the posture which favoured their designs, two Indians let
fly with their stone clubs which they call *itaizá* and struck his sainted
head such cruel blows that they stretched him dead on the ground
and shattered his skull and face to pieces with their clubs. (Plate 10).

"The saintly Father Alonso Rodríguez, who had been preparing to
say Mass, came out at this uproar, and was set upon and struck great
blows. Seeing his holy companion dead, he turned back to his hut, but
they went on raining such blows on the crown and sides of his head
with their stone clubs that they felled him lifeless by the church. They
then stripped the saints of their clothes and hacked Father Alonso's
body in two. After dragging the corpses round the hut for some time
and then into the church, they set fire to them. Whilst they were being
consumed, there came a voice from Father Roque's heart, from deep
within his breast, clearly and distinctly addressing them in their own
tongue and saying that he had come to their lands for the good of their
souls and adding—'Though you may kill me, my soul will go to
heaven, and punishment will soon come upon you!' This the murderers swore to, and 50 Indians who were captured with them declared
with one accord that the voice had spoken thus, and that they had
witnessed and heard it. This they swore in front of five priests and the
Spanish soldiers and many other Indians.

"This miracle should have been enough to win over those barbarians,
yet it failed to soften their stony hearts but only increased their fury
the more. 'What, can this deceiver still speak?' they cried, as they
cut open his breast, tore out the heart, and hurled it once more into
the fire, and the bodies likewise. But the heart was miraculously kept
from burning and remained quite whole and intact, so that it was
later found amongst the ashes pierced by an arrow.

"Nor did those barbarians' rage and fury against our holy Catholic
faith stop there. A most sacred picture of Our Lady, the *Conquistadora* of all these missions, was most cruelly torn to pieces, the
altar was overturned, the stem of the chalice smashed, the missal torn
up and its leaves scattered over the fields, the holy cross pulled down
and many other sacrilegious acts committed. When a good old *cacique*
in whose lands the Fathers had been living remonstrated to see them
treated in this fashion and upbraided the murderers for so misusing
the priests, they struck him on the head too and slew him with great
rage and violence.

"Then they went to report to Nezú that they had carried out his
orders. The same night he decked himself out in all his fine feathers,
leaping about and shouting and making out that he was a god, as was
his wont, whilst he addressed his hearers thus: 'I commanded the

tigers to kill the father who is in my lands, but in this they would not obey me. Go and kill him yourselves!' In the morning they went to carry out this command and found the saintly Father Juan del Castillo praying. 'What is this monkey saying?' they asked. The saintly father, who was a veritable angel and loved the Indians tenderly, answered that he was not saying anything, but that he was praying. Then they laid hands on him and began striking him roughly and crying out that they wanted to kill him. To this he replied that if it was his possessions they were after, they should take them all as a gift, and he would live amongst them and serve them as a slave. But they said that it was not this, but his death that they wanted, and that after killing him they would go to kill Father Alfonso de Aragón and his companion. Then the saintly father said to them; 'Take me with you then, and kill me together with them!' As he said this, they threw him to the ground, tied his hands together and dragged him for three quarters of a league or more across the rough and stony ground, and through a couple of streams, and when they reached the place where they burned him they found that he was not quite dead, so one of Nezú's Indian slaves finished him off with a stone club.

"Then the others broke his bones with heavy stones, and after they had tied his arms in the shape of a cross, they cast a lot of wood on the fire and burned him, so that there was scarce a single member of his body that was neither charred by the flames or pounded by the stones".

Father Romero went on to describe how some 50 of Nezú's Indians had then raided the Reduction of San Nicolás with the aim of killing the missionaries there and of burning down the church, but were beaten off by the neophytes. A few days later a much larger band descended on Candelaria, shouting out that they had come to kill "Granny"—for so they dubbed Father Romero on account of his long robes and mild manner. But the valiant missionary mounted a horse and with one other companion went out to face the invaders who "marvellous to relate, behaved just as if they had sighted an army a thousand strong", and turned tail. The Father ended his report by relating how a thousand Indians then rallied from the Reductions and, stiffened by a handful of Spaniards led by Captain Manuel Cabral, routed Nezú's Indians and hanged 12 of the murderers on the scene of their crimes. As for the great wizard Nezú, after presiding over a ceremony in which he sought to de-baptize his Indians by having them well scrubbed and their tongues scraped, he fled over the River Uruguay and into the obscurity of the forests on the other side.

Nezú's attempt to drive the white men from his lands had failed.

The Indians of the Reductions remained, for the most part, loyal to their missionary fathers. A few years later, the missions of the Guayrá, assailed by the still more destructive fury of the Brazilian slavers, were abandoned and their survivors, after an epic trek down the river, were resettled by the indomitable Father Ruiz de Montoya in the greater security of Paraguayan Mesopotamia. The Reductions which had been the site of the martyrdom of the three missionaries were repopulated and in time they too were moved to join the network of settlements between the Uruguay and Paraná. For more than a century these Reductions grew in numbers and prosperity, so that by the time the Jesuits were ordered out of Paraguay in 1768, they numbered 30 in all and, in their heyday, boasted a population of more than 140,000. The memory of the great founder and apostle was not lost. When the Indian neophytes piously gathered up the mortal remains of the martyrs from amongst the ashes, they found the miraculously preserved heart of Father Roque González. Though the Reductions have long since vanished, the relic is still venerated today in the shrine of the church of San Salvador at Buenos Aires—the generous heart which an Indian's arrow might pierce but flames could not destroy, a cherished symbol of those men who laboured so long and so fruitfully to build the city of God in the wilds of Paraguay.

CHAPTER 9

The Slave of the Slaves—
San Pedro Claver

AMONGST the institutions grafted onto the New World from the Old was one whose antiquity obscured its intrinsic iniquity—the institution of slavery. The indigenous inhabitants of America, it is true, might make slaves of one another; there are even cases on record of their making slaves of the white man who occasionally fell into their hands. But the use of slave-labour as the economic basis of human life in certain parts of America, particularly in Brazil, the Caribbean and what later became the South of the United States, was a lamentable consequence of the coming of the Europeans.

The evil might have assumed even more terrible dimensions. Columbus shipped back to Spain some 500 of the natives from the islands he had discovered with the intention of selling them as slaves. Few of them survived, but those who did were saved from slavery by virtue of Queen Isabel's momentous ruling that the natives of the New World were vassals of the Crown, not slaves. There were many who disregarded the royal commands and continued to capture and enslave Indians for toil in the pearl fisheries, the mines, and on the land. But, in law, the Indian was not a slave; only certain strictly defined categories, such as cannibals and obdurate rebels, might legitimately be reduced to slavery.

But if the indigenous population of America was protected from the wholesale depredations of the slaver, an attempt to find some substitute for quasi-servile native labour (which was economically inefficient as well as morally reprehensible) resulted in the large-scale importation of slave labour from another quarter. The Portuguese, in their penetration of the west coast of Africa, had hit upon an inexhaustible new reservoir of cheap man-power. Directed first to Portugal and Spain, the traffic in African slaves was soon extended across the Atlantic and began to transform the economic and demographic patterns of the New World. The Crown attempted to regulate the flow by issuing *asientos* or licences for the import of specified numbers of slaves, but attempts to curtail or to suspend the traffic altogether met with opposition not only from those who saw their economic interests adversely affected, but also from the well-wishers of the Indians who believed that the latter's lot would be alleviated by allowing negroes in to take over the most back-breaking toil. Thus we find the Hieronymite friars protesting to the King against the instructions which Cardinal Ximénez de Cisneros had issued in 1516 suspending the traffic. An epidemic had decimated the native population of Hispaniola, and the friars wrote—"Forbid the entry of negro slaves, and we certify that if this pestilence lasts two more months, the lands will be wholly depopulated". Las Casas himself, the great champion of Indian rights, advocated the introduction of negro slaves for much the same reason, though he came bitterly to repent having given this misguided advice. As he himself writes in the *Historia de las Indias:* "The priest, Las Casas, was the first to advise that permission should be given to bring slaves to these lands, not realizing how unjustly the Portuguese take them and make slaves of them; had he realized this, he would not have given them permission for anything in the world".

The attitude of the Church towards slavery in the 16th and 17th Centuries cannot but strike us as ambivalent. Admirable in taking up the defence of the Indian, the Church seems to have been curiously blind to the plight of the negro. Even after the Defender of the Indians had lamented his error in advocating the extension of the slave-trade to America we find him petitioning the Crown for permission to import four slaves for his own use. Perhaps he was conscious of no inconsistency here, for slavery was taken for granted as part of the inevitable order of things; a natural misfortune, such as plague or earthquake, which one could do little or nothing to prevent. In Spain, this assumption was particularly deep-rooted, owing to the century-long conflict between Moslems and Christians, when either might find themselves slaves of the other. Even when the Reconquista had been completed, Moslem corsairs would descend upon the coast of Spain and carry off Christians as slaves. Miguel de Cervantes, Spain's greatest writer, had been captured in battle and known the bitterness of slavery. The Order of the Mercedarians had been founded for the specific purpose of redeeming such Christian slaves. The victim might be succoured, and the worst horrors of slavery mitigated, but few called in question the institution itself.

It was an institution which the weight of tradition and authority seemed to support; the tradition not only of classical antiquity but of the early Church itself. Paul exhorts Philemon to take back his slave Onesimus with the love and forbearance due to a fellow Christian; he does not exhort him to set him free. 1,600 years later, Christian families, and even the monasteries and convents of the New World, would still see nothing contrary to their profession in owning slaves. Those who gave thought to the matter at all, were concerned that legality should be observed—the guide-lines had been laid down long ago in the *Siete Partidas*, the famous code of Alfonso the Learned—and slaves treated humanely. Las Casas' fellow Dominican, Fray Tomás de Mercado, who went further into the subject than most in his *Suma de Tratos y Contratos*, published in Seville in 1587, declares that "to capture and sell negroes, or other people, is a legitimate business and *de jure gentium*", though it was subject to outrageous abuse in Africa and led to inexcusable maltreatment of its victims by the slavers. Fray Tomás reaches two conclusions : "first, that buying and selling negroes in Cape Verde is in itself lawful and just; secondly, seeing the ill repute that the traffic has rightly come to deserve, it is a mortal sin to engage in it, and those who seek to transport negroes from Cape Verde do ill and live in great peril [to their souls]".

The slaves thus transported were brought to Vera Cruz and Cartagena, the only two ports in the New World authorized to receive them, and from there they were distributed throughout the Spanish domains. Cartagena, as we learn from the Annual Letter sent in 1605 to the General of the Jesuits in Rome, then numbered "probably more than 300 [Spanish] households, comprising 2,000 Spaniards who have in their service 3-4,000 negroes". Though the latter included a high proportion of women, children and men broken by disease, the presence of such large numbers of able-bodied negroes, snatched from their homeland and rendered desperate through ill treatment and the prospect of a life-time of servitude, constituted a menace which was a constant source of concern to the authorities who could count on a regular garrison of little more than 200 soldiers. Slave revolts and attempts at mass flights were frequent. Some succeeded and resulted in the runaway slaves establishing their own independent communities such as the settlement of San Basilio de Palenque, which has retained much of its African character to this day. The escaped slaves even launched an occasional raid on Cartagena. But the latter was constantly replenished with fresh ship-loads of captives—10-12,000 of them a year, we are told, in its heyday, giving a total of perhaps 1,000,000 during the whole time that the port served as the hub of the slave-trade.

*　　　*　　　*　　　*

In the year 1610 three galleons under the command of don Gerónimo de Portugal y Córdoba arrived at Cartagena from Seville.

Amongst the passengers who disembarked from them was a young Catalan novice of the Society of Jesus called Pedro Claver. He made only a short stay in the modest Jesuit College which was later to be his home and then continued overland to Bogotá, and later to Tunja, where he had still to spend another five years preparing for ordination. The novitiate may well have seemed long and his studies unnecessarily elaborate for the vocation to which he already felt called. Long before he had known the impact of the terrible institution of slavery, some intimation may have come to him of what that call was to be. "I must dedicate myself to the service of God until death", he had written on taking his first vows at the age of 24, "in the knowledge that I am like a slave wholly occupied in the service of his master". Willingly accepted slavery to Christ was to be the preliminary to a lifetime of dedication to the slaves of America. When at last as a young priest— for Claver was the first Jesuit to be ordained in the New World—he made his final profession in the Society on 3 April, 1622, he resolutely added to the customary vows one of his own devising and signed himself *Petrus Claver, ethiopum semper servus*—"Peter Claver, slave of the slaves for ever".

The seed had been sown in the heart of this quiet, sturdy farmer's son by an unexpected hand. Soon after starting his novitiate Claver had been sent to Majorca where he came under the influence of Alonso Rodríguez who had been serving for 30 years as doorkeeper in the Jesuit College of Montesión in Palma. By worldly standards, the old man could scarcely be accounted anything but a failure. He had been in business when young and had gone bankrupt. He had married, but soon lost his wife and children. Then he had been grudgingly granted admission into the Society of Jesus as a lay brother but had been regarded as incapable of anything but the menial duties of a porter. Yet Alonso Rodríguez was indubitably a saint. In the very obscurity of his office he saw the God-sent opportunity to practise those virtues of self-denial, obedience and humility which are the foundation of all sanctity. As he himself describes it: "When someone rang the bell, he would raise up his heart to God and say to Him; 'Lord, I shall open the door for you, for love of you', and he would open the door. When someone rang, he would make interior acts of gladness on his way, as if he were going to open the door to his God, and as if it were He who was ringing the bell, and as he went he would say to Him 'I'm coming, Lord!' When someone rang loudly and in a great hurry, his natural reaction was to get upset, but he suppressed this vigorously and by the time he had reached the door he had calmed down and he opened it as if the caller had only given a gentle ring". In short, as the old man recorded of his humble labours, "it seemed to this person that when he went to open the door, he went to open the door to his God". Today there stands in the courtyard of Montesión College a statue of the old porter, still hastening to answer the bell, above the inscription "I'm coming, Lord!"

Such was the man who, then well into his 70's, became Pedro Claver's spiritual mentor. The novice was allowed 15 minutes converse with him every day. This, together with the example of Alonso's childlike life and teaching, was enough to leave a profound impression on the younger man's malleable mind. The saintly doorkeeper's message, summed up in a number of short precepts which he wrote out and gave his pupil as a parting gift, was simple but uncompromising. Utter denial of self and subordination to God's purpose; "as one who is dead to the world and lives for God alone... making his will conform in every way to the will of God, and bringing it into such close union with Him that he not only rejects evil, but even the good which God may not desire". Absolute obedience to the Superior set over him in the place of God, neither questioning nor attempting to justify himself even if unjustly accused: "observing great silence, answering nothing, nothing, nothing at all, for in this way a man conquers himself, not defending himself, but for the love of God accepting everything that is not contrary to God's will and his obedience". Humility based on searching self-knowledge: "a man who knows himself despises himself". Complete absorption in God at all times: "There must be no more than God and you in all the world, for He alone must be all things to you". The fruit, a lifetime of service to others: "look for God in all men and serve them as images of Him". In a vision of the saints in glory the old man had seen an empty throne and it had been revealed to him that this was reserved for the young novice he was instructing. Alfonso, of course, said no word of this to his pupil, but it seems that he did confide his conviction that Claver's field of service was to be the New World. Claver learned his master's precepts by heart and absorbed his austere teaching so thoroughly that it became the basis for his own apostolate. When permission was given him, as he had requested, to leave for America, he at once set out for Seville without even taking leave of his family. "The good religious must be like Melchisedech without father or mother", Alonso had written: "he must have as little to do with them as if he did not possess them".

On reaching Cartagena Claver met the man who was to exercise the other great formative influence on his life and to initiate him into the practice of his vocation. Father Alonso de Sandoval was a young Spanish Jesuit, son of a Lima official and Claver's senior by some four years. He had been sent to strengthen the small Jesuit community at Cartagena and was at once appalled and fascinated by the challenge presented by the multitudes of pagan or nominally Christianized wretches dumped on the shores of the Caribbean with the arrival of each slave-ship. Sandoval had the curiosity of the scholar as well as compassion and missionary fervour. He realized that the only hope of alleviating this mass of human suffering and of saving souls for Christ was to begin by distinguishing between the very different African tribes and races engulfed in this common misery, to know something of their respective customs and mentality, to speak to them in their own language and in ways accessible to their simple and fear-ridden minds. His researches into these fields, published at Seville in 1627 under the title *Naturaleza, policia sagrada y profana, costumbres, ritos y superstiticiones de los Etíopes* mark Sandoval as a pioneer in African ethnology and the methods which he devised for the catechizing and baptism of his negro neophytes as a working psychologist with an unusual insight into the primitive mind. With both the theoretical and practical aspects of Sandoval's work Claver wholly identified himself. Having no calling himself for scholarly research, he nevertheless saw how essential it was to the success of their common apostolate, and in 1625 we find him writing to the General of the Society urging him to expedite the publication of Sandoval's manuscript. In their techniques of approaching and instructing the negroes, in their methods of catechism and simple exegesis, in their conviction that the slaves were as entitled as any other Christians to the sacraments of the Church and as capable of benefiting spiritually from them, the two missionaries spoke with one voice. They differed only in the field of their labours, Claver devoting his time primarily to Cartagena whilst Sandoval spent much of his visiting the outlying townships and plantations.

The first obstacle to any approach to the negroes—at least to those newly imported from Africa—was linguistic. In the course of his long ministry amongst them, Claver acquired some fluency in Angolese, the language spoken by the majority of them, but neither he nor Sandoval were ever credited by the hagiographers, as Luis Bertrán and other notable evangelists had been, with the miraculous gift of tongues. They had therefore to find and work through negroes who could act as interpreters. Sandoval started a register of such negroes, listing the tongues in which they were proficient and the Spaniards who owned them, and borrowed them from their masters when the slave-ships came in. The arrangement did not work smoothly, as the owners were often loth to part with their slaves. The missionaries needed permanent interpreters of their own. None questioned the propriety of a religious community possessing slaves; even poor houses, such as the Jesuit College in Cartagena then was, used them for agricultural or domestic labour. So Peter Claver, the avowed slave of the slaves, soon found himself a slave-owner. The paradox, however, was more apparent than real. Claver's slave-interpreters were treated as a privileged group. More than servants or even assistants, they soon became his most trusted friends and associates. On them, as indispensable fellow-workers in the propagation of the gospel, he lavished his tenderest affection and solicitude. He would spend hours patiently instructing them in the faith so that they could catechize intelligently. If one of them fell ill, Claver would give up his own bed to him and nurse him devotedly back to health. When they went on short mission tours outside Cartagena, Claver would let the interpreters set the pace and fix the daily programme. When catechizing newcomers from Africa, he would stand or squat with them on the ground whilst the interpreter sat in a chair in the middle of the group.

We learn from the Annual Letters sent to Rome by the Father Provincial that, by the year 1642, the College possessed no less than 18 of these interpreters. Some spoke three or four languages, others still more, and one was even reputed fluent in 11. The names and particulars of many of them are on record, for though one or two abused their position, most gave long and devoted service, some surviving their master to make their contribution to the testimony collected for the Process of his beatification; Andrés Sacabuche and Francisco Yolofo, both of whom worked with him for more than 20 years, Ignacio Aluanil, who entered his service as a lad of ten, José Monzolo, who had been so moved by Claver's charity when his slaveship put into port that he there and then begged the Father to buy him and keep him in his service. Claver had sometimes to fight hard for his interpreters. There were those, even in his own community, who resented the privileges accorded them and held that they should be at the general beck and call like any other slaves. Claver had to appeal to the General of the Society who ruled that, though they might learn some trade and ply it when not otherwise needed, they should remain primarily at the disposal of the Fathers for the work of catechizing their fellows. Without their willing and intelligent collaboration, the apostolate of Fathers Sandoval and Claver could not have borne its fruit.

*　　　　*　　　　*　　　　*

In their visit to Cartagena a century later, the young Spanish travellers Juan and Ulloa refer to the *tiempo muerto* or dead season of sweltering lassitude into which the Caribbean port would sink in the intervals between the arrival of the galleons from Spain with the attendant fairs which attracted buyers of slaves and merchandize from every part of the Spanish domains. Father Claver allowed himself no respite of the *tiempo muerto;* there were always the poor, the sick and the prisoners crying out for care. But whenever a fleet was sighted, his work reached a new peak of feverish intensity. If the ships proved to bring only Spaniards, the Jesuit showed himself strangely indifferent to the excitement which brought half the population down to the wharves. But if the arrival of a slave-ship was reported, "his eyes shone and his pale face flushed as red as fire". Brother Nicolás González, his companion for over 20 years, assures us that this was on account of the great "kindness and friendship" he felt for the negroes and his ardent desire to bring them the consolation of the gospel. But was it not also the saint's compassionate emotion at the prospect of those scenes of harrowing misery and degradation which he knew he must shortly confront? The matter-of-fact tone of one of Claver's own rare accounts, quoted by his first biographer, only throws the picture into starker relief :

"Yesterday", (he wrote in a letter to his Provincial on 30 May, 1627), "there came to land a great ship laden with negroes from the Rivers. We went there laden with two baskets of oranges, lemons and tobacco. We entered their house which seemed like another Guinea, piles of them on all sides; we made our way through till we reached the sick of whom there were a great number lying on the ground which, as it was damp and liable to flooding, was levelled up with sharp-edged pieces of brick and tiles, and this was their bed, where they lay naked without a stitch of clothing. We threw off our cloaks and sent to fetch planks from another store-room and we laid a floor there and carried the sick in our arms, pushing our way through the rest. We collected the sick in two circles, my companion taking the one and I the other".

Accounts of the arrival of the slave-ships can scarcely be read without a shudder. The negroes were chained together by long fetters called *corrientes* which were not struck off until they reached Cartagena. To the physical torture of the voyage were added the terrors of mind induced by the negroes' belief that "when they arrive they will be used to extract oil from or be eaten, so that about a third of those embarked die during the crossing, which lasts more than two months; so tightly packed, so filthy and so ill-treated that the very men who bring them here assure me that they come in sixes with rings round their necks, the *corrientes* and their feet joined by fetters in pairs, so that they are chained from head to foot; below decks, with no outlet to see the sun or moon, no Spaniard dares look through the hatches without feeling faint, nor be in with them above an hour without risk of grave illness in the stench, overcrowding and misery in that place [the hold]. The only relief and consolation they have is to eat, every 24 hours, nothing more than a platter of flour, maize or raw millet, which is like rice for us, and with a little jug of water and nothing else but plenty of beating and whipping and ugly words. . . With this kind of treatment they arrive like skeletons; they are then taken out naked and placed in a great court or yard. Then there come endless crowds of people, some from greed, others from curiosity, others from compassion, and among these the Jesuits ready to instruct, indoctrinate and baptize those who arrive in a dying state. And although they make haste they always find some dead".

In his chapter *Concerning the manner of examining the negroes when they arrive at the ports in the cargo ships and other necessary procedure before the catechism is taught* Sandoval describes how the Jesuits set about their daunting task. "When the ship arrives and the negroes disembark we must first of all go to meet them at once so as to find out how many there are, what they are like and from which lands and ports they come; what diseases they suffer from; how many and which of them are sick, chiefly those dangerously ill, and the children about whom diligent enquiry must be made to learn which of them are not baptized. . . We shall also find out the state of the sick, to what house they are taken to be cared for; how many there are and what ails those who have remained in the ships because they could not disembark, or those who are outside the town so as not to infect the other healthy ones, and how many healthy ones have stayed to guard and care for these sick people, and those who entered the town coming from the ship, in how many houses they have been distributed and to what houses the negroes brought in by other private individuals have gone, so that all may be duly attended to; afterwards they may be examined by means of trusty interpreters who can speak Spanish, according to the languages they use. . . Then those belonging to the different tribes are separated, the women on one side and the men on the other, and before all else the first thing to be done is to win their confidence, giving them some presents and making their master give them something, clothing them decently and bringing them some garment for this purpose, even if it is old. At other times, jugs of fresh water will be handed round—a very important thing, as they have not been able to get even salt water and they are parched with thirst, chiefly the women and children". Ignacio Angola, one of the faithful slave interpreters, adds that "as soon as Father Claver knew there was a ship in port, he was greatly delighted. He at once ordered the old interpreters to make enquiries and to greet them and bid them welcome in his name". Then he would hurry to the ships "carrying bananas, cakes, and other sweet things to give them, specially to the sick, and the interpreters were ready on the wharf to carry the injured in carts to the sheds".

These sheds were a couple of dozen gaunt rectangular buildings where the slaves were kept until being sold off. They were prisons rather than lodgings, each having a single door and one window high up in the wall, and with a few benches for their sole furniture. Some sheds were kept for the men, others for women, the sick, the diseased and even the dead lying pell mell amongst the emaciated bodies which still passed for sound. Sandoval relates his horror, on visiting the sheds each morning, to find always fresh corpses amongst the living, lying "stark naked on the ground, their mouths open and full of flies. . . The most worn-out mat was sought, they were wrapped in it and their bodies flung into a corner until they were buried, the latter now being done as a result of some slight reform. Before this they were left naked in the patios". Those who were deemed fit for work were generally hired out for labour on the public works and fortifications of the city, and there followed "some alleviation of life while they are there, because they are fattened so that they may be sold more profitably". But, in their overcrowded and enfeebled state, many who had survived the horrors of the voyage soon succumbed to the epidemics raging through the slave-sheds which "in a few days become a hospital full of the sick when the universe is peopled with corpses, some dying from severe pains in the side, some from high fevers, others from smallpox, typhoid or measles, or a sickness they call scurvy which is incurable. . . There they lie and there they normally die without anyone caring for their bodies or their souls".

What could the small band of men, the compassionate Jesuits and their helpers, do in the face of this immense wave of suffering and degradation? They went first where the need was greatest—to the sick and dying. Where famished bodies were beyond all remedy, they could do no more than hear confessions and ease the dying. Many, especially the children, had never been baptized, and the Fathers hastened to confer this sacrament upon them whilst their souls, if not their bodies, could yet be saved. Small wonder that, long after their first desperate thirst had been slaked, water remained for them, in literal rather than symbolic sense, the most precious of gifts. Sandoval relates how the eyes of one of his catechumens continually strayed to the water-jug, and it was only after he had drunk again and again of it, that "he straightened himself, cheered up and spoke and answered and was baptized, to the great solace of those present". At other times, after jugs of fresh water had been handed round, Sandoval would be amazed to find that when the baptismal water had been dispensed from a silver dish and was to be decently emptied after the ceremony, he found it quite dry and realized that "as the water fell into the dish from the head of those who were baptized, they were lapping it up without leaving a drop". From the reality of this consuming physical thirst the Fathers sought to make their flock understand the spiritual meaning of the sacrament. Just as parched bodies were refreshed by the longed-for draught of water, so would their souls now be refreshed and strengthened by the outpouring of God's grace.

We can hardly doubt that the Fathers were alive to the evils of slavery as an institution as well as to the sufferings inflicted on its victims; and if they stopped short of raising their voice against the institution itself it was, perhaps, above all, because they discerned the divine providence working through the inhumanity of the system to redeem humans who would otherwise be left in pagan darkness. The missionary, Sandoval declares, should console the wretched negroes by discoursing on "the great mercy of the Lord in bringing them to a Christian land, where it is better to be a captive than to live as a free man in their own country; for here, though the body suffers hardship in captivity, the soul rests in liberty through baptism" The argument may seem to us specious, but it was held by the Jesuits with passionate sincerity. If they found it up-hill work to convince the wretched Africans faced with the prospect of a life-time of slavery in a strange land, they brought at least the example of their own gentle compassion and selflessness to contrast with the blows, curses and callous cruelty which was all the slaves had as yet known from their captors. Without such witness of Christian charity, the Gospel message could have sounded in their ears as no more than a cynical fable, or at the best, a meaningless formality.

The first aim of the missionaries, once they had begun to dispel the terror and despair of the wretches unloaded from the slave-ships, was to bring them to a speedy and willing acceptance of baptism. This was an urgent matter, not only since they were liable to succumb so easily to disease and their souls thus be lost to all eternity, but also because, once they had found a buyer, they might well be carried off to some distant *estancia* in Central America or Peru beyond the reach of any missionary's labour. But the catechist had to resist the temptation to seek short cuts to salvation. Sandoval is insistent that the converts should be questioned and prepared "with great kindness, time and patience, putting up with the slowness of their replies, and their variety, very far from the point which is to be cleared up. They should be given time to think about the question and to quieten down". He stresses that "they should be spoken to gently, giving them to understand that one loves them greatly; being, as one is, Father and priest of God, whom all men respect and reverence (by reason of the tonsure he wears like a crown and which should be shown to them, for they are much influenced by these external signs), he must speak to them, caress them and tell them many things about God, great things that they must believe, take to heart and listen to with great attention".

The Fathers made liberal use of many such "external signs" to bring home the truths of the Christian faith to the simple minds of their African converts. When the latter were deemed ready for baptism, the missionary would "set up an altar on a raised place where they could all see it, and on it he placed a picture of Christ nailed to a cross painted on cloth, with a basin at His feet into which all the blood fell that flowed from his wounds, and beside the basin stood a priest wearing a stole and cope who was baptizing with this blood several negroes who looked very beautiful after they were baptized, whilst those who were not baptized looked very ugly. Some demons were standing near by with gaping mouths as if they would like to swallow them, and through the interpreters he [Father Claver] told them that those who were not baptized would continue to be ugly". Such is the account given by the lay brother Nicolás González who had often witnessed the scene. The negro interpreter Andrés Sacabuche adds : "The first thing he taught them was to make the sign of the Cross perfectly with the right hand. To the one who learned it best he gave a present of tobacco, and to the one who was slow about it he gave a little tap on the head with the stem of the crucifix he held. Then he taught them the Our Father, Hail Mary, the Creed, and the mystery of the Trinity. To explain that, he used to make a number of folds in a handkerchief and he showed it to them, and when they had looked at the folds he undid them and told them it was only one handkerchief; and in this way the negroes believed easily in the mystery. He took out a book he had in which all the life of Christ was shown in pictures. He spoke of the immortality of the soul, of hell and heaven, and showed them pictures, particularly of hell—a soul in pain and also a soul in glory. After the instruction, he took from his bosom a wooden crucifix and with great fervour made them all, through the interpreters, recite the following : 'Lord Jesus, Son of God, Thou are my Father. I am sorry for having offended Thee. I love thee very much', repeating it many times and striking their breasts. Then he raised his eyes to heaven and remained for a time rapt in prayer".

Brother Nicolás adds another graphic detail. After Claver had repeated "Lord, I have great love for thee, great, great. . ." beating his breast and weeping, he went on to explain that "in the same way as the serpent changes its skin, they must change their lives and habits, forsaking paganism and its vices so as to lose all remembrance of them, and as he said these words Father Claver, replacing the crucifix in his bosom, pinched his skin from forehead to waist with his hands as if he were tearing at his skin to pull it off, and the negroes did the same, and immediately afterwards he did the same with his arms and other parts of his body, the others imitating him with such fervour that it seemed as if they were really pulling off the skin and putting on a covering of faith. This was the new man".

Father Sandoval tells us that, in preparation for the ceremony, the converts would first have their heads washed "in two or more troughs of water", so that the baptismal water could pass through their hair to touch their skin. Then they would be formed into groups of ten and made to kneel down, first the men, then the women, "with all possible devotion" round a silver dish placed so as to catch the baptismal water. The priest, clad in his vestments, would first put a few simple questions and words of exhortation through the interpreter, and then "bestow on each of the ten a name which is common and easily pronounced, making them repeat it so that they do not forget it and that they may remind one another in case any of them forgets". They would then be solemnly enjoined to use it henceforth and to forget their former name "as it was that of a Moor or Gentile and a child of the Devil". One of the interpreters, or some other Spanish-speaking negro or negress of their own tribe, would act as godparent. Finally, a rosary with a metal medallion bearing the name Jesus on one side and Mary on the other would be put round their neck as a token that they had been baptized and to make sure they did not go through the same ceremony twice. The converts were generally impressed and delighted by the whole procedure. They would "embrace each other, telling one another the Christian name they had received", and delightedly seek out others who had been baptized with the same name.

Some 6,000 negroes are said to have been baptized in this way in Cartagena every year. Including those who slipped through the net— for many were smuggled into the country so that their owners could avoid paying import duty—and were later found and baptized on his missionary rounds outside the city, Father Claver estimated at the end of his life that he must have brought a total of some 300,000 souls into the Church. From such unremitting labours, observed Father Sandoval, "two conclusions follow—firstly, that these negroes are not brute beasts, as I have heard some say, for hereabouts they try to make out that they are incapable of being Christians, nor must they be reputed childish or mentally defective, because they are grown-up men and as such should be given baptism, preceded by an act of will on their part".

*   *   *   *

There were many Spaniards who disapproved of the Jesuits' work amongst the negroes. Some simply complained of the time spent by their slaves in receiving religious instruction, attending mass and keeping the feasts of the Church when they ought to be working. Others, particularly those who made their living out of the slave trade, resented the implied reproach at their exploitation of slave labour and the moral pressure which set limits to its severity. How could they be expected to accept that this piece of human merchandize picked up at some African port for a few ducats was the temple of an immortal soul, equal to any other man in the sight of God and to be treated with the consideration due to a fellow Christian? Besides, the Jesuits, even though counselling obedience, industry and good behaviour, were really putting ideas into the heads of the slaves which were dangerously beyond their station. Claver, with his simple medicaments and comforts and his patient vigils by the bedside of the sick, was "spoiling" the negroes. When he intervened with some cruel master on behalf of an offending or runaway slave he sometimes only added fuel to the master's wrath. But not always; there were those who were swayed by his arguments or moved by his dedication and even came to be numbered amongst his helpers.

There was opposition, too, at first from the clergy, and even in Claver's own little community voices of censure or scepticism were sometimes raised. Some objected on the grounds of "jurisdiction"— that fertile source of conflict between Order and Order, between secular and regular clergy. There were secular priests who claimed that Father Sandoval was trespassing on their preserves by baptizing and dispensing the sacraments to those theoretically within their own parishes. Claver had to face similar complaints but found an effective way of dealing with them. When he encountered a negro in need of baptism or extreme unction, he would himself seek out the parish priest and offer to accompany him. But the parish priests, who saw their duty primarily in ministering to the Spanish and Creole flock, generally had little stomach for such exacting work. When the question was referred to the Bishop, it was ruled that "the said ministry was more suited for penitent and mortified religious on account of the strong stench emitted by these negroes", and there the priests were content to let matters rest.

At certain periods of his life Claver had also to contend with misunderstanding and disapproval within his own community. The Society was, in general, a staunch advocate of missionary work amongst the negroes, and there survive a number of letters written to Claver by the General in Rome encouraging him in his difficult ministry and backing him on specific issues such as the dispute over the use of the slave-interpreters. But some of Claver's own superiors found his dedication to the cause of the slaves both misguided and embarrassing. One referred to him as "a Catalan, pig-headed and difficult". Another rebuked him sharply for spending too much of his time on the slaves and expecting too much from them, and for turning his cell into an unseemly storehouse piled high with clothes, food, even spirits and tobacco, as comforts for those who were sick or most in need. More serious still, the Superior disliked Claver's methods of instructing the negroes, particularly his use of crudely painted pictures. Claver tried to explain that such visual aids were the most effective means of approaching minds too primitive to grasp abstract truths. The Superior insisted and Claver, mindful of the silent obedience enjoined by his beloved Alonso Rodríguez, submitted. But events quickly proved him right. Deprived of their pictures and images, the negro catechumens proved quite unable to make progress and the Superior was obliged to withdraw his ban.

The attitude of a Jesuit who devoted almost his whole life to the negroes and actually seemed to prefer their company to that of the whites was regarded by some of his fellows not only as an oddity but as an affront. Claver would attend to the spiritual, no less than the physical, needs of the blacks with inexhaustible patience. "While there were negroes about", records Brother Nicolás, "it was useless to attempt to confess to Claver. After the slaves came the poor, and when they were lacking, the children from the school". Another witness, a lady prominent in Cartagena society, states that, "he loved the negroes so much that he was loth to confess Spaniards, and if any Spaniard asked him to hear his confession, he would answer that the negroes were in great poverty, that they had masters to serve, whilst Spanish ladies never lacked for confessors ready at their call; and in any case, he was fit only for blacks". To the great ladies of Cartagena, specially when wearing the fashionable farthingale which Claver held in particular abhorrence, the saint, so gentle and compassionate towards their slaves, could appear almost insultingly dour.

Brother Nicolás relates one scene of tragi-comedy, with its epilogue of apostolic self-abasement, resulting from his attitude. "One day in the Holy Week of 1644 there entered the church a lady dressed unsuitably for the religious season and wearing the detested farthingale. Claver was busy with some negroes near his confessional, but as soon as he saw her he went over and told her that she ought to respect the holy season. She thereupon went off to the chapel of the Virgin of the Miracle exclaiming that Claver had publicly insulted and gravely offended her. I tried to calm her as best I could and turning to Claver told him he ought not to meddle in these things, and that very soon the church would be empty because of him. The Rector, who was then Father Francisco Sarmiento, heard the commotion. He came down to the church and in the presence of everyone sharply reproved Claver, saying that priests were not reformers of female attire and that, in any case, the confessional, or even the pulpit if necessary, existed for such purposes. Father Claver made no answer. Next day, at four in the morning when I was saying prayers in the sacristy, he came in and falling to his knees kissed my feet. He called himself Judas at the feet of Christ. I tried to make excuses for my behaviour the day before, telling him that I was only worried lest fewer people should come to our church. Without saying a word, Claver rose to his feet and went to his confessional". Had he not learned from the saintly old doorkeeper of Montesión never to answer back, never to justify himself when reproved, "observing great silence, answering nothing, nothing, nothing at all?" Or as he himself once recorded in his note-book: "Whenever I fail to behave as a donkey behaves it is the worse for me. How does a donkey behave? If they speak ill of him, he keeps silent; if they do not feed him, silence; if they forget him, silence; he never complains, no matter how he is assaulted or maltreated, because he has a donkey's patience. That is how the servant of God must behave; I stand before you, Lord, as a donkey".

This practice of uncomplaining, almost beast-like submissiveness, punctuated by occasional outbursts of indignation at what he considered affronts to God or God's suffering creatures, could appear in a very different light to Claver's less spiritual contemporaries. His humility was sometimes mistaken for stupidity, his self-control for moroseness, his fervour for imprudence. Claver's thirst for self-abasement certainly unfitted him for any position of administrative authority. A brief term of office as "Minister" of the Jesuit residence proved disastrous, since his one idea was to take on all the most menial tasks—the sweeping and cleaning and washing-up—himself. A curious insight into what his Superiors thought of him is provided by the personality reports which they were required to send every three years to Rome. The earliest extant of these (1616) describes his *mental powers* as *less than mediocre,* his *instruction* as *slight,* and his *prudence* as *lacking,* though it was somewhat condescendingly observed that he was *useful for hearing confession and dealing with the natives.* After 26 years of unremitting labours, he was described as having made *good progress* in *instruction,* though his character had become *very melancholic* and his *mental powers* were rated only *mediocre,* whilst his *prudence* was still *lacking.* Five years before his death, his *mental powers and instruction* are recognized as good, and both his *advance in spiritual matters* and *mission work* are *excellent. . . outstanding in his dealings with the negroes.* But his *judgment* is still no more than *mediocre,* and as for *prudence and experience of the world,* his Superior can only report that it is *nil.*

Withdrawn and taciturn to the point of moroseness this dedicated man must have seemed to many of his compatriots. One of them declares that "the saint walked the streets with bowed head and greeted very few Spaniards; he spoke only to negroes". Yet he numbered Spaniards as well as negroes amongst his helpers; even gentlemen of quality like don Francisco Núñez de Quero, a knight of the Order of Calatrava, who used to go down to the slave-ships with him, and ladies like doña Isabel de Urbina, whose husband was commandant of the fortress at the Punta del Indio. These and many other pious and respectable folk gave generously in response to Claver's incessant appeals on behalf of the slaves, even if there were few who dared put their hand to the same plough. The negroes themselves, both slave and free, made up the core of Claver's active helpers. There was Margarita of Cape Verde, Isabel de Urbina's slave, whose task it was to cook special dishes for the sick and to prepare the banquets which Claver delighted to organize for the lepers and beggars of Cartagena. Angela Rodríguez, a freed negress, shared Claver's task of visiting the sick. Bernardina specialized in house-to-house collections for the hospitals and kept up her visits for 30 years. Justina and Martina took on the grim task of taking up the bodies of slaves which had been left lying for collection by the mortuary-cart and giving them Christian burial, whilst Claver said a mass for the repose of their souls. Antonia devoted her time to the lepers and Isabel Folupa to the spiritual preparation of her fellow-slaves wishing to receive com-

munion. These, and many other humble men and women, together
with the select band of Claver's slave-interpreters, trod valiantly in the
path traced by the saint.

It was a long and arduous path. For Claver, who began his ministry
under Father Sandoval in 1615 and continued it, despite the last four
years of virtual incapacity which preceded his death, it lasted for
nearly 40 years: It led relentlessly uphill, since the flood of human
misery which the saint and his devoted band strove to alleviate, was
replenished with the arrival of each new slave-ship. Only after 1640,
when Portugal recovered her independence from Spain and ceased to
export slaves in such numbers from Guinea, did the flow of traffic
through Cartagena begin to slow down. Sometimes, with the advent of
an exceptionally large contingent, the flow became a cataract and it
was then that the city would know its worst hours; overcrowding, a
breakdown in food supplies and epidemics. Of the latter, Claver
experienced four or five major outbreaks in his life-time. In 1633-4 the
smallpox raged. Only two years later, following the arrival of a large
fleet, more than a thousand patients were sent to the hospital of San
Sebastián alone. In 1639-41 there occurred another epidemic, and ten
years later, a still more disastrous visitation. "The negroes, forgotten
and neglected, suffered worst of all", writes Claver's first biographer.
"They were riddled with ulcers and worms, without bed or shelter,
and the pestilential stench which they gave off was so strong that it
went to the head and deprived of his senses anyone who ventured near
them. A monk tried to go in and got only as far as their door when he
collapsed in the infected air with such dysentery and nausea that he
did not completely come to for a couple of days. Another priest went
to give the sacraments to a negro but the stench was so nauseating that
it turned his stomach and for two days he could not swallow a mouthful, his head swam, and he could not go on with his work. This contagion lasted for more than three months and great numbers of
people of every class and condition died". In their despair and terror,
the citizens sought the protection of the miraculous image of the
Virgen de la Popa and bore it in suppliant procession from her hill-
top sanctuary down through the streets of the stricken city.

Much of Claver's labour was devoted to succouring the neediest victims in these recurrent crises and the intervening periods of neglect and
chronic suffering. The slave-sheds, the hospital of San Sebastián run
by the brothers of San Juan de Dios to whom he gladly offered his
services in the humblest of tasks, the leprosarium of San Lázaro, the
compounds of the Capitolio, where the disabled and incurable found
the roughest of shelter, the isolated huts in which infected slaves were

left abandoned to their fate—these were the saint's familiar haunts. We do not read of Claver, as of Martín de Porres, that he was skilled in the use of herbs or had any special gift of healing. Often he could do no more than soothe the last hours of the dying or bring the fruit and simple comforts which, to the abandoned and hopeless, might do as much good as any medicine. We hear of him constantly tending and washing the sick, dispelling as best he could the degrading squalor, cleansing their sores, often with the compassionate touch of his own lips. "I saw the Father close to those disfigured faces and repulsive ulcers which he kissed devotedly", declares don Francisco Núñez de Quero who frequently accompanied him. "Not only did he cleanse those plague-ridden ulcers with the two cloths he kept for that purpose, but he did not hesitate to press his lips to them". Other contemporaries bear witness to such sublime and horrific acts of compassion, instances of which are also recorded in the lives of St. Catherine of Siena, St. Francis Javier and other saints. But with the slave of the slaves, according to another witness, Francisco Caballero, the mayor of Cartagena, such acts "became a habit in the holy father, which he did not only in the infirmaries for the negroes, but in the hospitals and still more often, in the leprosarium".

*   *   *   *

Cartagena, with its torrid heat and teeming slave population, became a fertile breeding ground for the ancient scourge of leprosy. At the beginning of the century, only a dozen cases or so were known, but in 1627 more than 70 were admitted to the leprosarium, whilst many more could be found at large. The leprosarium of San Lázaro was a wretched collection of huts which scarcely merited the name of hospital. It stood at some distance from the city, beyond the gate of the Half Moon. The inmates were in danger of losing even this inadequate shelter owing to its ruinous state, and Claver took it upon himself to mobilize a work-party of negro masons and carpenters who would rehouse them. He himself showed absolutely no fear of the disease, and would gather the lepers around him for his little homilies, taking the sick as tenderly in his arms, and lavishing the same care upon them, as upon his other patients. His message was of the simplest. Suffering, if accepted for the love of Christ, could be the surest path to Him; a disfigured body was of no account so long as the soul was pure. The lepers found renewed hope in the Father's words and looked forward to his coming. He always brought gifts for them; honey and fruit, particularly the famous "Father Claver's dates", picked and preserved by his own hand. Sometimes there would even be tobacco and wine, or practical gifts like a set of mosquito nets which Claver had made with the assistance of his negro helpers. The most eagerly awaited of these visits were the banquets which Claver would organize from time to time to mark some feast of the Church and to bring a touch of warmth and gaiety into their grey lives. Then Margarita would work day and night in doña Isabel's kitchen preparing food, and Claver, who had the true Catalan's love of music, would get together a band to play to the lepers whilst they sat at table.

Another grim place where the Jesuit, with his medicines, his basket of food and other gifts, was a familiar visitor was the city gaol. Sometimes he would bring with him a lawyer to help some wretch whose case, as well as his person, languished there forgotten. At others, when Justice had spoken, he could do no more than help the condemned man to prepare for death, accompanying him to the place of execution and inspiring him with his own fortitude and serenity. Once, when a murderer called Melón was sentenced to be executed, a Moslem galley slave was ordered to act as hangman. He had no heart for the job and fumbled it badly. The condemned man expired at last in Claver's arms, the grisly affair having an unexpected sequel in the conversion of the Moslem hangman who later left an account of it in his own words. "I was the king's slave and they told me to be Melón's hangman. I did not want to, and fled to Boca Chica. The soldiers caught me. The execution took place in the main square. Father Claver brought wine in a glass which he gave to the condemned man, and to me too, which gave me strength to go through with it. I made up my mind to be converted through Father Claver's charity. He kissed me and taught me the mysteries of the Faith. I lived all this time in the College, and Father Juan Bautista Fajardo, a priest of the Cathedral, baptized me there".

A special category of prisoners were those who had fallen foul of the Inquisition. The Indians, as infants in the faith, mercifully exempted from the attentions of that institution. Not so the negroes; though, since most of the latter were penniless slaves, there was no material inducement for the Holy Office to pursue them with fines or the confiscation of goods, and because they were without social influence, their errors hardly threatened to contaminate the community at large. The slave-owners moreover had every reason to resent interference by the Inquisition. If a slave was imprisoned, his master not only lost his labour but was supposed to pay for his food in prison and other expenses. As for the punishment inflicted on him, the slave had generally less to fear from the Inquisition than from his master, and his lot might even be improved by his committing offences which brought him within the jurisdiction of the Holy Office. A slave condemned by his master to a flogging had only to cry out at the first stroke *Reniego a Dios!*—"I deny God!"—a common oath deemed tantamount to blasphemy, which was supposed to bring the offender automatically into the clutches of the Inquisition, for the flogging to be stopped and the culprit handed over to the inquisitors. The latter were likely to inflict a less severe punishment or even let the culprit off altogether with a reprimand. The result was that masters and inquisitors commonly turned a blind eye to such misdemeanours on the part of the slaves. For the mass of the latter, moreover, the Christian faith was only skin-deep; the old habits and mentality of their ancestral religion remained deeply ingrained. This was particularly true of those who passed rapidly through Cartagena to spend the rest of their lives in remote *estancias* or mines.

One survival from their pagan past to which the negroes remained firmly addicted was the practice of witchcraft. As this was an evil widespread too amongst the white-skinned Christians, the Inquisition had sometimes to take cognizance of it and attempt to punish its practitioners. At the *autos da fe* which Claver witnessed in Cartagena, many stood accused of this offence, though none was called upon to pay for it with his life. Witchcraft was most flagrantly practised amongst the large numbers of negroes who laboured in the gold mines of Zaragoza in Antioquia. Here things reached such a pitch that the Inquisitor, Juan de Mañozca, reported to the Suprema of the Holy Office in Spain that the witchdoctors killed or crippled their victims at will and were impervious to the influence of the missionaries sent to them who, in any case, were themselves of very low calibre and generally more interested in seeking gold for themselves than with the spiritual welfare of the slaves. To arrest and call the guilty to account for these evil practices, Mañozca observed, would require an operation altogether beyond the resources of the Holy Office and he recommended that the civil authorities should take over the responsibility for it.

Father Claver had his own more modest methods for weaning his negro converts from their pagan practices. He particularly deplored the traditional wakes which they held in honour of the dead, when they would dance throughout the night, in a veritable orgy of drinking and dancing and sexual licence. At such times the Jesuit would appear amongst them, crucifix in one hand and scourge in the other, wrathful as Christ driving the money-lenders from the temple, and put an end to their impious revels. The drums used for the ceremonies he would carry off and leave in the keeping of some shopkeeper with orders that they were only to be returned when their owners had paid a fine of a peso or two as alms to the poor lepers of San Lázaro.

If the Inquisition and the slave-owners turned virtually a blind eye to the continuance of such traditional practices and superstitions, it was a very different matter with any suspected taint of Lutheran heresy. Not that the soil was favourable for such dangerous weeds to flourish. Mañozca reported, with some exaggeration, that the Spanish and Creole population, from the Governor down, were wholly given to the pursuit of gain. There was consequently no intellectual vigour, no questioning of orthodox beliefs, and thus little inducement to error. During all his years in Cartagena, Claver saw only two heretics burnt at the stake. One was a Portuguese shoemaker accused of secretly practising Judaism, the other a young English protestant, whose name figures in the records as John Edon. He had been sent by an English merchant to buy tobacco in Cumaná where he had been apprehended in 1619. For two years he stoutly resisted all efforts to wean him from his errors. Claver and another priest reasoned long and earnestly with him but to no avail. His fate was therefore inevitable and he met his end, with unflinching fortitude, in the solemn *auto da fe* of 13 March, 1622—the first victim to perish at the stake in Cartagena. Inquisitor Mañozca, reporting that "this ceremony was, we may hope, to the honour and glory of God", declared that the Englishman "persisted in the defence of his errors and died for them in the fire with so much obstinacy that his blindness amazed all those present, for without being bound, he seated himself upon the bundles of faggots and remained motionless there without moving so much as a foot".

Claver had other encounters with English heretics which ended more happily. The Spanish galleons sailing from Cartagena, and the port itself, were exposed to attack by Dutch, English and other raiders who found in the smaller Caribbean islands excellent bases from which to launch their operations. From time to time the pirates would fall into the hands of their enemies and be sent, if not executed on the spot, to Cartagena where not a few were reconciled to the Catholic faith and some even took service under the Spanish flag. The biggest haul of freebooting heretics was made in 1639-40 when a fleet under Don Federico de Toledo managed to flush them out of their lair on the island of Santa Catalina, off the coast of Nicaragua, and brought some 600 prisoners back to Cartagena. Father Claver turned ardently to face this new challenge and played a leading rôle in the conversion of the heretics. His first biographer writes that "Father Claver sought out Catholic interpreters and filled a ship with monks". They set about proselytizing the Protestants who were being kept under guard at sea, whilst Claver himself parleyed in Latin with "an old man of respectable and venerable aspect, with white hair and a long beard", variously described as their "bishop" and as "the Archdeacon of London". The Jesuit "spent many hours with the English churchman, striving to lead him to the path of the Catholic faith and almost convinced him". Finally, after the old man had fallen mortally sick and been brought ashore to hospital, Claver succeeded and the "Archdeacon of London" was received on his deathbed into the Catholic Church. The great majority of his compatriots in time followed suit. The prisoners were taken ashore where they lived wretchedly and were frequently to be found at the lodge of the Jesuit College. There at least they could always count on receiving their fill of bread and water and an earnest welcome from Father Claver. Some succumbed to their wounds or to epidemics, but many were eventually reconciled to the Church—"so many, that the Commander of the fleet, on Claver's persuasion, admitted them as soldiers of the King, with pay according to their rank", so that—we learn from Claver's biographer —"from infidels they were turned into good Christians, and from enemies into friends and vassals of His Majesty, a regiment being formed from them more than 1,000 strong, which gave most loyal service by land and sea".

To take over the doorkeeper's duties so as to give him a rest would not be many people's idea of relaxation. But for Claver the hours spent in the college lodge held a special charm. Here he was accessible to all, at the disposal of beggars, vagabonds, heretics, and children, free to listen to their troubles, to teach them, to help them with advice and to dispense alms and foods. On important feast days such as Christmas, Easter, Lady Day and the Feast of St. Ignatius, he would get together singers and musicians and have special meals prepared for his motley guests and would wait on them himself at table. Ignacio Angola, one of his interpreters, recalls that "there was music while we ate, and my heart was stirred to see Father Claver sitting on the ground whilst the beggars sat on chairs". Such occasions recalled those hours of long ago, so fruitful for the development of his own spiritual life, when he had talked with old Alonso Rodríguez in the lodge at Montesión. Had not the humble calling of doorkeeper provided his revered master with the means of achieving that utter self-renunciation and dedication to the needs of others which is the foundation of sanctity? It is said that when Alonso was having difficulty in obtaining admission to the Society, the Father Superior decided the matter by remarking, not without a touch of irony perhaps, that if he could not be expected to become a priest, then he had better become a saint.

The pure in heart have a disconcerting way of taking such injunctions literally.

With such an obsessive concern for serving others, Claver, we can imagine, may have had difficulty in observing the statutory hours of recreation. One favourite pastime was to make rosaries by threading together fruit-stones in place of beads, a task in which his helpers gladly joined. Another was to prepare certificates for the negroes and negresses who had made their prescribed confessions in Lent. An innumerable quantity of these scraps of paper, covered with the saint's neat handwriting, was discovered in his cell when he lay dying and eagerly carried away as relics. The cell itself, until illness put an end to Claver's customary activities, presented an extraordinary spectacle, more like some corner of an eastern bazaar. There the Father kept whatever he had been able to get together for the slaves; baskets filled with oranges and lemons, casks of wine and spirit—until ordered by his Superior to have those placed under lock and key in the college storeroom—food and tobacco, bales of cloth and bundles of cheap dresses, for each new slave-ship discharged its human cargo stark naked on the quayside. Claver's bed was little more than a mat, but even that would often be occupied by some sick patient whom he was nursing back to health. His wardrobe too was of the simplest. Few knew that under his habit he wore a long and very rough hair-shirt, though they might note the scourges hanging on the wall. At night these would be joined by his threadbare cloak—the famous cloak which he used as a shroud for the dead and blanket for the sick, the cloak which had sometimes to be washed half a dozen times every day after contact with so many infected bodies but which never smelled other than fresh and wholesome and came to be reputed miraculous.

Innumerable, indeed, were the miracles attributed to the saint; healings which folk vowed could only be supernatural, stories of corpses brought back to life so that the sinner might confess and be absolved before returning to the other world, unspoken thoughts read from a man's soul as from an open book, future happenings predicted —the common stock-in-trade, it may be said, of the man of God. But there are others which, had they not been vouched for by more than one witness in the Process of Beatification, might be smiled away as picturesque legends, and which show the saint in an attractively human light. One of these is the Miracle of the Eggs, recounted in slightly differing versions by two witnesses at the Process. According to one account, a young negress slave was walking along with a basket of eggs on her head when she was jostled off the pavement and her load sent tumbling to the ground. The other version has it that it was an old Indian woman who had the basket knocked off her head when passing under a low balcony. At all events, the result was the same. The precious eggs were sent flying and their owner set up a great lementation which led Claver, who happened to be passing, to enquire what the matter was. After learning the cause and seeing the woman's distress, he walked over and righted the basket with his stick as he gently admonished her to put her trust in God who protects the poor. To her amazement, and that of the bystanders, the woman looked again and found that not a single egg had been broken; each was as whole and fresh as before.

The poor and defenceless knew they could always turn to Claver whether their troubles were great or small. The negresses who kept stalls in the Plazuela de la Hierba might discover that their takings for the day had somehow fallen short, and fearing a good beating, would come sobbing to Claver who would either make good the short-fall himself or intercede with their master. A slave chained to the wall in solitary confinement for some offence would find Father Claver beside him, unpacking food and tobacco from his basket and preparing to spend the long evening by his side. The sick, abandoned in some hut or attic, would be cheered by the Father's unexpected visit, though no one had told him of their plight. In a word, as one citizen of Cartagena records, "he often reproved the slave-owners, he interceded for the slaves, he took them to the College, he protected runaway slaves and sought good masters for them".

Yet Claver was more than an indefatigable social worker; he was first and foremost a priest, striving to win souls and nurture them in the faith by teaching and the grace of the sacraments. From five o'clock to eight every morning he would be in the confessional. In Lent, his labours were intensified and he might spend the whole day hearing confessions and then passing to each of his negro penitents the voucher which they could then present to their parish priest. The cell where he heard these confessions was by the door, exposed to the full glare of the tropical sun. A lurid picture of a soul in torment, and a well-thumbed book of prints depicting Christ's passion, helped to induce a mood of contrition in his penitents. They came in their hundreds, the women by day and the men at night. His labours left him so exhausted that Claver had sometimes to be carried up to the refectory where a frugal dish of rice, or some bread dipped in wine and water and followed by a banana, helped to revive him.

Of the intense spiritual life which sustained this toil we know little. Prayer was undoubtedly the inexhaustible power-house. The saint, we are told, never allowed himself more than three hours sleep at night. Brother Nicolás, who had a cell next to his for eight years and would come rushing in to his neighbour when frightened by the tropical thunderstorms, invariably found him praying or reciting verses from the psalms or gospels. One of the negro interpreters confided that he had once entered Claver's cell and been terrified to see him suspended in the air rapt in prayer. He had helped him back into bed and been made to promise to say nothing of what he had seen. We know that mystical works were among the saint's reading, particularly Luis de la Puente's *Meditations on the Mysteries of the Holy Faith, with the practice of mental prayer,* a work much studied at the time in the Society of Jesus. But the strictly mystical element is not prominent in Claver's life. The latter was so utterly dedicated to his active apostolic calling, and the saint's humility and reserve were so great that we can catch no more than a glimpse into the intimacy of his private devotions. Moreover, Claver left almost no writings of his own. The few jottings which survive breathe the spirit of Alonso Rodríguez and his concern with self-renunciation and the glad acceptance of suffering : "To follow Our Lord Jesus Christ in the love of souls, we must persecute ourselves. To be His, we must cease to belong to ourselves. We must accept whatever is bitter as if it were sweet. Of all the afflictions which befall us for His sake, there is no higher path for life, nor anything more pleasing to God, than to suffer willingly for Christ". The most treasured of Claver's few possessions was his *Vita Domini Nostri Jesus Christi,* an illustrated Life of Christ by Fray Bartolomé Ricci. Brother Nicolás tells us that "whenever he prayed he chose the picture of the mystery upon which he intended to meditate, so that it might inspire him". His favourite subject for meditation was that of the Passion, and then "so great was his fervour that his eyes dwelled upon the picture the whole day; he used to leave the book open at this place on a little table. . . . It was never out of his hand or out of his sight".

The suffering which Claver saw around him and so fervently embraced for himself left its mark upon his physical appearance. He had the Catalan peasant's robust constitution and was of medium height, but he stooped a little as a result of the heavy loads he so frequently carried and his habit of walking with downcast eyes. His brow was broad but deeply furrowed, as was his whole face. His eyes, beneath thick eyebrows, were large, dark and melancholy. His complexion was sallow and he was seldom seen to smile. Yet he was not a man wholly bereft of humour, provided it was at his own expense and not that of others. His extreme modesty made him feel uncomfortable even to be called "Father", and when so addressed he would open the leather bag he carried with him and remark wryly : "Let us leave the 'Father' in this pouch". (Plate 11).

*   *   *   *

For nearly four decades Claver's sturdy physique and strong will allowed him to sustain his arduous ministry. But the time came when his exhausted body could no longer respond to the demands made of it. Collapse came when Claver had reached the banks of the Sinu river on one of his missionary tours. He struggled back to Cartagena to find the city smitten with one of the worst outbreaks of plague in its history. The Jesuit College lost six priests and three assistant brothers —nearly half its total strength. Claver was stricken with a palsy; his malady developed into what seems to have been Parkinson's disease. His body was seized with uncontrollable twitchings and tremblings and he lost the use of his limbs. They carried him to a room built on the city wall and overlooking the sea and harbour. It was next to the sacristy, through which he could be helped down to the church to attend mass. Very occasionally he felt strong enough to say mass himself, and then, in devotion to the divine office, his tremblings were seen to be momentarily stilled. Often he could do no more than remain seated in a chair by the altar and beg alms from others for the charitable work he was no longer able to perform himself. The last sacrifice required of him was the surrender of his active apostolate, and his apparent uselessness in God's cause weighed heavily upon him.

It was now that Claver was to suffer the full rigour of his vow to be the slave of the slaves. The small Jesuit community, decimated and exhausted by the ravages of the plague, could not give the chronic invalid all the attention he needed. Father Sandoval, who had initiated him into his apostolate, had himself succumbed after a painful illness. Brother Nicolás visited the sick-room when he could, and once brought Claver a present which gave him a moment of joy—a copy of a *Life* of Alonso Rodríguez published in Madrid not many months before. But in general Claver was left to the none too tender mercies of a slave recently imported from Africa, who had been given the name of Manuel Moreno. By some freak of fortune, the young savage found that he had a white man at his mercy. Instead of a master to give him harsh orders, here was a fumbling old man who could not feed or dress himself and would not even utter a word of protest when, as frequently happened, Manuel shook and shoved the invalid into his clothes, forgot or simply could not bother to bring him his food or his drinking water. Manuel stole the titbits for himself and let the swarms of flies gather round the uncleared garbage of the sick-room. He was, in short, a sloven and a bully. Claver, who had devoted so much of his life to relieving the suffering of the slaves, could now only suffer in silence at the hands of this unthinking negro, suffer as the defenceless donkey suffers—"if they speak ill of him, he keeps silence; if they do not feed him, silence; if they forget him, silence".

During the last four years of his life, Claver seems to have been all but forgotten by the city in which he was once so familiar a figure. Perhaps folk thought that he had been carried off, like so many others, by the plague. On three occasions only, during this last phase of his life, did he leave the sick-room to pay farewell visits to those who were most dear to him. Once, to doña Isabel de Urbina, the most devoted of his helpers in the Spanish community, who had herself been ill and besought the favour of his final blessing; once, along the familiar road leading through the gate of the Half Moon to the lepers of San Lázaro; once, to witness for the last time the arrival of a slave-ship from Africa. He had to be carried down to the wharf in a litter and could not hold back his tears at the sight of this new wave of human misery which he was now powerless to alleviate.

A few days before his death, the city suddenly became aware once more of his presence. Now that it was about to be taken from them, folk began to extol the treasure of his sanctity and to vie with each other in eagerness to secure some shred of it for themselves. The little room on the city wall overlooking the harbour became a place of pilgrimage. Monks and merchants, soldiers and beggars, men of quality, negro freedmen and slaves, the pious and the merely curious, all came hurrying to the Jesuit college. The Governor of the province came and the captains of the galleons. "Some of these persons were of such authority that they could not be denied admission," reported the Rector. "His cell was soon crowded and stripped of anything associated with him; only his bedclothes were left. . . . People went in and out as if it were a church on Maundy Thursday, whilst groups of children and negroes came crying out 'Let us go to the Saint! The Saint is dying!'." Before this hue and cry started, Claver had made over to Brother Nicolás the few treasured objects which had nurtured his devotion—a small notebook of his own, a print of Alonso Rodríguez and the precepts which the latter had given him as a guide to his spiritual life. These he asked Brother Nicolás to convey to the novices of the Jesuit seminary at Tunja with his fervent prayer they should turn them to better account than he had been able to do. The final sacrifice which Claver was called upon to make was the surrender of the crucifix which he wore round his neck and which had been "his physician and physique throughout his life". The Rector brought a distinguished visitor to the bedside of the dying man—no less a personage than the Marqués de Mancera who was on his way back to Spain after completing his service as a Viceroy of Peru. At the request of his Superior, Claver took the crucifix from his neck and gave it to the visitor without a word.

Pedro Claver died peacefully in the early morning of 8 September, 1654. "We all joined in praying for his soul," declared the Rector, "and between one and two in the morning he gave it up to God, without the slightest movement or gesture, dying with the same peace and serenity with which he had lived." Brother Nicolás records that "I only realized he had died when all at once his pale, thin countenance shone with extraordinary brilliance and loveliness, so that I knew his soul was in the presence of God". The people of Cartagena at once acclaimed him as a saint, though two centuries were to pass before the Process of Beatification was completed. His canonization followed a few years later—in 1888—together with that of his beloved Alonso Rodríguez. The Slave of the Slaves had become the Saint of the Slaves.

Cartagena raised its monument to his memory. The coloured folk, as they saw how the white stone was weathering to a dusky hue, told each other: "See, he was truly one of us!" But Claver's achievement was more than the transcending of the barriers of colour and caste. A still greater miracle was the transmuting, in the hearts of those moved by his example, of the bitterness born of racial injustice into charity and compassion. Some 80 years after his death, Juan and Ulloa paid a surprising tribute to the people of a city so long the hub of the slave trade. "Charity," they wrote, "is a virtue in which all the inhabitants of Cartagena, without exception, may be said particularly to excel." They noted the plight of the "poor whites" who had come to the New World in the vain hope of bettering their lot, and how "the negro and mulatto women, moved at their deplorable condition, carry them to their houses and nurse them with the greatest care and affection". Thus well had the descendants of Andrés Sacabuche, Francisco Yolofo, Ignacio Angola, Isabel Folupa, Margarita of Cape Verde, and countless others learned their lesson from the saint.

A CALENDAR OF SAINTS

	Born	Died	Beatified	Canonized	Festival
Luis Bertrán	1526	1581	1608	1671	9 October
Toribio de Mogrovejo	1538	1606	1679	1726	27 April
Francisco Solano	1549	1610	1675	1726	14 July
Roque González	1576	1628	1934		17 November
Martín de Porres	1579	1639	1837	1962	5 November
Pedro Claver	1580	1654	1851	1888	9 September
Rosa de Santa María	1586	1617	1667	1671	30 August
Juan del Castillo	1596	1628	1934		17 November
Alonso Rodríguez	1598	1628	1934		17 November
Mariana de Jesús	1618	1645	1850	1950	26 May

BIBLIOGRAPHICAL NOTE

THE literature in English on the missionary activities and early history of the Catholic Church in South America is limited. J. M. Mecham's classic study *Church and State in Latin America: a history of politico-ecclesiastical relations* (Chapel Hill, N.C., 2nd rev. ed., 1966) and John A. Mackay's protestant view—*The Other Spanish Christ: a study in the spiritual history of Spain and South America* (New York, 1932) deal mainly with later aspects of Catholicism in Latin America. Chapter X, "The Church in America", in Clarence H. Haring: *The Spanish Empire in America* (New York, 1947; paperback, 1963) provides a good summary of the institutional structure. The rôle of the Church in defence of the Indians has been studied by Lewis Hanke in *The Spanish Struggle for Justice in the Conquest of America* (Boston, Toronto, 1965) and *Aristotle and the American Indians* (London, 1959). Useful documentary material on the *patronato real* will be found in W. Eugene Shiels: *King and Church—The Rise and Fall of the Patronato Real* (Chicago, 1961). Antonine Tibesar: *Franciscan beginnings in colonial Peru* (Washington, 1953) is a useful specialized study. J. L. Phelan: *The Kingdom of Quito in the Seventeenth Century* (London, 1967) contains useful material on church matters in that area, whilst the same author's *The Millennial Kingdom of the Franciscans* (John Hopkins, 1970), together with Charles S. Braden: *Religious aspects of the Conquest of Mexico* (Durham, N. C., 1930) and Robert Ricard's admirable *La Conquête Spirituelle du Mexique* (Paris, 1933), though dealing primarily with an area falling outside the scope of the present study, throw useful light over a wider canvas. The extensive and often highly polemical literature dealing with the Jesuit missions in Paraguay is similarly of far more than local interest. The fullest study in English is M. Morner: *The Political and Economic activities of the Jesuits in the La Plata region in the Habsburg era* (Stockholm, 1953).

The literature in Spanish is naturally more extensive. General studies include Ybot León: *La Iglesia y los eclesiásticos españoles en la empresa de Indias* (Barcelona, 1954), Lucas Ayarragaray: *La Iglesia en América y la dominación española* (2nd ed., Buenos Aires, 1935), Constantino Bayle: *El clero secular y la evangelización de América* (Madrid, 1950). There are several useful works dealing with the origins and early development of the Church in Peru; Rubén

203

Vargas Ugarte: *Historia de la Iglesia en el Perú,* 1511-68 (Lima, 1953) and Fernando de Armas Medina: *Cristianización del Perú, 1553-1600* (Seville, 1953), Roberto Levillier: *La organización de la Iglesia y órdenas religiosas en el vireinato del Perú en el siglo xvi* (Madrid, 1919). Some of the Orders, particularly the Dominicans, Franciscans and Jesuits, have well-documented histories of their Latin American provinces (e.g. Antonio Astraín: *Historia de la Compañia de Jesús en la Asistencia de España,* 7 vols. (Madrid, 1912-1925).

For the "pseudo-saints" and deviant religious movements the literature is most abundant with regard to Brazil. Da Cunha's vivid portrait of Antonio the Counsellor can be read in S. Putnam's translation *Rebellion in the Backlands* (Chicago, 1944) and there is an excellent study of Father Cicero and Brazilian popular Catholicism in Ralph della Cava: *Miracle at Joaseiro* (Columbia University Press, 1971). For studies in Portuguese, see Maria Isaura Pereira de Queiroz: *O Messianismo no Brasil* (São Paulo, 1965) and Abelardo Montenegro: *Historia do Fanatismo na Ceará* (Fortaleza, 1959).

The literature with regard to the canonized saints is in the main hagiographical rather than strictly biographical or historical. A useful general bibliography on this subject, though now out of date, was compiled by the great Chilean bibliographer, José Toribio Medina: *Ensayo de una bibliografía extranjera de santos y venerables americanos* (Santiago, 1919). The official Processes of beatification and canonization, containing sworn statement by contemporaries, are an indispensable source for any serious study of the lives of the saints, though not easily accessible for consultation. The publications of the Bollandist Society, *Acta Sanctorum,* also constitute an inexhaustible quarry.

The sources which have been found useful in preparing essays on the individual saints are as follows :

San Luis Bertrán

St. Luis Bertrán's first biographer was his disciple and fellow Dominican, Fray Vicente Justiniano Antist, who had the advantage of a long and intimate acquaintance with the saint in Spain but wrote without first-hand knowledge of his years in America. His *Verdadera Relación de la Vida y Muerte del Padre Fray Luys Bertrán* (Pampplona, 1583) is still the main source for our knowledge of the saint's life. Another Dominican, Fray Bartolomé de Abiñón, or Avignon, was appointed Procurator by the monastery at Valencia to further the cause of his canonization and was able to draw on the statements submitted for the Process; his book was published in an Italian version in Rome in 1623. There are numerous hagiographies in Spanish, a biography in French by Jean-Batiste Feuillet (Paris, 1671) and one in English by B. Wilberforce, the *Life of St. Lewis Bertrand* (London, 1882). There are also two more recent works in Spanish: Alvaro Sánchez—*El Apóstol del Nuevo Reino, San Luis Beltrán* (Bogotá, 1953) and V. Galduf Blasco—*Luis Bertrán, el santo de los contrastes* (Barcelona, 1961).

San Toribio de Mogrovejo

The fullest and most scholarly work, based on a thorough study of the archival sources in Rome and Spain and containing annexes comprising some of the contemporary statements prepared for the saint's Process of beatification, is the two-volume study by Vicente Rodríguez Valencia: *Santo Toribio de Mogrovejo, Apóstol y Organizador de Sur-América* (Madrid, 1956). This supersedes the earlier work of Carlos García Irigoyen, *Santo Toribio* (Lima, 1906-7, 4 vols.) which nevertheless contains much interesting material and has the advantage of being written with a full knowledge of the local Peruvian background and sources.

Of the early biographies, the most interesting and reliable is the *Vida* by Antonio de León Pinelo (Madrid, 1653; Lima, 1906), an official of the Council of the Indies, who was commissioned by the *cabildo* of Lima to write a life of the Archbishop in connection with the Process of beatification.

San Francisco Solano

The first Life of the Saint was written by Diego de Córdoba Salinas, official chronicler of the Franciscan Order in Peru, and published in Lima in 1630. A new and expanded edition, containing material relating to the saint's beatification, was published in 1643. More recent lives have been published by Bernardino Izaguirre (Tournai, 1908) and Antonio Santa Clara Córdova (Buenos Aires, 1949). There is a short but useful essay by R. Vargas Ugarte in Enrique T. Batra, *San Toribio de Mogrovejo* (Lima, 1964).

San Martín de Porres

The first Life of Martín de Porres was written by the Dominican Bernardo de Medina, whose *Vida Prodigiosa del venerable siervo de Dios Fray Martín de Porres* (Lima, 1673), now very rare, was reproduced with slight modifications in volume 3 of the *Tesoros Verdaderos de las Indias—Historia de la Provincia de S. Juan Bautista del Perú del Orden de Predicadores* (Rome, 1862) by Juan Meléndez. Alfonso Manrique's *Perfessión Cristiana* (Venice, 1697) contains a life of Fray Martín on similar lines. These earlier works were used by José Manuel Váldez for his *Vida Admirable del bienaventurado Fray Martín de Porres* (Lima, 1863). A Latin version of Medina's work was published by the Bollandists in their *Acta Sanctorum* for November, Vol. 3 (Brussels, 1910).

Modern studies of the saint include the short but useful *Blessed Martín de Porres* (London, 1953) by C. Ryan, *Social implications in the work of the Blessed Martín de Porres* (Washington, 1941) a doctoral thesis by L. M. Preher, and R. Vargas Ugarte, *El Beato Martín de Porres* (Buenos Aires, 1949).

Santa Rosa de Santa María

The first biography of Santa Rosa was written by one of her confessors, Pedro de Loaysa (reprinted as *Vida de Santa Rosa de Lima,* Lima, 1937). Most subsequent biographies have been based on the *Life* by Fray Leonardo Hansen, first published in Latin in 1664 and used for the Life of the saint in the Bollandists' *Acta Sanctorum* (1868). There is a Spanish version of Hansen's *Life* by Jacinto Parro (reprinted, Lima, 1929). The second volume of *Tesoros Verdaderos de las Indias* by Fray F. Juan Meléndez (1681) includes a delightfully written life of St. Rosa which is a modified version of an earlier biography by Fr. Andrés Ferrer de Valdecebro.

The extensive modern literature on the saint in Spanish includes Rubén Vargas Ugarte: *Vida de Santa Rosa de Lima* (Lima, 1951, 3rd ed., Buenos Aires, 1961), María Weisse: *Santa Rosa de Lima* (Lima, 1922) and César Miró: *Cielo y Tierra de Santa Rosa* (Buenos Aires, 1945). D. Anguló: *Santa Rosa de Santa María* (Lima, 1917) contains useful bibliographical material and Luis G. Alonso Getino: *Santa Rosa, Patrona de la América* (Madrid, 1943) an account of the author's discovery in 1923 of the manuscripts left by the saint.

There is no adequate modern Life in English. Recent studies include M. Storm: *Life of St. Rose* (Santa Fe, New Mexico, 1937), Frances Parkinson Keyes: *The Rose and the Lily* (New York, 1961 and London, 1962). Sheila Kaye-Smith: *Quartet in Heaven* (London, 1952) contains a slight but perceptive essay on the saint.

Santa Mariana de Jesús

The first *Life* of Mariana was written by a Jesuit, Father Jacinto

Morán de Butrón, and first published in Lima in 1702. A second and expanded edition appeared in Madrid in 1724. There have been several subsequent editions, the latest being the *Vida de Santa Mariana de Jesús*, Quito, 1958. Morán de Butrón's work was followed by the *Compendio histórico de la prodigiosa vida . . . de Mariana de Jesús* (Madrid, 1754) written by Father Tomás de Gijón y León, the Procurador sent by the Province of Quito to further Mariana's beatification Process in Rome, and is the basis for all subsequent biographies. Those published in recent years (all in Quito) include the *Lives* by Augusto Arias (1944), Enrique M. Villasís Terán (1946), Germania Moncayo de Monge (1950), Wilfredo Loor (1954) and Aurelio Espinosa Pólit (1956). An essay in English on Mariana is contained in *The Rose and the Lily*, by F. Parkinson Keyes (London, 1962).

Roque González, Alonso Rodríguez, Juan del Castillo

There are two good collections of contemporary documents in Spanish relating to Father Roque González and his fellow martyrs. They are—José María Blanco : *Historia documentada de la vida y gloriosa muerte de los Padres Roque González de Santa Cruz, Alonso Rodríguez y Juan del Castillo* (Buenos Aires, 1929) and the volume prepared for the Congregation of Rites : Bonaeren—*Beatificationis seu Declarationis Martyrii Rochi Gonzalez, Alfonsi Rodriguez et Joannis del Castillo—Positio super introductione Causae* (Insulae Lire, 1932).

There are also two short modern biographies based on these documentary sources : J. M. Blanco : *Los Mártires del Caaró y Yjuhí* (Buenos Aires, 1931) and Gaspar González Pintado : *Los Mártires Jesuítas de las Misiones del Paraguay* (Bilbao, 1934).

San Pedro Claver

The first Life of Claver appeared in Madrid in 1657 under the title *Vida del Venerable y apostólico Pedro Claver*. The author's name is given as Licenciado Gerónimo Suárez de Somaza, but the book is generally attributed to Father Alfonso de Andrade of Bogotá who based it on letters from the Provincial of New Granada and other correspondence and conversations with those who knew Claver personally. The biography of Father José Fernández, *Apostólica y penitente vida del venerable Padre Pedro Claver* (Zaragoza, 1666), follows the earlier work but incorporates material from the Process of Beatification. It is the basis of most subsequent biographies of the saint. An expanded version of this book was published in 1888, the

year of Claver's canonization, by Fr. Juan María Sola in Barcelona.
Modern studies include Gabriel Ledos : *Saint Pierre Claver* (Collection
Les Saints, 1923), Mariano Picón Salas, *Pedro Claver, el santo de los
esclavos* (Mexico, 1949) and *El Santo que libertó una raza—San
Pedro Claver* by Fr. Angel Valtierra (Bogotá, 1954). The latter book
draws on a wide range of historical sources and is available in English
translation (*Peter Claver—Saint of the Slaves*, London, 1960).

INDEX